A MARNE MIND

A SOLDIER'S WAR WITH RECOVERY

CY MULHOLLAND

WESTBOW
PRESS
A DIVISION OF THOMAS NELSON

WestBow Press books may be ordered through booksellers or by contacting:

WestBow Press
A Division of Thomas Nelson
1663 Liberty Drive
Bloomington, IN 47403
www.westbowpress.com
1-(866) 928-1240

Because of the dynamic nature of the Internet, any web addresses or links contained in
this book may have changed since publication and may no longer be valid. The views
expressed in this work are solely those of the author and do not necessarily reflect the
views of the publisher, and the publisher hereby disclaims any responsibility for them.

Any people depicted in stock imagery provided by Thinkstock are models,
and such images are being used for illustrative purposes only.

Certain stock imagery © Thinkstock.

ISBN: 978-1-4497-3749-8 (sc)
ISBN: 978-1-4497-3750-4 (hc)
ISBN: 978-1-4497-3751-1 (e)

Library of Congress Control Number: 2012900964

Printed in the United States of America

WestBow Press rev. date: 01/28/2012

CONTENTS

PREFACE

I was a member of the 3rd Infantry Division (Mechanized) for the first ten years of my Army career: also known as the Marne Division. The 3ID earned its nickname in the First World War following the Second Battle of the Marne, which was a major turning point in the conflict. The battle began with the last German offensive and ended with the first allied offensive, which began at the Marne River in France in the year 1918. That is why, to this day, the 3rd Infantry Division Motto is "Rock of the Marne."

I am glad to have served in the 3rd Infantry Division, and I am very pleased that PTSD (Post Traumatic Stress Disorder) is drawing more and more attention all the time. There is a growing public interest and, because of this, it is becoming more possible and effective for those who are still suffering and those who are in need of skills that will assist them in sustaining and maintaining recovery to receive the help they need.

"A Marne Mind" began as a coping skill for me: a therapeutic means of allowing myself to put my thoughts and emotions down on paper, as I struggled mentally with Post-Traumatic Stress Disorder. Before it was "A Marne Mind" it was only poetry that I began writing while receiving treatment for PTSD, which I had developed early on during my childhood. My PTSD symptoms became more severe as an adult, due to multiple overseas deployments while serving in the United States Army. During my treatment, at about the two and a half year mark, I met a gentleman named Rich: a Vietnam Veteran who introduced me to the idea of writing poetry. Once I began writing, I never looked back.

Initially, I had no aspirations of writing a book, and even after sharing some of my poetry and being told by others that I had talent for writing and that I should consider writing a book, I still never imagined it would be possible. It wasn't until I had written somewhere around twenty to thirty poems that I thought were decent that I began thinking I might actually be able to put something together and call it a book. The more I wrote, the better I seemed to feel. I discovered that I was making leaps and bounds in my recovery and most of my success was due to my spiritual reconnection and my ability to see how I truly felt about the things that were going on in my mind when they were directly in front of me, on paper, where I could read and process them whenever I wanted. Writing gave me the ability to sift through bad memories and figure out a more positive way to deal with them. I learned that by doing this, I was able to open up and talk about the things I had experienced in a much more positive manner. After making a great deal of progress, I was able to effectively begin my journey back to my roots: my Christian upbringing.

It was then that I realized what kind of book I was actually called to write. "A Marne Mind" is a book of repetition and growth, because it is my experience that the more I see something, the more I will become familiar with it and the more I will act on it. It is my hope that it can do the same thing for someone else struggling with PTSD. Too often, we see too much negativity, whereas this book draws something positive from something negative. The chapter titles coincide with the poetry, and much of my poetry is a reflection of who I was and who I am today because of my success with recovery. "A Marne Mind" is probably different from what most people typically read; however, in this book are the things that have worked for me and how my mind operates.

There are two sides to every war, and therefore there are two sides to the war that goes on inside the soldier or any other militant or civilian who has experienced a traumatic event. In a different aspect, there are two sides to recovery until eventually victory is achieved by learning and acquiring the skills necessary to be successful in recovery and getting as close to a normal life as possible. Throughout the contents of this book, it will be made clear that the poetry reflects my real thoughts of the things I have experienced from my darkest times, as well as my hopes for the future, while the narratives shine light on the details of my experiences and explain my growth and views on my personal recovery as a Christian. I know the details of this journey will be beneficial to anyone.

As you read through the contents of this book, you will be able to see that, as I grew more successful with recovery, the poetry developed from a dark and worldly view into motivational and influential poetry. These join the narratives to become a combined positive outlook. I hope anyone who reads this book will find something helpful in it for his or her life: something that will help in the journey that is recovery. It sure helped me. I hope and pray the war within will be won for those still fighting.

ACKNOWLEDGMENTS

I will be forever grateful to GOD for his patience and love and for putting His Son and people, places, and things in my life to help me in my journey toward recovery: particularly, my Lord and Savior JESUS CHRIST. I am grateful for the opportunity to be counted among His children and the multitude of answered prayers which have only strengthened my faith. I appreciate the fact that many of the prayers have been answered in very obvious ways, further proving His existence. Thank You, JESUS, for taking human form and dying on the cross for all mankind's sins. Thank You for Your HOLY SPIRIT. I love You and I will forever remain in communication with You, through prayer.

I want to thank my wife. I am grateful that GOD blessed me with such a beautiful, loving, selfless and strong-willed woman. She is my best friend and I don't know where I would be without her in my life. She is my soul-mate and I know with all my heart and soul that we were destined to be together by GOD Himself. She truly has stuck by my side through thick and thin, the good times and the bad and the terrible. She is a strong woman and the only one I know that can put up with me in my worst times. Our marriage survived five overseas deployments, along with various other training exercises. Our marriage has survived all of the many negative aspects of Post-Traumatic Stress Disorder. I look forward to spending the rest of this life with her. She is a great mother and the Lord has blessed us with three awesome children, who I love with all my heart and soul, and I am eternally grateful for them as well.

I want to thank my dad, Rodney Mulholland, who has always been there for me. He is the primary influence, second only to JESUS CHRIST, in shaping me into the man I am today. He has always been there to give me advice when I needed it. Many times, he was the only one who could help me get my feet on the ground when I was drifting off course. He showed me the importance of family and instilled in me the same values and morals which had been taught to him. He taught me manners and respect and what it means for a man to love his family. He gave me guidance and was the first one to introduce the idea of resilience to me. I am grateful for my mom, Gayla Mulholland. She is a good example of what it is to be a woman who stands by her husband, as well as a loving mother.

I would like to thank my in-laws, Scott and Diana Mortensen. They have always been there for my wife and I and our children, and without them I wouldn't have my wife or our children. I would like to thank Pastor Gregg Curtis of Stithton Baptist Church, who has been there for my spiritual guidance. He helped me better understand GOD's plan and taught me a great deal about the Bible. I would like to thank Dr. Andrews for listening and helping me better understand and figure out what was going on within me. He helped me get back to a proper frame of mind. I would like to thank my friend Rich for his service in Vietnam and also for introducing me to the most effective coping skill I have: writing poetry. I would like to thank Christy Faulkner and Kat Forader of Operation Resilient Warrior for all their kind support and all they do for soldiers and soldier's families. I would like to give an extra special thank you to Elizabeth Boylan for her help and amazing hard work editing this book.

I want to thank the thousands of service men and women and their families who have sacrificed so much in the name of freedom, both in the United States of America and abroad. I will remain forever mindful of the thousands of innocent lives lost on 9/11 and their families. I would like to especially thank those with whom I served in the 3rd Infantry Division. The men and women of the Marne Division are a large part of me having the ability to come home to my family. I will never forget those who made the ultimate sacrifice. I will never forget.

In Loving Memory

of

SSG David Julian

and the many

Men and Women

of the

Marne Division

who

Sacrificed Everything

in

Defense of Freedom.

CHAPTER ONE

BATTLEFIELD MIND

———

So much is captured on the battlefield by the mind and brought home to the battlefield in the mind.

I REMEMBER

I remember the day SGT Lamie died. It hurt my heart. It hurt me deep inside.
Then I remember the day I rode up that Baghdad Hill.
The sound of my coax was quite a thrill.
It was 2003. Sometime in March, I think.
The smell of a cooked corpse frozen in place didn't even stink.
I saw a man in a crowd holding a rifle.
I was so excited, but I didn't smile.
Arroyo yelled, "Fire" without delay and with an "On the way" I began to spray.
Never again would they pray on a rug, 'cause with my help they gave the pavement a hug.
I remember the day SSG Julian died.
Just before we left, he made Erin his bride.
They had a daughter together. He met her on leave.
Then he returned to Baghdad, but only to bleed.
A man with a vest laid him to rest.
I will always miss you, Dave. You were one of the best.
Then I remember rolling down those city streets.
With seventy tons of steel, I felt I couldn't be beat.
All of a sudden, out came a little white truck
With a pathetic mounted machine gun that had to suck.
As soon as they saw me, they dismounted and ran.
Then I put a heat round in that piece of shit can.
By that time, the three dismounts had jumped a tiny wall.
They didn't get far. My rounds helped them fall.
I remember the day SSG Cimmarusti died.
You were one funny Mexican, so full of pride.
We deployed many places together. It was one wild ride.
The day you lost your life changed something inside me.
I lost something too. I lost the old me.
I miss the times we used to cut up and laugh.
I will always remember the good times from the past.

I remember the day we assaulted that hotel.
We killed many. We sent them all to hell.
I remember the day SPC Gudino died.
It was Christmas day when your tank was fried.
That EFP that you never did see cut right through you and set you free.
I watched for hours as your tank burned to the ground.
The radio was loud, but I couldn't hear a sound.
Your crew got out and I knew you were still in there.
You were the best soldier I knew. How was this fair?
What was once your driver's hull was now your tomb.
It won't be long, brother. I will see you soon.
Christmas will never be the same and I'm trying to change.
I will remember the good time we all shared down range.
I've been a soldier for twelve years now. Where'd the time go?
The only way I can remember, the only way I can show
Is to remember my brothers, those who stay and those who go.
For some reason, by the grace of GOD, I'm still here.
And I've finally decided not to drown myself in beer.
For if I am one chosen to carry your memory through.
Then I must strive to live more like you.
The LORD, our GOD took you because it was time.
And I believe it's through the SPIRIT I came up with this rhyme.
I love all my brothers. I will never forget.
I will always remember. I will never regret.
I will be a better man for my wife and my kids.
'Cause while you were on this earth, that's what you did.
I'm here for some reason. I'm here for some purpose.
I must get rid of the guilt. Bring it all to the surface.
No matter the position. No matter the test.
You, my brothers, were man enough to ride the Marne Express.
And so this is my promise. I will live without regret.
I will always remember. I will never forget.

Cy Mulholland

I deployed to Iraq three times throughout my Army Career. We, the 3rd Infantry Division, crossed the Kuwait border and invaded Iraq in 2003. I didn't know what to expect, but I knew it was going to get messy. I returned to Iraq in 2005 for a year and again in 2007 for a fifteen-month tour. I prayed every day for my wife and kids back home and prayed that God would let me return to them.

Of course, I prayed for their well-being much more than my own. There was a helpless feeling I kept with me all the time when I was away from them. It was the feeling that I had no influence over their daily life and that I could not protect them. I couldn't stand the thought that I might not make it home to them and that my kids would never fully understand the sacrifices that have to be made in order to keep this great country that we live in free. Many people I knew made such sacrifices. Some of them were just soldiers I would see in passing, or maybe worked with at some point in time in the motor pool or during a training exercise. Others were drinking buddies, or "drinking associates," as I call them, that I would hang out with from time to time. And then some, a few, were close friends of mine: The type of people I could count on.

There was one noncommissioned officer, a staff sergeant named David Julian, who was killed in action during my third and final tour in Iraq. He was my friend. He was a natural born leader and I looked up to him. We were both from Wyoming and we had plans of returning there to work and raise our families. I lost other close friends to the war, both when I was deployed with them and when I was not. Every time a soldier that I know lost his life, I lost another piece of myself. I will never forget the ultimate sacrifice that my brothers and sisters have made.

Every time I went to Iraq, I kept a copy of Psalm 91 in my breast pocket. It gave me strength to carry on. It strengthens me to this day, but little did I know during my days in combat that I would bring the war home with me.

However, my struggle with post-traumatic stress disorder began long before the war. From as far back as I can remember, the hardest thing for me to endure has always been losing those I love and care about. I will refer to this several times, as I will the fact that I am a man of repetition, both in the wrong and in the good that I have done. It will be stated within the context of this book why, even as a child, I was set up for failure by someone who I loved dearly: I will explain the immense impact my brother's suicide had on my young and impressionable mind.

Looking back and pondering what I experienced as a child, I find comfort in what God tells us in His Word about taking care of the children. Even though some feel the burdens of this world and the pain they've experienced mentally, emotionally, physically and spiritually is too much to cope with, they do not have the right to harm themselves or the children in their lives, as my older brother did when I was a child. Some who have attempted suicide and lived through it, such as a few who have jumped off of the Golden Gate Bridge, stated that as soon as they jumped, they changed their mind and tried to reach back and grab on to something, but it was too late. It's amazing how lives can be changed in a matter of seconds, minutes, hours, or days.

Lord, help me to remember that you have a plan for my life and always, Lord, I pray that Your will be done. In JESUS' name I pray. Amen

21 DAYS

Open desert for miles.
Hard faces. No smiles.
Down range, I see four black and white tiles.
My bore site is tight. The firing line is ready.
The Black Knights are now prepared to rock steady.
Crossing the border, the Patriots have our back;
Forming a wedge begins the attack.
Miles are traveled before any contact.
This is the place where heroes will be made
For the land of the free and the home of the brave.
Nasiriya, Najaf, Karbala, Highway nine.
Twenty-one days is a mighty long time.
Five hundred or more to Objective Saints.
None of these boys will ever be the same.
Sixty-four will bring the thunder and many will run.
This is a war that will never be won.
More blood flows in Baghdad than water in canals.
That city is the place where I lost many pals.
Twenty-one days in a smoky haze: so much death, in so many ways.
I knew at the time this was only one phase, but the war changed my life
in twenty—one days.

After Operation Desert Spring in 2002, and somewhere around fifty-four days of leave back home and seeing my second child born, I found myself back in the Kuwaiti desert. We were preparing for war. We had been in the desert for seven months, preparing for the war that was to come prior to going back home for a short stay.

It would be more than seven months from that point before I would have the chance to see my family again, if I survived. Nonetheless, there I was with my crew, preparing our tank for battle.

I was the gunner on a M1A1 Abrams Main Battle Tank. It weighed more than seventy tons with a combat load. It had a 120mm main gun, a 7.62mm coaxial machine gun, a .50 caliber machine gun for the commander's weapon station, and another 7.62mm machine gun for the loaders hatch. It only knew how to do one thing. Kill. Friend or foe, it didn't matter, and as long as any potential crew member kept that in mind, any potential crew member could most likely make the machine work for him. The rest of my crew consisted of a middle-aged Puerto Rican man who fought in the Gulf War and two brand new soldiers straight out of basic training. I remember thinking it felt good to have combat experience on the crew, but Lord have mercy, two brand new trainees to train in such little time. Long story short: they ended up being pretty good tankers.

We had a solid crew and a solid platoon. We were the Bravo Company Black Knights from the 1st of the 64th Armor Regiment. We were Desert Rouges and we were attached to Baker Company 1-15 Infantry out of Fort Benning, Georgia. We were normally a part of 2nd Brigade out of Fort Stewart, Georgia, where the majority of the 3rd Infantry Division is based. We traveled hundreds of bloody, war torn miles to Baghdad over the course of twenty-one days.

We were, and always will be Marne Soldiers. Many lost their lives and those who didn't lost part of who they were prior to the war.

Lord, let me never forget where I've been and where I'm going. Let me always seek your will and your purpose for my life. In JESUS' name I pray. Amen

I Killed Me

Honestly, most definitely, what I tell you is true.
I've killed more than one, more than two, more than a few.
What you might not know, but it's a fact, is that I'm dead too.
Every time I took something, I lost something.
Every time I lost someone, I felt done.
Oftentimes, I wonder why I wasn't the one.
Most often, I feel life is no longer fun.
Most days, I feel like I'm coming undone.
Maybe this war within me is one that won't be won.
I refuse to end this trip with a gun.
O.M.G. this is me, instituted, no longer free.
It seems this is the way it's s always going to be.
Smiling on the outside, but dead on the inside.
Listen to me, carney; I want off of this ride.
Me, myself and I can no longer coincide.
I tried to cope. I mean it, I tried. No matter what I do, my mind feels fried.
I've killed more than one, more than two, more than a few.
I tried to take myself out by drinking too much brew.
I'm a dead man walking, but I'm still talking.
In my mind, it's me that I'm still stalking.
I need to sit down, I can barely stand.
Internally I killed me, with my own two hands.

C ombat stress is a stress that is all its own. There are other forms of trauma out there that are very extreme, but I have personally felt the brunt of combat. I remember being in the combat zone and at the time, I was so tuned into what was going on. I was in my element. It's who I was. I was constantly receiving orders from my leaders and providing purpose, direction and motivation to the noncommissioned officers and soldiers that were under me. In the combat zone, I was always keyed up and ready to react to whatever came our way. I was poised under pressure, and when things got real intense, I was able to keep my guys level-headed. This was all true for the most part, but by the time I had deployed to Iraq for the third time, Baghdad and its stressors had caught up to me and it began to show.

We were a little more than half way done with our tour. We were operating in a Sunni town called Aadimiya in Baghdad. My crew and I had been hit six times by various weapon systems and I had lost several of my close friends. My mental state was getting worse all the time, and I began spending part of my time while out on missions looking for alcohol to purchase from the locals. They were more than happy to oblige.

At the same time, I began to be harder on my soldiers and was very short-tempered. I had a short fuse and I would ride them very hard for simple mistakes. It wasn't long before the crew that once had been so loyal and looked to their tank commander for solid leadership felt they had no choice but to report me to command. So that's what they did. I was relieved of my duties as a tank commander and a section sergeant: A job that I loved so much, but was no longer capable of doing to the best of my ability because the war had taken its toll on me.

Besides missing my wife and kids back home, the only thing I could think about was the fact that my friends were not coming back. They were gone forever. I would think about the good times, but I would focus on the fact that we wouldn't have any more good times. Some of them I had known for years and we had deployed many places together. With others, I had lifelong plans of staying in touch. So many of those guys had wives and children that they were forced to leave behind. While trying to process all of these things, I would let myself get down and depressed, and when I made it back home, my own family would suffer the consequences. It wasn't until I got help with my Post Traumatic Stress Disorder (PTSD) and alcoholism that I learned positive ways to cope. I will always miss those guys, those brothers, but I can't allow it to be my undoing. I must honor them by living a fulfilling, worthwhile life. There are certain times of the year that are harder than others, but I cope. I will never forget.

Lord, grant me the strength to honor my brothers by celebrating their lives and not living a life of grief. In JESUS' name I pray. Amen

Have You?

Have you ever seen a head explode?
Have you ever seen a fresh off the fifty-cal one legged man hop across the road?
Have you destroyed a house, not fully knowing what's inside?
Have you put two in his chest when he's trying to hide?
Have you kicked in someone's door and slammed him on his face?
Have you trashed his entire house because there's no time to waste?
Have you zip-tied a man in front of his wife and kids?
Have you done what you had to do? That's what we did.
Have you accepted that some were at the wrong place at the wrong time?
Have you ever felt that it was a crime?
Have you seen the enemy stand there and seconds later, nothing's left?
Have you been the one that put a main gun round in his chest?
Have you felt like taking life was the decision that was best?
Have you felt that it was ok to send those souls to their unrest?
Have you aimed to kill while looking down your sight?
Have you lost five friends when a vest ignites? Have you killed ten others trying to make it right?
Have you laughed and cried at the same time?
Have you imprisoned a man's brother because he dropped the dime?
Have you chased the enemy with rounds from your gun?
Have you felt badly for it? Have you felt that it was fun?
Have you sacrificed anything? Have you had to lose?
Have you served your country or watched it on the news?

Oftentimes, I've had mixed emotions about the things I've seen and done in combat. At times, I felt one way about certain things and then felt another way about it. There have been times when I have felt guilt over some of the things I've done that I had to put to rest. It took a long time for me to make peace with myself over a few instances I experienced. I had to come to terms with some of the engagements I had participated in and that wasn't easy, but today I have peace.

I didn't feel guilt because I committed any crimes. I felt it because I had taken life, and I have a conscience and I'm not an evil person. For me, for a long time, it wasn't a matter of it being ok, because soldiers to my left and right were being killed by the enemy. It was the "What Ifs" that gave me so many issues. I believe these "What Ifs" contributed to my flash-backs and nightmares and made me so angry and hard and irritable most of the time. What if a house or a building that I engaged with a 120mm heat round had more than just the enemy inside? What if enemy combatant vehicles such as trucks and SUVs contained more than just insurgent forces in them? What if I killed someone innocent on the battle field that was in the wrong place at the wrong time?

These are things I used to beat myself up over. And that was wrong of me to do to myself. For years, my wife and my dad and others tried to tell me that I shouldn't hold that against myself, but at the time my thought was, "You can't tell someone who has been there what to think about it." But they were right. It just was not that easy to shut it off. I didn't know how to leave the war on the battle field in Iraq, until I got help.

I'm glad to see that PTSD has become more recognized for how serious it is today. Many soldiers are getting the help they need, because there are more resources available. For ten years and five deployments with the 3rd Infantry Division—three of those tours being to Iraq—I went without any treatment for my issues. I came to Fort Knox and finally began getting the help I need. My recommendation to anyone that has ever deployed to a combat zone would be to get checked out by a professional at a minimum, to see where that person might stand after experiencing combat stress. It took me a long time to realize that I had issues, but I'm glad I got help. I'm a better man because of it today. There are men and women out there, military and civilian, that really care about our well-being and want to help. No one should be too proud to ask for help and no one should hold back from talking to others if they seem to be suffering. Someone's life or the lives of his or her family members could depend on it. No problem is too big to find a solution for. For our own sakes and for the sakes of those who love us, we must try until the problem is identified.

Lord, bless and comfort those men and women who have stood and fought or supported those who fought and experienced traumatic events in the name of freedom and their families. In JESUS' name I pray. Amen

Identified

Identified, I got 'em. Identified, I caught 'em.
Gunner, coax, troops and identified, I shot 'em.
Identified, fire is the order. Over and over, like a recorder.
It's easier, I figure, to go ahead and pull the trigger.
By the way, on the way, and that is how I ruined their day.
Identified, a body falls. A man with no legs only crawls.
A man with one leg is ok to hop. The bleeding will stop—another body will drop.
Identified, they tried to hide. It's already known that you are inside.
A sabot round and your tank is fried.
Identified, you tried to run.
The flight of the round has already begun.
Identified, an ammo truck. Up in smoke: that had to suck.
Superior equipment or your bad luck?
Identified, a technical through my spectacles.
You are suspect, I am skeptical.
You run away—I burned your truck today.
I followed you up with a killing spray.
Identified, it is a hotel.
Full of instant death winners who win a trip to hell.
Identified, again and again. Some are warranted and some are sin.
If I were asked if I'd do it again? I'd tell you, damn right I would, my friend.

As I mentioned, after the invasion, I struggled for a long time with guilt and regret. I didn't have survivor guilt, but I still felt a guilt that ate away at me every day. I felt so much regret for some of the things I had to do in combat. I thought the only way to cope with the pain was to drink alcohol, but drinking only made things worse. The things I had going on in my mind and in the depths of my soul were tearing me apart.

During the invasion, I was a tank gunner on a M1A1. From time to time, throughout the next few years after the invasion, even after my other tours to Iraq, I would see my old tank commander and I would ask him if we'd done the right thing. We would have a conversation and he always reassured me that we had indeed done the right thing. I would nod my head, as if I had been convinced and felt some sort of relief, but I didn't feel any better. I continued to try and drink the pain under the table, but the pain always beat me down.

My loved ones never fully understood what exactly was going on with me. I didn't put a lot of effort into explaining it to them. I simply told them that they would never understand. It is impossible for someone to understand unless they have been there and done the things we in the military have done. Experts understand what is going on inside the brain and it does help for them to explain and break down the chemistry of PTSD, but they can't understand that immense feeling in a person's core, after they have taken a life and second-guessed themselves.

That being said, it is still helpful to listen to those who care about you, instead of shutting them out. My dad could relate to me, because he is a wise man and understands the world. I learned more from him than anyone else on this earth. I don't know where I'd be without my wife by my side. She is the one that has always been there to pick me up when I was down. So many times, she cleaned me up and put me to bed after a long night of trying to cope with the memories. She loves me so much, that she was able to forgive me after I broke her heart. She is always there for me. She listens and she gives me worthwhile advice. I don't know where I'd be without her.

Though it is very important to seek help for PTSD, it is equally important to maintain the bonds a soldier holds with his or her family and to make a conscious effort to get well. On more than one occasion throughout my time in the war, I found myself in situations where I had to engage the enemy in spite of any collateral damage. I won't go into detail about the things that took place, but I know in my heart that I did the right thing. I did what had to be done to protect the men that fought with me and they did the same for me. Today, I know that I am forgiven by GOD for all of my short-comings and I have peace by no longer blatantly living in sin.

Lord, thank you for putting people, places, and things in my path to help me realize that You are in control and that I am forgiven. In JESUS' name I pray. Amen

Sin Bomb

A sin-bomb exploded and I caught the debris.
I can blame no one else. No he or she: just me.
I was only a child when I felt the first blast.
These memories still haunt me, though they are from the past.
I did not see it and I was miles away.
In my mind the pain is stuck on replay . . .
Or should I say, used to be that way?
Or still is, but I'm in denial?
It's been a while, but every now and then I smile.
Another sin bomb hit me in close proximity.
There was shrapnel in my mind, in my eyes and in my knee.
Listen to my words: they speak to you figuratively.
In my own head is the worst place for me to be.
I caught a one-way flight to there from across the sea.
The explosion caused erosion and so I became one, too.
A sin bomb that impacts others, possibly even you.
My blast has impacted many, especially the members of my crew.
The fires are getting weaker; I'm trying to put them out.
The fires burn slowly. They are of anger, fear and doubt.
It's hard to see through the smoke. I've had to do without.
It makes it hard to breathe—what is this all about?
I must find a positive release; it scares me when I shout.
I will catch the next sin bomb and throw it back at the source.
The objective here is getting close to a normal life, of course.

My behaviors changed when I was a child, following my brother's death. He took his own life when I was just twelve years old. It's amazing how much of an affect a single, isolated incident can have on a person, especially a child. My son is ten-years-old and I can't imagine him making the mistakes that I made at such an early age, following my first traumatic experience. It would be hard to discover one day that my little boy had lost his virginity at the same young, preteen age that I did. It would be hard to find drugs in my son's backpack or bedroom or to receive a call and be told that I needed to pick up my drunken son, because he and a friend drank some other parent's alcohol. Those were the types of things that were typical of me at the young age of twelve. I didn't know what was going on with me at the time, but looking back I realize that I had PTSD as a child, following my brother's suicide.

Part of me wishes that my parents had kept a better eye on me when I was younger. The other part of me understands that everyone in my family was hurting the way I was. My parents did a great job raising us kids. Yes, we are imperfect beings and there are no perfect parents, but I can only hope to be as good a parent as my parents were to me.

I learned a lot from my parents about the responsibilities of parenting, and, although I didn't know it back then, I learned a lot from myself as a child about parenting as well. I learned just how essential it is for me to teach my children the importance of not making the same mistakes that I made. It is my duty to show them positive ways to deal with negative situations, no matter how bad things might be. I must help them discover positive ways to cope with loss, because when I was their age I didn't know how to deal with that hardship. Losing the ones I love or served with has always been the hardest thing for me to cope with and I don't want that for them. I want my kids to know that they can always depend on and talk with both me and their mother. I will no longer allow my struggle with things I have experienced in my life to negatively affect my children.

It is especially important for any soldier that has deployed or is deployable to communicate effectively with his or her children. It's hard enough as it is on children to have to be away from a parent for such a long period of time. They do not understand, regardless of their age. It's important for us as military parents to find effective ways to maintain a close relationship with our children. So much valuable time can be wasted when we don't put our children's needs above our own. I for one was guilty of this. For so long, I didn't realize that while I was self-medicating with alcohol, I wasn't dedicating the time I should have been to my kids. I was selfish. I put my wants before their needs. Though I was hurting inside, I was selfish because I didn't seek the help I needed, and my kids and my wife paid for it. I let PTSD take over my life, but before it was too late I took my life back.

I know now that I can remember those who have fallen and still have peace. I remain aware that some have to tell their children that their mother or father is never coming home. This is something my children do not have to know, because I came home. I honor the fallen by cherishing the time I have with my children. I thank GOD I was able to find a way to unwind my Marne mind.

Lord, I thank you and praise you for allowing me the time to realize Your purpose for my life. In JESUS' name I pray. Amen

DAVE

Today is Memorial Day, the day I remember my fallen brothers;
Most of all SSG Julian, though I remember the others.
He and I had plans, but we cannot follow them through.
He was and is a brother to me. I will never forget you.
We are both from Wyoming and we were going back.
That was until the day you fell under attack.
You gave your life in defense of our country.
You sacrificed everything and were taken away from your family.
Left behind were your wife and your daughter.
I am thankful to GOD you were able to meet her.
One of these days, when I get past my issues, I'll go see her again.
I want to make sure I honor you by being a good friend.
I will never forget the good times we had.
There are only good memories: none of them are bad.
We shared the same views and you were so funny.
I'll never forget how you always quoted Bill O'Reilly.
I remember you, Dan and me hanging out, drinking beer.
Things will never be the same. I haven't seen our friends in years.
When it came to soldiering, you were the very best.
No bar could be set too high: you always passed the test.
Something I never told you, but to this day is true:
I wanted to be the best NCO I could be, just like you.
You loved your family and country so much, and for these it was your
life you gave.
I love you so much, brother and I will never forget you, Dave.

My biggest problem with this disorder I'm dealing with was learning how to properly grieve and being able to talk about my friends that have fallen in combat in a positive manner. Not only that, but it has always been hard for me to hear news of any tragedy related to the war. It used to be that it didn't matter where I was: if I heard of a service member getting wounded or killed, my entire day was ruined. My mood would change. I would become angry and agitated. I would create separation between me and those I love. Basically, I would shut down emotionally because I didn't know how to handle the stress of the news I was hearing. As soon as I heard the bad news, I was already forming a plan to get away from everyone and everything, so that I could get a drink and isolate myself, in order to cope with the pain.

The memories from the friends and fellow soldiers that I lost in combat were continuously brought to the front of my mind, no matter how hard I tried to block out those painful memories. I drank as an attempt to once again block them out, but this was never the case. I never seemed to learn my lesson, and instead of achieving the effect of feeling better about my issues, things only got worse. It was always only a matter of time before I ended up in jail. The sad thing was that it didn't always have to be news of someone being injured or killed in combat.

I remember one morning I went to church with my family and everything was fine. One of the units was preparing to deploy from Fort Knox and a large portion of our church congregation were members and family members of this particular unit. The pastor asked the soon-to-be-deploying soldiers to come and stand in front of the rest of the congregation to be recognized and prayed over. I didn't realize it at the time, but because I knew they were deploying soon and I knew that it was probable that not all of them would make it home, my subconscious mind was already looking for a way to feel better, because I was already struggling with the idea of tragic events that hadn't even occurred.

Shortly after leaving church and returning to our home, my wife asked me to run to the store for a few groceries. I was more than happy to oblige, due to the fact that I was already savoring the first drink in my mind. I left the house with my short grocery list, and before heading to the store I stopped at the local shoppette to purchase a beer. I then drove to my favorite parking spot where no one could bother me, while I consumed my forty-ounces of ice cold malt liquor. I was then ready for my task at hand. To make a long story shorter, I purchased the groceries and took them home, where I had my son come out to the car and get them, and then I was off to purchase a second bottle of beer. Then onto the third, the fourth and the fifth forty-ounce bottle of beer, because to me this was the best way to cope with the pain.

Later that night, when I was making what I thought would be my last run for alcohol, I started an argument with a Military Police Officer who called for back-up, due to my being belligerent and I was once again arrested. I was placed in a holding cell, where I continued to act completely irrational, yelling at the top of my lungs and banging on the windows like a crazy person. At one point, I noticed the end of a cable poking out of the wall, where an intercom speaker had been. I walked over to it and began pulling on it. After I had several inches of cable hanging out of the wall I began pulling it up the wall, tearing through the dry wall, making an absolute mess of the cell I was in. One of the MPs rushed to the door to tell me to stop what I was doing, but I paid him no mind and continued on with my destruction of, technically speaking, government property.

I eventually had a couple of feet of cable hanging from the wall and I proceeded to wrap the cable around my neck in order to make it appear as if I were suicidal. Of course, I was not suicidal. Though I was completely irrational, I still was aware of the consequences of taking my own life, due to my Christian faith. It was my way of getting the MPs' attention, because I was tired of being in the cell for hours. I definitely got their attention.

Several MPs rushed in, put me on the ground and hog-tied me, in a manner of speaking. I continued to yell and carry on. They called an ambulance and I was carted off on a stretcher. As I was being carted from the MP station to the ambulance, I noticed one of the officers and a senior NCO (non-commissioned officer) from my unit standing outside and I yelled at them to, "F*   *   * off!" I would later be held accountable for all of my actions, but I didn't care at the time. I was taken to the hospital, where I was diagnosed as a threat to myself and then taken to the Lincoln Trail Behavioral Health Hospital in nearby Radcliff, Kentucky, where I spent the next 30 days.

Looking back at the events that took place that day, I realize that, however unfortunate, it was necessary in order for me to get the help I needed. Going to the hospital was another step toward recovery, and I am grateful that no one was hurt and that I got more of the help I needed. Desperate times do indeed call for desperate measures. I would hope that anyone reading this would reach out and help someone in need, if they know anyone in this type of predicament and realize that in order to have freedom, there is a cost.

Lord, I am grateful to You and the aid that You send, because I know that all good things are from You. In JESUS' name I pray. Amen

The Cost

Tomorrow is Independence Day, and all I can think about is the cost.
My mind is like a runaway movie reel, picturing all my brothers who were lost.
I must honor them by being the man I'm supposed to be.
I hope in the midst of the fireworks, everyone takes a moment to reflect why it is they are free.
I give thanks to GOD that I'm learning to cope with PTSD.
Most days are better than the few days and my family is happy.
I've learned not to regret and I'll never forget.
I still get anxious, to the point that I sweat.
The cost of freedom is so high. Some have to die while loved ones ask why.
The price tag, the bar code was put in place by those who would snuff out freedom.
They are the evil ones who allow Satan to lead 'em.
Just like in the movies, good always conquers over bad.
And just the same way, both have scenes that are sad.
It's still hard to put myself out in the crowd.
There are so many people and the sounds are too loud.
I feel like a prisoner in my own land.
Only those who have been there can truly understand.
I thank GOD every day for my kids and my wife,
And I am grateful to GOD that I still have my life.
That doesn't discount the pain that's still here.
I know I have to let it go and not live in fear.
Tomorrow, I'll put on a smile because it's the fourth of July.
I'll make it a point not to let my family see me cry.

The cost of freedom is indeed very expensive in many aspects. War costs money, time and most of all, lives. It's amazing when you put things in perspective: the fact that there are men and women who are willing to sacrifice everything in defense of freedom. It doesn't matter who you are: in my opinion, no one goes through the pain and suffering of not only rigorous training, but also the chaos of combat, for a small paycheck and benefits. It is much more than that. It is the American Spirit and it's what makes our country the best in the world, even among our many faults. That is not an irrational statement. Though less than one percent of Americans account for our military, it still goes to show that this country is worth fighting for: Not to mention the fact that so many Americans were willing to answer the call, after we were struck on 9/11. The unity that was felt shortly after the attack was amazing and expected. That's what we do in a crisis. We come together and those of us who can stand tall hold up the ones that can't and lend a shoulder to cry on, all the while persevering in and demanding justice. I love this country and I am proud that I was able to serve. I only wish that the kind of unity experienced during traumatic events was common.

Why does it seem to fade away, with the exception of a few holidays where we remember the cost? Those in denial would probably say that everything is fine and I realize that things could be much worse, but why is there so much anger in our country today? Nobody seems to have any patience any more. It seems as if the Golden Rule has been lost forever for most people. What happened to loving your neighbor as yourself? I have to admit, my heart had been hardened by combat for years and I had lost focus on these very principals. Now that I am coming back to my senses, I am reestablishing the importance of little things that mean so much and I thank GOD because I am responsible, with my wife, for teaching three little people what is right and wrong. While I am relearning what my core values are and what is morally sound, I instill these beliefs and this faith in them. Most of all, I show them the importance of loving everyone. As a realist, and more importantly as a Christian, I understand that this world is going to progressively get worse and that this entire place is going to eventually burn, but that doesn't mean that we can't do our best to create chain reactions of love and kindness.

As I said, I am coming back to my senses—my roots if I may—and I make it a point to respect my elders. When I open a door, I hold it open for those following close behind. When I'm in line at the grocery store and another aisle opens up, I let those waiting in front of me take their rightful turn instead of rushing over ahead of them. I stand firm in what I was taught and let ladies go first. I try my best to smile when someone is rude to me: I keep in mind that I don't know his or her story and how bad they may have it. Who knows, maybe some of these rude individuals are suffering from PTSD, just as I have been for so long.

Don't get me wrong—I still have plenty of bad days. This disorder demands a lifetime of preventative maintenance. I am, however, so grateful for being so blessed and being able to achieve the level of recovery that I have. I realize that adversity is coming, and I remain ever watchful. When I am faced with such hard times, I hope and pray that I will have the strength and courage to love.

Lord, thank You for helping me find my way out of the darkness and when I am faced with adversity, please remind me to love and to let this light that You have filled me with shine bright for those around me to see. In JESUS' name I pray. Amen

CHAPTER TWO

ENEMY ANGER

———•———

Fear is balanced by anger in battle and anger creates fear when the battle is brought home.

I Hope It Hurt

If even for a split second, I hope it hurt before you died.
It's not enough for me to know your family probably cried.
I hope you felt that spinning metal burning inside you.
What was once enemy soldiers smoking next to a T72 is now a fried crew.
I get the satisfaction of knowing I did that to you.
That's for innocence lost in two burning towers: so, to hell with you.
I can only hope that for every American, many of you died.
To know what you're really made of, I have to see you on the inside.
It's just as I thought: you're made of evil and darkness.
Wait a minute; you're just burnt from the sabot that sparked this.
Nevertheless, it was fun making you well-done.
I'm going to do a little preventative maintenance and get rid of more
than one son.
I know it hurt when I coaxed you bear-crawling hide and seekers.
You can't outrun my 7.62mm heaters in your sneakers.
I hope it hurt and I know it did when I blazed the crooked crowd.
I was inside my tank, but I didn't have to hear to know your screams
were loud.
I'm hurting you because you hurt me when you killed innocence in the
land of the free.
We do it right and bring a real fight and we don't kill your innocent out
of spite.
For every one of you I killed, I would do something that might not be
something I should.
I would bring you back to life and kill you again; hopefully before you
got me—knock on wood.
Laughing out loud, I'm at home away from the fight.
I'm still angry and vengeful; it doesn't feel right.
Who knows if this war will ever end inside?
I'll sleep now and fight you in my nightmares, until you've hurt again
and died.

I mentioned to someone once that if the path ahead is dark, then let your light shine on it. I guess throughout my recovery, I have always appreciated little tidbits of knowledge such as this . . . but is it possible? Is it possible, for example, for light to shine on a path when it is as dark as the path to healing from PTSD? So often—as was the case with me for years—we reject every possible resource of help and advice we are given. Even if it comes in the form of constructive criticism, help and advice—as broad as those terms may be—it should simply be love manifested into extended arms and opened hands, at a minimum. It is the inability of the hurting individual to help her or himself that creates distance between loved ones. Instead of reaching out, we turn our backs. Thank GOD for gifting people with patience, because I know I have tried the patience of everyone who has ever loved me, but for the life of me I can't think of a single one who has given up on me. I know I am very fortunate, especially since, in the vast majority of the world, it is trendy to be impatient. Nonetheless, is there a way for the lost (in my case, the PTSD sufferer) to turn from a wicked and harmful lifestyle without hitting rock-bottom first?

Both options are possible. It's not a matter of somehow intervening in some loved one's descent: It's a matter of loving the loved one unconditionally. The hard reality is that the individual suffering with this disorder is going to have to make a choice: The choice of what his or her rock-bottom is going to be. There were a few different occasions throughout my life when I thought I had hit my rock-bottom. Thankfully, I had enough people around me who never gave up on me and a GOD who has a plan for me and I was able to recognize these blessings. By His grace, I was able to use my GOD-given free will to come around and make the better choice, eventually.

On the other hand, there will always be suicides and penitentiaries are going to get filled. Innocent lives will be claimed by various means and mental hospitals and emergency rooms are not going out of business any time soon. The important thing to keep in mind is love and everything that comes with that four-letter word. Giving up on a loved one, though an option, is never the right choice. It is when those hurting feel lonely and unloved that they pick up speed in the descent toward rock-bottom.

For the one who is loving and hurting while watching a loved one suffer with this disorder: it is possible to love without enabling and it is necessary to love without being codependent. The law of gravity works in relationships as much as it does anywhere else—when two people are in any relationship, and one is physically or psychologically addicted, while the other is physiologically dependent on a substance or activity, the two together will indeed plummet to their rock-bottom at a much faster rate of descent, than if they were struggling alone. It takes recognition through resources, such as this book and the many others out there, to learn how to dig out of the black hole we so often get stuck in. It takes listening and accepting help. There is a world of useful knowledge available to us all. That is one of the things I had to learn. It takes listening to others when they say things that are true, but at the same time hard to hear. If someone who loves us tells us something that is meant to be helpful, then we should try to listen and weigh our options logically.

Granted, the people we love and who love us possess the ability to over-step boundaries and say hateful and hurtful things. This isn't a true manifestation of love and when this is the case, though forgiveness will be in order later, at least a temporary distance may be established. It is unwise to remain a part of any situation which is going to be counter-productive to recovery. My advice to anyone reading this is to be loving and giving, while seeking and accepting help.

Lord, let me never forget the importance of the gift that is love. I pray in JESUS' name. Amen

In America

In America, we do things that would blow your mind.
In America, we are free to search the next find.
Here we are free to stand up for our rights,
While others are free to try and take away our rights.
Here we are free to pass laws and later amend them.
It's not ok to break these laws . . . but it's ok to bend them.
In America, we're free to tax the poor and give breaks to the rich.
Here we are free to do things backwards. No, it's not a glitch.
Here we are free to print money every single day.
And each and every single day, we are free to throw it all away.
We are free to elect who we see fit, according to the book.
In a dying country, every politician is a crook.
We were free to build this nation with the use of our guns.
Now those who are trying to take them from the fathers are the sons.
In America, a man is free to marry another dude.
Not only is it unnatural: it's just plain crude.
Parents are responsible for teaching children to behave.
Our forefathers are probably turning over in the grave.
In America, we are free: there's not a single slave.
In America, we are free to do right or be read our right to waive.
This is America, the land of the free and for some of us, the home of the
brave.

I used to get so angry watching the news every day and night while I was stationed at Fort Stewart, Georgia. I would come home from work and spend hours upon hours watching the news: isolating myself and watching T.V., when I could have been spending quality family time. I used to let all of the information I would hear make me so angry. I couldn't stand to hear that the nation I had been defending for years was going down the drain. That was my irrational thought process.

I mean, it is true, the quality of our nation is decreasing all the time, morally and ethically, but that doesn't mean we are going to fail. Or we may, but there is no way that I can tell that. The point is, I would let all of the negativity I saw on television ruin most of my days, because of my irrational thought. PTSD and my inability to keep things in perspective and to think rationally led me to get angry and stressed-out, which ultimately led to drinking every single day.

I wasted a lot of time that I could have been spending more wisely, but I didn't waste too much time. I didn't refuse to see that there is another life: a better life that exists without alcohol, a life that exists without self-medicating. Today, I can say I'm an alcoholic, but I'm a nondrinker. That sounds and feels so good. I don't watch the news on a daily basis anymore, because it just doesn't put me in a good mood. Instead, I glance at the news from time to time when I'm flipping through the channels. I exercise rational thought by keeping things in perspective. I communicate effectively with my wife and we have many productive conversations throughout most of our days.

This is all possible because I was willing to change; I was willing to get help. I was willing to open up and get out of my own head. I was willing to acknowledge the importance of identifying my enablers and I got rid of them. It is my advice to anyone with this problem to find out what your enablers are and remove these things from your life or confront them and establish the changes that must be made. I made a choice, and that choice was mine and my family's well-being. We aren't perfect. We still have problems, but we are happy and we have a warm, caring, loving household because we are more spiritually-sound.

Lord, thank you for your direction and your love. Thank you for all of your many blessings. Thank you for my wife and children. I pray in JESUS' name. Amen

CORRUPT

The world is corrupt. It's bound to erupt.
Everywhere I look, I see another crook.
Women have babies from more than one dad.
It's only for an income and that is just sad.
Time and again, adults mistreat girls and boys.
Leave them alone, you. Those kids aren't your toys.
The elected official is not beneficial.
He has a hidden agenda because he is a pretenda.
The thing that hurts the very most
Happens right here at this very post.
Soldiers like me go out and fight wars.
Soldiers like me settle other men's scores.
Soldiers return home like government whores.
They say, "Hey soldier, what did you see while fighting for the free on the other side of the sea?"
The soldier saw many things, blood and death.
He watched many brothers take their last breath.
They say, "Soldier, you will be ok. We're sending you to war again in a few days."
The soldier struggles. He's in his own head.
All he can think about are those that are dead.
The soldier has trouble and then he is read.
It's time to be punished, when he needs help instead.
I realize now that I'm all alone. I realize now it's time to go home.

My alcohol use and abuse has caused me more than enough trouble throughout the years. Unfortunately, I didn't always realize that the fault was my own in every situation—that didn't come until a later point in time. That's how I work sometimes. The important thing and the only thing that mattered to me when I wrote the previous poem was that I had a pen and a pad to write on, because when I write I feel better.

It doesn't matter what the situation is or what emotion I am feeling at any giving time. When I write, I feel better. It doesn't matter if I'm angry, sad, confused, lonely or any other of the multitude of emotions humans are capable of feeling. Whenever I express myself through poetry, I am able to calm down and relax. When I'm happy and I write, I become happier. It's true. It is my escape and it is my release. It is a positive way for me to cope with the pain, the memories and the nightmares that come with my Post Traumatic Stress Disorder. It's something I really enjoy doing. It's my favorite way to express my thoughts and feelings and I would recommend that everyone at least give it a try. Even if it's just writing in a journal or maybe writing a book or short stories, it doesn't matter. It's a great coping skill and it's just plain fun.

When I wrote the previous poem, I was mad at the world. I hadn't yet accepted that I was the one responsible for causing my own misery once again. My excuse to myself was that I didn't cause my PTSD, which caused my drinking, which caused my arrest, which led to my hospitalization. The fact of the matter is, it was just that: an excuse. I allowed myself to use my trials with PTSD as a reason to get into trouble. Somehow, that was supposed to be ok. Yeah. Right. That way of thinking is absolutely insane.

The bright side is that, due to this situation, I went to get the help I needed. The other upside is I received the punishment I deserved and I learned from it. PTSD and alcohol are definitely not a good combination.

Lord, help me to always be mindful of others and their differences and their feelings. Help me to remember the importance of not being judgmental. I pray in JESUS' name. Amen

Stupid People

Is this irrational thought, or do they exist?
Not only are they here, but they also persist.
Now granted, it's irrational at the same time.
The stupid people here are so quick to drop the dime.
The stupid people here are why I write this rhyme.
One gets in another's business for absolutely no reason.
They seem to be everywhere I look. It must be stupid people season.
They're like gremlins: If you get them wet, they start to multiply.
Don't feed those stupid people after midnight, or we all will die.
Yes, I'm talking to you crook staff, though a few of you are cool.
It would be irrational for me to trust any of you. I would have to be fool.
I came here to get the help I need. I'm trying to do my best.
Most of these stupid people aren't here to help; they put me to the test.
I try to prepare for them every night by getting plenty of rest.
Here at the crook, every single day is stupid people fest.
Just about all of the social workers are ok.
I'm not quite sure if that's enough reason to stay here another day.
Stupid people are counterproductive; it might be time to go home.
I wouldn't mind staying and getting the help I need, if the stupid people
would leave me alone.
It's too bad that all who work at a place that's supposed to help cannot
be on the same page.
Some of you need a new career. Stop only collecting a check. You actors,
get off of the stage.

Cy Mulholland

I once attended an anger management class for about eight weeks with my wife, because we both were having issues with anger at the time. We would go back and forth bickering at each other over the dumbest things: Things that could have been resolved by peaceful means and could have saved a lot of time from being wasted. We attended anger management at behavioral health on Fort Knox, Kentucky, which is where a lot of my early recovery took place. Anger management proved to be a helpful tool for both of us, due to the fact that anger is a PTSD symptom. Later on in this book I will discuss how spouses and children can also acquire PTSD as a result of a mother or father, husband or wife deploying to a combat zone.

The biggest tidbit of knowledge I took away from that group were insights about irrational thought, speech, and actions. I came to realize just how much I utilized these irrational behaviors in my day-to-day life. I realized just how quick to judge others for their speech and actions I was on a daily basis.

Let me break it down "elementary-style" for everyone. For example, (and so many of us are guilty of this) I could be anywhere, such as a grocery store or the local park and see someone walking by, minding their own business, but at the same time wearing something I felt was inappropriate or carrying themselves in a manner that I disagreed with. Instantly, I would say or think something like, "What a moron." Now, was the individual actually a moron, and, if so, what made he or she a moron? The answers are no and absolutely nothing, but that was the type of thought-process that I was guilty of on a regular basis. For all I know, any given individual that I was judging for their appearance or behavior could very well be judging me for my appearance or behavior at the very same time. Just because I view things a certain way doesn't mean that's how they are.

Thanks to the valuable lessons I learned in anger management, I now have a greater respect for others and the way they carry themselves. Another thing I keep in mind is not to judge others, because I don't know their story and what makes them the person that they are. I don't know if they are hurting or angry, or what they may be feeling because of what they may have been through. I keep in mind that there are people in the world that have had a much harder life than me and I need to remain understanding and respectful of everyone at all times. It all comes down to being a good Christian and behaving myself the way my Father in Heaven would have me do. Today, I try to keep in mind the importance of letting others see the light in me through my actions. I still make mistakes, but I try to correct them and learn from them. The previous poem was an example of my irrationality and I'm proud to say that I look at things in a different light today.

Lord, help me to be mindful of my surroundings and let my first thought be to help others and not to tear them down. I pray in JESUS' name. Amen

Red Band

Come on man, red band?
You're trying to put that on my hand?
I only sat down. Why are you wearing that frown?
What was it that I did that caused you to talk to me like I'm a kid?
I came to this facility with humility to achieve peace and tranquility
And this is how you are going to treat me.?
What was it that I did? What was my offense?
What ruined your night and made you so tense?
If this is how you handle things, you must be dense.
But it's ok. You won't derail this train.
I won't allow you to get inside my brain.
But work your program, I will not do.
With your program, I am through.
Part of me wants to say what I really think of you.
But it's cool. It's fine. You won't put me behind.
You asked me to move and move I did.
I just need to take a moment and unwind.
It wasn't that serious. You must be delirious.
It doesn't make sense. With your reasoning, I'm curious.
I'm glad I stopped myself before I got furious.
Enough talk about you. Life definitely goes on.
I can't wait to go home and it won't be long.

The second time I was hospitalized was at The Brook DuPont Hospital in Louisville, Kentucky. I found myself once again struggling with alcohol because of my PTSD. I was having trouble with the memories from combat. I was constantly thinking about situations, both where I had killed and where my fellow soldiers had been killed. I was having nightmares every night and I was waking up in cold sweats. Previous to that, I refused to drink at home around my family, so instead I drank while I was away throughout the day to help cope with the pain. At least, that's what I thought I was doing. The truth was that I was making it worse. It was just a matter of time till I spiraled out of control and wound up in jail or the hospital. The following is an account of what happened the last day I had a drink.

I was in the Warrior Transition Unit (WTU) on Fort Knox, Kentucky. I went to formation that morning, and then, because I had no appointments that day, I had nothing but free time until it was time to go back for a mandatory briefing about a new policy that was being put into place. I left formation and, because I was already feeling down, I bought some beer and went off to my favorite place to isolate myself and drink: A little spot on post where no one would bother me and where there were plenty of trees to park my car under. I went there often throughout any day that I was feeling down.

This particular day, I drank 'till I was heavily intoxicated and then proceeded on to my briefing, where a few of the senior NCOs from my unit noticed me staggering and had a hunch that I had been drinking. They politely asked me to step outside, where they could smell alcohol on me and then it was off to the Military Police Station, where I blew a .079 into their breathalyzer. A couple days later, I was in the hospital for treatment once again.

The previous poem is one of many that I wrote while I was an in-patient at The Brook Hospital. There was a situation one night where the majority of the adult patients in the hospital were attending a group that took place twice a week. No one had informed me that there were seating arrangements for the groups, so I chose a random seat amongst some strangers and sat down. It wasn't long before one of the Techs stood up and came over to me and informed me that I was to move to a seat that was designated for the patients. I, being fresh off my alcohol for only a few days and still feeling cocky and rebellious, made an issue out of it. (My negative attitude came out on a regular basis. The thought-process of being

Cy Mulholland

untouchable and rebellious to any form of authority is common in those of us who have PTSD.) I could have kept quiet and done as she asked right away and there would have been no issues, but at the time that little devil on my shoulder had other plans. Anyhow, later that night, around the time I was settling down for bed, a nurse on duty came into my room and informed me that I had been put on red band status, as opposed to yellow band. If a person had a red band it meant that he or she was restricted to his or her unit in the hospital and could only participate in groups and not activities. Once again, I got what I deserved.

Lord, help me to remember that I am to remain humble and never to be aggressive. Let me remember the importance of working with others and not against them. I pray in JESUS' name. Amen

The Crook

It's all I see, it's all I can do.
It takes everything in me just to cope with you.
I had no idea this is what I was getting myself into.
You pay no respects: you only collect checks
Off of each and every one of these government prospects.
There's no need for you to play fair: you're raping Tri Care.
For you to think about your actions is so very rare.
This place is counterproductive; it's so funny.
Few of you are here to help: you're here to make money.
You want to fill the beds so you can fill your pockets.
And your bottom-feeding staff resembles a light socket:
Plug anyone in where you see fit.
If they can take your vital signs, they must be legit.
Man, I quit, I'm no longer cool with it.
I could go anywhere else and get treated like shit.
I'm the one who volunteered for you to help me.
This program is completely backwards, you see.
Think about it: I left my place of solitude, the place I felt free,
With the thought, at the time, this was the best place to be.
Only a handful of you people even understand PTSD.
I'm convinced I was wrong; this is my sad song.
No one in this place ever gets along.
I'm going to keep to myself; I'm not going to call my mama.
You were supposed to help me cope, but you only create more drama.

This poem is another prime example of me reacting irrationally through my anger, at a point in time before I'd fully changed my thought process to one where I remain conscious of rational thoughts and behaviors. I had a disagreement with a couple of the staff members at the hospital and didn't catch myself before I reacted negatively. Not too long after that incident, I realized I needed to make a change. I had to come to realize that everywhere I go there are going to be people that have different views than I do. I had to realize the importance of understanding that people have different beliefs and thoughts than mine. This doesn't mean I have to agree with them or even understand why they have them, but simply that they are important to them. It's a matter of respect and staying away from misperceptions. It is important for me, personally, to maintain my "cool," regardless of what is said, how it is said and how I perceive it. So much time can be wasted if I am careless, as I have been in the past.

I used to spend every day walking around with a chip on my shoulder. Simple things, such as a look from a stranger, someone standing to close to me, or one of my many misperceptions, could easily set me off. This always led to some form of altercation. I had to realize that, in an angry and dying world, there are always going to be those out there who feed off of conflict, as I used to do. There are always going to be people out there who wish to make others feel as miserable as they are feeling. For me, it is vitally important to stay focused and see something positive in every situation and, for those that may listen, I try to spread a positive message. It's a message of allowing your glass to remain half full on the worst days and allowing your cup to overflow on the better days.

Lord, help me to be an example of something positive in such a negative and angry world. Remind me, Father, daily of my purpose and allow me to be an outlet for Your message that others might hear. I pray in JESUS' name. Amen

The Gone Zone

You have now entered the gone zone.
Look to your left and right: you're not alone.
I hope you didn't make any plans; you're not going home.
Here, the objective is to peel back your dome,
Or jack you up so bad that you're never be the same.
Look down your sight and pull the trigger.
If my calculations are correct and it's like I figure,
Someone has a bead on you and he's going to squeeze it quicker.
Your odds will improve if you drink some liquor.
Ah, there you go. That's better, right? Now, do you see your future getting bright?
When you're feeling down, just have a sip.
I'm laughing out loud, because I know you'll never quit.
Now go on, get out there, and get on your way.
There's much to be done. You're going outside the wire today.
I really hope, but I never pray that your punk-ass gets killed while your mind is grey.
And if not you, I'm bound to get someone. I'll claim one of your brothers: it'll be so fun.
After all, you know the extent of the damage I've done.
You don't want to live anymore. Come on with me, son.
I've taken many like you, several million or so.
I've taken your friends, though I couldn't take their souls; but I was sure glad to see them go.
I blew them up. I shot them down. I sent their bodies back to the ground.
Listen to me. Join me in the unknown.
You are never, ever leaving the gone zone.

n my mind, life is like training by various means. We have the obstacle course that never ends, the strength training that is most definitely required, and of course, in order to be serious about any training regimen, we have to eat right. Spiritually, it is the same. We are called to be trained and to train. GOD has a purpose for us all and with our GOD-given free will we make the choice to live either for the world or for the Father. A common worldly deception is that PTSD cannot be overcome, but with the proper treatment and self-help it can be cured.

In order to strengthen your heart, you must commit yourself to regular and vigorous cardiovascular workouts. The harder you train, the more fit you will be, and the healthier your heart will be. The same is true when it comes to spiritual fitness. Life is an uphill battle, with the fortunate occasional plateau, but the fact of the matter is that obstacles and challenges will never cease to be thrown in our direction. They come from out of nowhere and if you're spiritually obese, then you're setting yourself up for failure.

PTSD, in a manner of speaking, is like running up a very long hill. Perhaps it would be beneficial to get on a treadmill and max out the incline and run only uphill for a couple miles. It's probably safe to say that if we run uphill for a month or so and then finally go for a run on level ground, it will be easier. One would most likely be able to run the same distance in a faster time. Is it not the same for us spiritually?

Everything we do in this life requires planning, training and execution: especially when it comes to recovery from PTSD. Of course, very often, people just shoot from the hip, but those individuals generally aren't the ones that end in success and if they do, it has been given to them by the world. The point I am making is that, in order to achieve all-around success, we must be well-rounded. In order to be well-rounded, we must be spiritually, physically and mentally fit. Anyone who already knows this can attest to the fact that you can have all or part of these, but without spiritual fitness you can have nothing after this life. It is important for me to mention that with spiritual fitness, as I call it, it is easier to have the other two. Sure, the sin-natured world can offer anyone physical and mental fitness, but it would do no one any good to inherit the entire world if they don't have JESUS in their hearts, as the Bible clearly states.

Too often, we become our own obstacles. There are various types of obstacles and I am guilty for having let much of this block my path for the majority of my lifetime thus far. My biggest obstacle throughout the years was burden. For far too long, I made every attempt to carry a burden that was far too heavy for me carry on my own. Over the course of my life, my burdens continuously piled up on top of each other until my knees gave out. I was told all of my life how to get rid of the burden, but for some reason I would never let it go. It seems that I felt as if I was *supposed* to have this burden. These deceptions come from the evil one, who is Satan. I am grateful today that I no longer carry that load.

Another obstacle that individuals place in front of themselves is greed. There are so many different forms of greed: more than the average person realizes. The stereotypical versions of greed are greed for money, women, cars and fame. We are all well aware of those, but there is a greed for time as well. This greed is common with parents and oftentimes goes hand in-hand with burden. I have to admit, I have been guilty of this also. This ugly form of greed shows its face in the form of isolation or self-absorption. Often, burden drives us to isolation, but that is not the sole cause.

There is another form of deception that comes from Satan. An example of this is when a father or a mother creates distance between themselves and their children and/or spouse until he or she altogether gives up on their commitment. The children are not the cause of their parents' decision, but often parents are deceived by the evil one in this manner: that life can be easier without the stressors of having a family. Often, individuals become just that: individuals. Some people become so self-absorbed that nothing else in life matters, not even family. This self-absorption goes hand in hand with greed and so we can clearly understand that everything mentioned works together.

I was once told by someone close to me that a rich man who this person knew told his own brother, "Money is thicker than blood." It is appalling that someone could feel that way about family, but it is not uncommon. Deceit becomes a lifestyle of sin and for many that deception comes in the belief that there is no GOD, while others believe that they somehow are a god. If there is no GOD, then there is no reason to be held accountable. If there is no GOD, speeding tickets become far more aggravating, getting married three times in one's lifetime is no big deal and planning the perfect murder is that much more possible. The Truth is that if we block out GOD, life is miserable and we do it to ourselves. But we have the choice.

My brothers and sisters, there is a GOD. He is the creator of all things. He loves us and He wants what is best for us and, given the chance, He works in our lives. He gave us free will and if we make the choice to come to Him, we then see what a real and amazing difference there will be. My challenge to anyone reading is to let go and let GOD. Talk to someone who knows about this freedom in CHRIST JESUS and get into the Word. Research and pray and ask whatever can be asked, but let it glorify GOD. This is not a message I choose to share because I think it sounds good or because it may be faddish. No, I'm sharing this because JESUS lives and He is working in my life and I want everyone to know of this freedom found in Him. Don't just take it from me, though: every Truth one could ever need in his or her life can be found in the Holy Bible. Amen

Lord, may all that I do glorify you, Father. Help me to be better today than I was yesterday. I pray in JESUS' name. Amen

Echo Motions

It's days like today when I can't control my anger.
They shouldn't have to, but my family looks at me as if I'm some kind of
stranger.
It's sad when the head of the home provides a feeling of danger.
My judgment is poor; I always do the wrong thing.
I'm so pissed off; I just have to break something.
I'm so mad, I could come out of my skin.
Instant gratifications followed by guilt follow sin.
I feel so bad and need to feel good.
My plan is to do wrong, not what I should
Then turning to the ones I love just to push them away.
The guilt brings me down again; there must be a better way.
Guilt turns to anger and distance is created.
Alone, I carry my burden; I feel so over-weighted.
A loving family is what I have to provide my every need.
In my mind, it's not enough to satisfy my greed.
So many attempts to fill the void, until I feel regret.
Somehow, for some reason, she hasn't left me yet.
Sadness to anger, and greed to guilt;
The more damage I cause, the more the family will wilt.
Still, there is pain and emptiness burning inside me.
I've given up on all reason and the one who guides me.
I hate it so bad; I can't stand the loss.
Defiant of all authority: no one is my boss.
Senselessly, I am the cause of so much commotion.
I must somehow get control of my emotions.

One very important fact that I have learned in the recovery process is that it is ok to be angry: however, it is *not ok* to allow my anger to negatively impact others. Learning this takes practice: a lot of it. I have been practicing for a long time and I still have plenty of room for growth. It's a matter of repetition, and gaining the ability to call yourself out when you're wrong and swallowing your pride so that apologies can be made. Whether we are forgiven or not, though important, is not essential. To better combat the things that make us angry, we have to take an in-depth look at what it is that makes us angry. What is the root cause, the source? Why is anger a common response to trauma?

According to the Department of Veterans Affairs, anger is often a large part of a survivor's response to trauma. It is a core piece of the survival response in human beings. Anger helps us cope with life's stresses by giving us energy to keep going in the face of trouble or blocks. Yet anger can create major problems in the personal lives of those who have experienced trauma and those who suffer from PTSD. One way of thinking is that high levels of anger are related to a natural survival instinct. When faced with extreme threat, people often respond with anger. Anger can help a person survive by shifting his or her focus. The person focuses all of his or her attention, thought, and action toward survival.

Anger is also a common response to events that seem unfair, or in which you have been made a victim. Research shows that anger can be especially common if you have been betrayed by others. This may be most often seen in cases of trauma that involve exploitation or violence. The trauma and shock of early childhood abuse often affects how well the survivor learns to control his or her emotions. Problems in this area lead to frequent outbursts of extreme emotions, including anger and rage. So how can anger after trauma become a problem?

The VA states that in people with PTSD, their response to extreme threat can become "stuck." This may lead to responding to all stress in survival mode. If you have PTSD, you may be more likely to react to any stress with "full activation." You may react as if your life or self were threatened. This automatic response of irritability and anger in those with PTSD can create serious problems in the workplace and in family life. It can also affect your feelings about yourself and your role in society.

Researchers have broken down posttraumatic anger into three key aspects, discussed below. These three factors can lead someone with PTSD to react with anger, even in situations that do not involve extreme threat:

AROUSAL

Anger is marked by certain reactions in the body. The systems most closely linked to emotion and survival—heart, circulation, glands, brain—are called into action. Anger is also marked by the muscles becoming tense. If you have PTSD, this higher level of tension and arousal can become your normal state. That means the emotional and physical feelings of anger are more intense. If you have PTSD, you may often feel on edge, keyed up, or irritable. You may be easily provoked. This high level of arousal may cause you to actually seek out situations that require you to stay alert and ward off danger. On the other hand, you may also be tempted to use alcohol or drugs to reduce the level of tension you're feeling.

BEHAVIOR

Often the best response to extreme threat is to act aggressively to protect yourself. Many trauma survivors, especially those who went through trauma at a young age, never learn any other way of handling threat. They tend to become stuck in their ways of reacting when they feel threatened. They may be impulsive, acting before they think. Aggressive behaviors also include complaining, "backstabbing," being late or doing a poor job on purpose, self-blame, or even self-injury. Many people with PTSD only use aggressive responses to threaten. They are not able to use other responses that could be more positive.

THOUGHTS AND BELIEFS

Everyone has thoughts or beliefs that help them understand and make sense of their surroundings. After trauma, a person with PTSD may think or believe that threat is all around, even when this is not true. He or she may not be fully aware of these thoughts and beliefs. For example, a combat Veteran may become angry when his wife, children, or coworkers don't "follow the rules." He doesn't realize that his strong belief is actually related to how important it was for him to follow rules during the war, in order to prevent deaths.

If you have PTSD, you may not be aware of how your thoughts and beliefs have been affected by trauma. For instance, since the trauma, you may feel a greater need to control your surroundings. This may lead you to act inflexibly toward others. Your actions then provoke others into becoming hostile towards you. Their hostile behavior then feeds into and reinforces your beliefs about others. Some common thoughts of people with PTSD are:

"You can't trust anyone."

"If I got out of control, it would be horrible, life-threatening, or could not be tolerated."

"After all I've been through, I deserve to be treated better than this."

"Others are out to get me," or "They won't protect me."

How can you get help with anger?

In anger management treatment, problems with arousal, behavior and beliefs are all addressed in different ways. Cognitive-behavioral treatment (CBT), a commonly-used therapy, uses many techniques to manage these three anger problem areas:

For increased arousal

The goal of treatment is to help the person learn skills that will reduce overall arousal. He or she may learn how to relax, use self-hypnosis, and use physical exercises that release tension.

For behavior

The goal is first to look at how a person usually behaves when he or she feels threatened or stressed. The next goal is to help him or her expand the range of possible responses. More adaptive responses include:

- Taking a time-out
- Writing thoughts down when angry
- Talking with someone instead of acting
- Changing the pattern "act first, think later" to "think first, act later"

For thoughts/beliefs

Clients are given help in becoming more aware of their own thoughts leading up to becoming angry. They are then asked to come up with more positive thoughts to replace their negative, angry thoughts. For example, they may learn to say to themselves, "Even if I don't have control here, I won't be threatened in this situation." Another example would be, "Others do not have to be perfect in order for me to survive or be comfortable." Role-play is often used so you can practice recognizing the thoughts that make you angry and applying more positive thoughts instead.

(Chemtob, C.M., Novaco, R.W., Hamada, R.S., Gross, D.M., & Smith, G. (1997). Anger regulation deficits in combat-related posttraumatic stress disorder. Journal of Traumatic Stress, 10(1), 17-35.)

There are many ways to help people with PTSD deal with the high levels of anger they may feel. Many people have all three of the anger problem-areas listed above. Treatment aims to help with all aspects of anger. One important goal of treatment is to improve your sense of flexibility and control. In this way, you do not have to feel as if you're going through trauma again each time you react to a trigger with explosive or excessive anger. Treatment may also have a positive impact on personal and work relationships.

There are many valuable resources available to help those who are suffering with PTSD and all of these resources have been put in place or allowed by GOD himself. It is clearly stated in the Word that nothing touches us that doesn't first pass through GOD's hands. In the same light, all good things are blessings that come from GOD and it is His will that we should all seek Him first in our lives. It is through Him that we should pray and ask for forgiveness, healing and wisdom and through His mercy, we will receive all of these things.

Lord, let me never lose focus of who I am because of who You are. I pray in JESUS' name. Amen

CHAPTER THREE

THE ADDICTION DISPOSITION

A deception of the evil one, a floodgate for painful memories,
and a misconception that sorrow can be masked.

Self-Medication

Did anybody notice? Could anybody see?
No one ever told me this could happen to me.
I knew what I was doing, but I didn't know why.
I knew I could get help, but I wouldn't even try.
A Marne Soldier for ten years with five deployments under my belt;
"Fight the war" and "Don't be weak" are the cards I was dealt.
So what does one do? Self-medicate or die.
To make the pain go away, I drank and got high.
High is a feeling that can be achieved in so many ways—
I consumed alcohol, smoked dope, and ate pills for many days.
There was another high that I chased for years.
It brought on the most pain and to this day brings tears.
My wife has always given me everything I need.
Yet I continued to chase the ultimate high with my greed.
For years, I went outside our marriage for sex.
I was addicted, but I didn't realize its harmful effects.
When the truth came out, it was like many train wrecks.
Self-medication, it seems, was not the way to go.
I was not aware of the symptoms that I would show.
All I knew is what I thought made me feel so good—
The rush of doing wrong and not what I should.
The feeling of knowing I still had IT.
What is IT and who gives a shit? There was intense guilt, but I wouldn't quit.
Self-medication is my complication.
There are PTSD-filled soldiers all over this nation.
It's overwhelming to think of what they expect from us.
Three trips, five trips, the greater good, get on the bus.
I've met soldiers with seven deployments plus.
There's no Zoloft or Prozac that will matter to him.
It's too late. He'll self-medicate and his future is grim.
Your chances of bringing them back to a normal life are slim.
Fortunately for me, I have a strong supporting cast.
With proper treatment, I'm on my way at last.

A couple hospital stays and intensive out-patients have past.
Along the way, there has been the occasional relapse.
Now I know how to pick up the phone and use the right apps.
Just playing, but really now I use my resources.
Instead of self-medication I take proper action, the right courses.
I utilize the proper people, places and things for my sources.
It's all about finding your very own coping skills.
You have to get away from hiding and exploring cheap thrills.
Let Tri-Care pay for your treatment and you take care of your bills.
Self-medicating has proven to be deadly: it kills.
Asking for help is not a weakness: it shows you are strong.
Reaching out can save your life: you cannot go wrong.
Listening to others is what I should've done all along.
Take my words for it. I'm a veteran of all the above.
Don't depend on self-medication: depend on love.

I was sitting around the house one weekend in the afternoon, not doing anything other than thinking, which is normal and a regular occurrence for me. I find that it is good for me to set aside time for myself to process everything going on in my life, while ensuring that it doesn't turn into isolation. I remain fully aware of what my positive intent is and I do not let it turn into separation from my family.

As I was sitting there at my desk, I was wondering what it could have been that made my lack of interest in school as a child so extensive. I already knew that the majority of the problems I encountered as a child were obviously due to my brother's suicide, but why did I never turn from my negative ways and find new interest in the things that mattered most in my life? Then it hit me. When my brother died, my young, impressionable, maturing mind had been, in a sense, paused where it was during the time-frame in which I experienced the traumatic event.

As I began to put the pieces together with the help of the "experts"—most notably, Dr. Hoge, who wrote, Once A Warrior, Always A Warrior,—I realized that the only time in my entire life that I finally received any form of relief for my PTSD symptoms was when I finally received treatment as an adult. The only reason I received treatment was because of the traumatic events I experienced during combat.

With the help of therapy and medication, I was able to begin my journey toward a normal life. Though I came to realize that the reason I struggled throughout my childhood in school was due to the loss of my big brother, it wasn't only a matter of my subconscious mind holding in place, but I was also grieving and giving up in other aspects. I went from being a bright young kid who excelled in school to not caring enough to feel motivated about some subjects and not being able to comprehend the things I was being taught in other subjects. I especially struggled with more technical subjects, such as math and science.

It was because my subconscious mind was, in a manner of speaking, stuck on pause as far as the age of understanding was concerned. Instead of advancing mentally along with my peers, I stayed behind when it came to the ability to process technical, detailed information. On the other hand, it only makes sense that due to this same fact, I grew stronger in other subjects, such as English, where I was able to process the thoughts and emotions that were on my mind. This is what the experts tell us is one of the most productive forms of therapy. Writing poetry became the most useful and helpful tool I have in my tool bag.

I had always enjoyed writing as a kid, but I didn't really know why. When it came to writing essays and reports, I always scored very well. One of my favorite classes in school was one where I participated in creative writing. Now I understand why I enjoy writing so much. Some people play instruments, some sing, and others read, but I write. It's what I love to do. It is the best way for me to express myself, because it allows me to put my thoughts, feelings, emotions and opinions on paper, which in turn allows me to see it directly in front of me. It is the most effective way for me to process both the memories from my childhood and the war.

My writing poetry is not only beneficial to me, but to those around me as well. My family can be around a more calm and level-headed dad and husband because of the treatment I have received and the coping and survival skills I have acquired. Now, when I go out in public, I don't feel confrontational. I make it a point to have some kind of conversation with a stranger or to help an elderly man or woman reach something. I notice that as time passes, I grow closer and closer to a normal life. Yes, I still prefer to sit with my back to the wall while dining at a restaurant and I always know where all the exits are, but this is normal and recovery takes time. The truth is, recovery with PTSD lasts a lifetime: however, with proper treatment and the skills necessary for successful recovery, it does get easier.

The most important thing we can do in our recovery is to build a relationship with JESUS CHRIST. I know from first-hand experience, the more I pray and seek His guidance and make sound, moral decisions, the better off I feel and the smoother my daily life is. I've mentioned this more than once, but I will be forever thankful to GOD for allowing me to meet Rich, the Vietnam Veteran at Lincoln Trail Behavioral Health Hospital, because he is the one that introduced me to my favorite hobby and most valuable coping skill.

Lord, I pray that You will guide the many out there who are in need of help and healing, due to the trauma they have experienced, to resources that can point them in the right direction: toward a normal life. I pray in JESUS' name. Amen

Burden to Bourbon

Burden to bourbon, sloppy and slurring;
Drinking so much that the vision is blurring;
The feelings inside that here is no hope.
Turning to the drink in order to cope:
Instant gratification with my liquid dope.
So begins a wild ride down this slippery bourbon-lined slope.
Burden to bourbon and then the other way around.
Bourbon to burden when I hear that siren sound.
So many arrests, so much money down the drain.
The thought that next time won't be the same is insane.
Pain and misery, no one else to blame;
Helpless and hopeless, this demon I cannot tame.
Something has to change. I don't want things the same.
The night is for sleep and not for the drink.
It's in the Word, not only what I think.
The drink, the drug and the high till I die.
The alcoholic cannot, it does not matter why.
The deceit, the cheat and the never-ending lie—
The countless times we make our loved ones cry.
Burden to bourbon and all of the other booze,
Nor any other drug of choice is any path to choose.
Bourbon leads to burden; if I drink, I will lose.
I'm a drunk and an addict: I will not use.
When I'm clean and sober, I'm no longer confused.

went through a phase about a year after I came home from my third tour in Iraq where I only drank bourbon whiskey. It didn't really matter what kind it was and, though I had a favorite, I'm not about to advertise an alcoholic beverage. It was just another way for me to drown my memories.

During this phase of my struggle with PTSD, I hadn't yet begun to isolate. I would stop at the shoppette every day after work and purchase a fifth of bourbon, if I didn't already have a bottle in the refrigerator. Then, I would go home and drink and hang out with the family until I decided to go to bed. The problem with this was, most of the time, I drank to the point that I was drunk and I would get angry, which led to me yelling and possibly breaking things in the midst of my drunken tirade. Often, once I became mad enough, I would leave the house to drink and drive, simply because I thought it was fun. I didn't think twice about the fact that I was putting other people's lives in danger. Somehow, I managed to never hurt anyone and somehow I never got arrested for drunk-driving.

Perhaps I would have learned my lesson sooner if I had. The truth is, I would not learn my lesson until I received the treatment that I desperately needed. If I had not gone to therapy and taken the medication I was prescribed and if I had not gone to anger-management and not been hospitalized more than once, chances are that I would still be a mess or dead or in jail today. For people like me, getting into some kind of trouble is what it takes to initiate the long journey toward recovery.

Unfortunately, many who suffer don't get into trouble and receive it as a wake-up call. Many do not listen to the advice of loved ones or co-workers. An organization that I will not reference refers to these individuals as "unfortunates" and states that they must have been born that way. However, though some are unfortunate, nobody is destined to live as a drunk for their entire life. It is a choice that is made by a weak and burdened mind. Satan has powerful influences and though you can't see it, he tells us, the alcoholics, that the best way to forget about our problems is to drink them away, because for a little while the problems *will* go away.

This deception of instant gratification is just that: a deception. I don't know of anybody who has experienced a traumatic event of some kind and resorted to alcohol as a means of coping, and somehow their lives became more manageable because of it. The opposite is true. When these individuals—such as myself—resort to alcohol and/or drugs for a cure, more times than not these chemicals we put into our bodies act as a gateway for the painful experiences and memories to come pouring out, in the form of negative speech and actions. I was too stubborn for so long and wouldn't listen to those around me when they told me I had a problem and needed help.

My recommendation to anyone reading this who knows someone suffering in these ways would be to never give up on them and, though it may be difficult to watch and tiresome to accomplish, to keep in mind that if these individuals are not somehow reached, they could end up in jail, or worse.

Prayer is the most valuable tool a person can use when trying to help someone in need. Prayer, combined with love and lots of effort to reach into the depths of the mind and soul of the individual hurting, is a great place to start when trying to help.

Lord, thank You for putting people in my life that truly love and care enough about me to not give up on me and who continuously make efforts to pick me up when I am down. I pray in JESUS' name. Amen

Temptation

It comes from the tempter when I'm unaware.
I leave clear thought for not having a care.
He attacks me in so many ways, throughout all of my days.
It's spiritual warfare with these games that he plays.
Others seem so strong, where I am so weak.
I have a hard time controlling my thoughts, actions and the words
that I speak.
It used to be that I struggled with drugs and alcohol.
When it comes to drugs, I've pretty much tried them all.
When he realized he could no longer get me with that,
He hit me with alcohol and sex like a bat.
It's been that way for the majority of my life.
I've always been an alcoholic and I even cheated on my wife.
I received some education and realized I was addicted to sex.
That's what the world says anyway, but I know it's his hex.
I pray every day and I no longer drink or cheat.
I stopped looking online for girls I could meet.
I have a beautiful wife. She's everything I want and need.
There's no peace or happiness when giving in to Satan's greed.
One thing is true, and that is he will never stop.
The seeds have been sown, but he's trying to steal the crop.
He comes at me with things such as energy drinks and credit cards.
I know it seems strange. I know it sounds bizarre.
He tells me it's a great idea to go out and buy a new car.
From now on, I'm going to do what's right, because I'm not lost by far.

The most important thing, that most of us forget, is to love with every single thing we say and do. When we speak we should speak love. Our actions should reflect love. Everything we do should be done in a loving manner . . . but it's not something that can be acted out. No, it must come from the heart.

It took a lot for me to realize what this truly meant, but I understand it now. I came to the realization that when I yell at my wife or kids, it is not loving. When I isolated myself from them, it was not loving. When I wasted all the time that I did with drinking, I did not love. When I cheated on my wife, I did not love. Every violent act of fighting, cursing, scaring, road raging, threatening, were not out of love. Every time I was disrespectful to any form of authority, it was not done in a loving manner. When I have been rude, sarcastic and arrogant, these things were done in a hateful fashion and no doubt my actions made others not want to love me back. The most important thing in this world we are all called to do is to love.

That being said, the most forgotten thing in this world seems to be the importance of loving everyone. We are not perfect beings and we never will be. We should not expect ourselves to be perfect or we will only set ourselves up for disappointment. The most important thing we can do is strive to be our best and not discount ourselves. An honest effort is just that: an honest effort.

However, just because we know we will make mistakes doesn't mean we have the right to. There was a time when that was how I thought. I would act out now and ask for forgiveness later. To willingly do wrong and have a preplanned apology and repentance is to knowingly and acceptingly create separation: Separation between kids, wife, mother, father, best friend, any other loved one, but most importantly GOD. Not only that, but by lying to yourself this way, you lie to GOD and imply that He is not all-knowing and all-powerful. It is the worse form of disrespect anyone could ever show, because it is disrespecting our Father in Heaven, our Creator. I am guilty of this and I realize now the severity of my wrong-doings. I also know that GOD loves me more than I could ever fathom. I know how much I love my children and He loves us all more than that.

Another very important thing to remember is that, when people achieve this awareness and understanding, they are that much more accountable for their actions: meaning that to know something is wrong and do it anyway and later feel guilty about it is different than being fully aware of

GOD's purpose for one's life and willfully defying Him. He sent JESUS to die for our sins and it is heinous to state through our actions that we are willing to take JESUS, who loves us more than we can ever imagine, and nail him to the cross all over again. That sounds intense because it is, and I was guilty of carrying myself that way for years. "I'll just do this and do that and ask for forgiveness later," was my thought process. As if I was sneaking anything passed my Father!

Today, I am fully aware of who I am and I fully understand what LOVE isn't. It is not words. It is so much more. Love doesn't discriminate. It is not concerned with how a person looks or how a person talks or what a person does. It doesn't agree with everyone, but it remains true. It is never hateful, because it doesn't possess the ability to be. Real, honest, true love is just that: love. We are called by GOD to love.

Lord, I can never put into words just how grateful I am for your love and, though it still doesn't compare to how much You love me, I can honestly say that I love You, Father. I pray in JESUS' name. Amen

Anti-Sober

Today, I received news that my friend went back in.
I don't know what happened, except that he drank again.
I was at home, actively participating in sobriety.
I wish my phone had ringed, but he didn't call me.
I would have been there, to lend a helping hand.
We could have had a conversation, man-to-man.
If there is one thing I know, it's we must put our sobriety first.
We must reach out for help to overcome the thirst.
I hope you make it back. Only time will tell.
I fear if you don't live sober, you'll end up dead or in jail.
I know you are going through a very tough time.
Not everything comes easy; to get to the top, you have to climb.
It kills me to know that you knew what would happen after.
Most likely, now you will finally have earned that chapter.
Where will you go from here? What path will you choose?
I don't think she's coming back, but will you continue to lose?
Will you blow off sobriety with excuse after excuse,
All because you love the pain of self-abuse?
You still have two young men that look up to you.
Every son needs their dad around and we both know that's true.
You need to wise-up and realize you probably don't have a wife.
All I can offer is an ear and maybe some advice.
I hope you'll talk to someone and before you drink again, think twice.

Everyone I know (including myself) who has experienced trauma, not only initially looked for negative ways to cope, but also later took on a new attitude. We become more abrasive, edgy, short tempered and angry. We become independent, but not in a good way. We become known for the chip on our shoulders, rather than for what in many cases used to be smiles and a kind demeanor. We become this way, because our hearts have become hardened and cold and the way back to normal is anything but easy.

What about when we get close to our normal lives and things are feeling good? Some who are reading might not yet be there, but rest assured, when you get there it will be worth the hard work. For those that are close to good or normal or whatever you would call it, you know exactly what I'm talking about. It's that point in recovery where all of the treatment is starting to pay off and a new sense of awareness is achieved. Medications have been worked out between patient and doctor, and the proper chemical balance now allows the patient to think, focus and concentrate with an ability that used to be strange. Coping skills are so much more than coping skills: they are a blessed discovery and can even become an enjoyable part of life. It is important not to become complacent, and self-contingencies have been established for stressful situations that arise or triggers that are observed.

It's almost as if there are no obstacles that could block the patient's path, but sometimes, in the midst of all this success, something happens. A button is pushed that was partially unexpected and for a moment that thought that you have grown to reject enters your mind, accompanied by a feeling of doubt. Why and how is this possible, when we are leaning forward in the saddle and things are going so well? First, the obvious fact about the world we live in: The deck is stacked against us and these negative situations are different for all of us.

For example, the other day I went to work and I was feeling great. I hadn't thought about having a drink in days and, let's face it, we all think of the negative coping skill of our choice once in a while, whether it be a beer commercial or alcoholic beverages on a store shelf. Either way, I was feeling great, until another individual said some hateful and rude words to me. After that, for a large portion of the day, I felt down and my mind began to wander. For a moment, I thought about a drink and I quickly dismissed it. But what if I had been weak in that moment?

Let me back up to the root of my problem that day. My mistake was the very second I gave that other individual power over me. We have to remain in control of our train of thought. It's hard work at times, but it is essential. The subconscious mind still does and always will crave any addicts' drink or drug of choice. Experts such as Retired Colonel Charles W. Hoge explain in detail how powerful the subconscious mind is. It is crucial for those in recovery to focus on, maintain and constantly strengthen their will-power. How do we do this? We become better educated.

This can be done in more ways than one. It's more than just reading various books about our disorder, because many of us are already doing this. For those who are not researching their disorder, I strongly encourage them to do so. There is a world of knowledge out there on PTSD and it gets more and more attention all the time. I appreciate reading other peoples' experiences and what works for them in their recovery. Another way—and I will mention this more than once—is to seek higher academic education. From personal experience, I can say that going back to school has been very beneficial for me and my recovery. Due to the fact that I first experienced trauma when I was just eleven-years-old, I lost the desire to excel in school as a child. As my recovery progressed and I began to feel and realize that I was indeed getting closer to a normal life, I regained the desire to go back to school and that's exactly what I did.

Turns out, I'm actually good at it. I'm much better at school now at the age of thirty-two than I was as a kid, because I no longer have the disconnect that existed in my brain for so many years. Where my traumatized mind rejected school, ditched school and failed classes intentionally, my clear mind now strives to do the best I can. I do my very best to get the best grade I can. I study hard and I even do extra credit assignments. My worst subject throughout my entire childhood was math, but as an adult and after much treatment, I now love math and I'm actually pretty good at it. I am currently pursuing a bachelor's degree as a radiologist assistant. It is very exciting and it is my recommendation that everyone strive to further their education. For me, it is a feeling of accomplishment and I learn something new every day.

By educating ourselves, listening to the experts and achieving a higher academic education, we are able to strengthen our minds and repair our mental capacity, which helps us grow toward a normal life. By building ourselves up physiologically instead of tearing ourselves down, we are able to once again become excited, motivated, and emotionally in tune with our loved ones—and that alone is worth the effort.

Lord, thank You for the strength and courage to turn away from temptation and deception. I am grateful to You for the spiritual growth I am experiencing on a daily basis. I pray in JESUS' name. Amen

I Don't Remember the Time

I don't remember the time so many things took place.
I cannot recall much of that, which was a waste.
Drinking associates have told me stories of my past.
I consumed so much, that my senses didn't last.
It's not even funny how I've acted like a fool. I hate to admit it, but at
the time I was a tool.
Thinking I was so cool, trying to be the party's life.
There have been so many fights. I even slept with another's wife.
So many arrests and waking up in random places.
So many expenses and waking up next to strange faces.
Returning to my home and not remembering how I got there,
Or coming home just before the sun comes up and my wife is still
sitting there.
I used to be the host with the most when I lived near the coast.
Trust me, I'm not trying to brag. I don't mean to boast.
What I'm saying is I supported peoples' habits that I didn't even know.
I wasted time and money, putting on a lame show.
I exposed my family to people, places and things they didn't need to see.
And I can't even remember it all. The blame falls on me.
I wasn't where I should've been, but this is what I know.
Today, I'm clean and sober. It's time for us to grow;
To grow in love, have peace and harmony and be free.
Free-spirited as a group is the only way to be.
Looking toward the future with faith and hope,
Their love is my drug. I don't need liquid dope.

I t's funny now to think back to some of the times when my drunken behaviors were absolutely ridiculous. Then there are some that were not funny at all. When I see others in passing or from a distance who are drunk and appear to be having a tough time, even if they think they are having a good time, I am saddened. I am saddened because I know all too well what those behaviors can lead to. It's usually not hard to decipher a normal drinker from an alcoholic, especially when one is a sober alcoholic. It's well-known that we alcoholics have plenty of stories. Here is one of mine, and every single one of my stories is a testament of why not to drink, if you has a traumatized mind.

There was a time, like so many times, when I left my wife and kids at home to go out and drink with what I call "drinking associates," due to the fact that more times than not, they are not true to the term "buddies." So there I was, leaving the house and on my way to Savannah, Georgia to meet up with a couple other unfortunate individuals. Already visualizing the first drink in my mind, I could almost taste the alcohol. As I exited I-16 and pulled into Savannah, I called one of the guys and we arranged a specific bar at which to meet. Once there, I ordered up a beer, followed by a mixed drink, followed by a beer and so on. Mixing beer with hard liquor was typical for me. It made for a quicker buzz and my mission was always to get as drunk as I possibly could. Isn't it funny how we do that to ourselves, knowing how painful the next day is going to be? Much of the time, we can't even remember half of the fun we supposedly had, so it is entirely not worth it. Of course, the alcoholic who is in denial will disagree with me and for that person I am hopeful.

We kept things simple at first, while hopping from bar to bar, having a drink or two at each one. As the night wore on, the two guys who accompanied me began to tell me a story of a Lieutenant who went by the nickname "The Terminator." They explained how he would hang out with some of the guys from their unit on occasion at a local bar and he would buy all the drinks. It didn't sound like a bad idea, but they went on to explain that he bought the drinks one after the other and everyone had to pound the drinks as soon as they were placed in front of them. They told me how "The Terminator" had literally punished soldier after soldier, who thought they were up to the challenge. Being the arrogant and cocky drunk that I was, I stated that they should give him a call and see if this Terminator would meet up with us. The only thing on my mind was getting endless free booze. I had no idea what I was getting myself in to.

The call was made and less than an hour later this guy, whose reputation preceded him, was sitting at the same table we were and the onslaught of drinks began immediately. We pounded drink after drink and I could feel that I was getting very highly intoxicated, but my false sense of pride would not allow me to be drunk under the table. At one point in time during the fiasco, I noticed that the one purchasing all of the drinks was buying a different kind of alcohol than he was buying for the rest of us. I called him out on it and switched his drink with mine, but it was too late.

The last thing I remember was walking down the steps and out of the bar. Apparently, I immediately got separated from the people I was with and I wandered aimlessly for the next couple hours, losing my wallet, shoes and cell phone. At one point, I stopped to urinate on a tree while a Savannah Police Officer was looking right at me. Of course, I was arrested and taken to the Military Police Station on Hunter Army Airfield, where I was placed in a holding cell. From there, my 1st Sergeant was called and he came to pick me up. Needless to say, he wasn't very happy, because he had to drive forty-five minutes from Fort Stewart. We pulled into Fort Stewart as the sun was coming up and drove to the unit where we worked. I called my wife to come and pick me up and I went home and went to bed. A few weeks later, I was standing in front of a judge in my dress uniform, where I pled guilty to public intoxication and something along the lines of public indecency, for the fact that I had made a neighborhood tree my urinal. My fines totaled somewhere close to five-hundred dollars: five-hundred dollars that I took away from my wife and kids.

This is only one story of many like it and I'm happy to say that I don't act like that today. With the useful tools that I have learned to combat triggers and temptation and a strong will that has been fine-tuned by many mistakes and a lot of help, I will never again find myself in a complacent state of mind. I will avoid setting myself up for failure and I will achieve success by a constant drive within the depths of my soul to be the father and husband I am called to be. I will pray that someone out there in the world who is reading my experiences will stop and make the decision that I and millions like me have made: It is my hope that someone reading this will make the decision to live a fulfilled, worthwhile life of accomplishment, as opposed to continuously tearing him or herself down and living miserably. There is so much more to life than the pain and the suffering that goes along with it and there is a lot to be said about doing what is right and good.

Galatians 6:9
Let us not become weary in doing good, for at the proper time
we will reap a harvest if we do not give up.

2 Thessalonians 3:13
And as for you, brothers and sisters, never tire of doing what
is good.

Lord, let the words in this book help someone struggling the same way I did, or similar to that, to learn from my experiences and find a better life through You and Your Word. I pray in JESUS' name. Amen

Scary Thought

Without a doubt, I thought I had it figured out.
Turns out staying sober is a life-long bout.
Next week, my family is going out of town.
Can I handle the effects of having nobody around?
It's a scary thought to question myself on how I will feel.
I must come up with a plan. This thing is for real.
This stuff is serious. There is so much at stake.
There are so many factors in my life that can't afford another mistake.
My family is visiting our old home and asked me to come along.
Going with them is a scary thought . . . so much could go wrong.
Old friends and old drinking buddies—they all drink most of the time.
Because I care, I won't go there. To drink would be a crime.
I will stay home and yes, I will be alone.
The temptation will come and I will pick up the phone.
A loved one will definitely talk some sense into me.
I'll keep my sobriety and remain burden-free.
I have a plan, without a doubt and that is what it's all about.
With this kind of attitude, I'm headed down the correct route.
It's a scary thought to have a one-track mind.
And an eight-track mind is hard to find.
So I multi-task and plan ahead.
My best bet is to stay home, as you've already read.
So with one additional phrase, I'll end this thread.
I'll stay alert and stay alive, as opposed to becoming complacent and dead.

For some of us, will-power is something that is very hard to strengthen. For me, if it wasn't one thing, it was the other. I would take away drinking and add multiple sexual partners. I would take away the sex and I would add drugs. I would take away drugs and go right back to alcohol. This was my cycle. It never failed. I would become motivated about stopping one, without taking into consideration that I was already destined to fail with another addiction. Even before I quit doing something in excess, my subconscious mind was already processing how to make the loss of those feel-good chemicals better with replacement chemicals. Once an individual is down and finds something that instantly makes everything better, that individual then craves whatever it is. Even if it was sex that my mind was craving, there was still a chemical reaction there that made me feel good when I was down. And with sex, it was more than just the sex itself—it was the rush of putting the whole thing together and doing something that I wasn't supposed to be doing. It included getting on online dating websites and searching for just the right female to have a secret encounter with. It was also very stressful, keeping these behaviors from my wife.

It all seems ludicrous, and that is because it is. Who in their right mind goes outside of a happy marriage to be with another woman he found on the internet? The answer is, in cases such as this, nobody in their right mind does these things. However, a man or woman who is hurting from a traumatic experience, in desperate need of instant gratification, does do these things and needs real help, instead of self-medication.

I was actually diagnosed as a sex-addict during my first visit to the Mental Health Hospital and I will refer to this on occasion, throughout the contents of this book. As a Christian, I both agree and disagree with this label of sex-addict. Don't get me wrong: an individual can just about be addicted to anything and it's true we do indeed become addicted to various things. The thing I have a problem with is the misdiagnosis of the underlying problem.

We all know that everything that takes place in our bodies and minds is a chemical reaction to something else. When we drink coffee, we are stimulated. When we eat sugar, we get hyper. When we are in a fire-fight, we are capable of doing things we wouldn't normally be able to do. Based on the sensation or intensity of these things, we often want more of it. Everything that takes place within us is, in one way or another, due to some kind of chemical reaction, but it is not only a chemical reaction and it is not the cause of the problems, the troubles and the heartaches we inflict upon ourselves and others.

In fact, these issues do not begin with us; they begin with he who deceives: Satan. For those that are reading and aren't familiar with Christianity or the Holy Bible, know that there is indeed an evil spiritual entity who tempts us all to make bad decisions. However, the fault is still our own. We knowingly make the decision to do right or wrong, good or evil. The chemical reaction that one's body and mind are experiencing the moment a thought enters a person's mind telling he or she that this person needs a drink or drug or sex goes hand-in-hand with what is happening within the individual spiritually: Meaning that Satan influences us with a temptation that we are vulnerable to and we willfully accept and indulge. Obviously, this occurs with more than sex, drugs and alcohol, but given the nature of this book, I won't go into details about those. I will mention that the murderer is affected spiritually and chemically, as well as the gambler, who gets a certain rush or high from betting whether he or she wins or loses: Thus, these individuals are addicted in the same manner.

These are all examples of spiritual warfare and it does exist. For some, this is too much to fathom, but I can tell anyone from first-hand experience, once an individual has felt the HOLY SPIRIT working inside he or she, it is no longer a matter of being able to fathom the possibility that GOD, JESUS and the HOLY SPIRIT are real or not. It is then factual and undeniable and something that everyone should seek with all of his or her heart and soul through prayer, the Bible and research. GOD does not allow us to be tempted to the point where we cannot turn away from it. GOD tells us in His Word:

1 Corinthians 10:13

No temptation has overtaken you except what is common to mankind. And God is faithful; he will not let you be tempted beyond what you can bear. But when you are tempted, he will also provide a way out so that you can endure it.

So much damage can be avoided if we just give GOD a chance to work in our lives. If we would listen to what some call a "voice" when it comes time to doing right or wrong and go toward the right, there is much more gratification in that. The problem for me for so long and for others still is that we refuse to give GOD a chance to work in our lives. For so many, it is just too much to process and often the question is raised, "Why would GOD let all of these terrible things happen in the world if He is real?" but what we have to realize is that from the beginning of time we have been given free will. Like I mentioned, it all comes down to a decision we make ourselves to do right or wrong, good or evil. It is not GOD's fault that the majority of the time we choose the wrong path and, though we are all guilty beyond a reasonable doubt, He still gave us hope by sending His only Son to die for all of the wrong things we have done. Once we accept this fact and repent and turn away from a willfully sin-natured life-style and strive to be as good as we can be without making excuses, we have redemption through CHRIST JESUS.

Unfortunately for millions of people, it is just much easier to not be held accountable for their actions and for many they are having way too much fun to change and/or cannot grasp the concept of GOD or agree with it, as I mentioned before. I challenge any nonbeliever out there to give GOD a chance to work in their lives: To make an honest effort and find out if the answers you may or may not have been looking for are in the Holy Bible. Either way, I can promise anyone that if that person would turns his or her heart and soul and life over to the will of GOD, that person will find answers, whether he or she is searching or not. We all have an opportunity to turn away from pain and suffering and to have peace.

Lord, I thank You and praise You for Your blessing of the HOLY SPIRIT, which You have bestowed on my life. May all my thoughts, speech, and actions glorify You, Father, and always I pray that Your will be done. I pray in JESUS' name. Amen

One Time

One time, but not only one time, I drove while I drank.
Thank GOD I never killed anyone while my mind was blank.
I drove under the influence and somehow never went to jail.
Maybe I should have been shown sooner what it was to fail.
One time, but not only one time, I drank in inappropriate places,
With drunks that were as bad as I and I can't even recall their faces.
In movie-theatres and on the job, I was sloppy.
Drinking from a Styrofoam cup with a straw was my favorite hobby.
One time, but not only one time, I got drunk before the party.
I had no boundaries and I was overly-friendly and naughty,
Constantly making passes at women and starting fights;
Passed-out or throwing-up early on, for many of my nights.
One time, but not only one time, I turned my home inside out.
I took my anger and sadness and turned it into my family's fear
and doubt.
So many times, my actions forced them to leave.
Most of my problems are from not knowing how to grieve.
One time, but not only one time, I was arrested.
Over and over again, the patience of various authorities I've tested.
I butted heads with almost every boss I ever had, because I had a chip
on my shoulder.
The more time I spent in combat and the more I lost, the more I
grew colder.
One time was never only one time. It became most of the time and onto
all of the time.
Every time led to jail time, which let to in-patient for a long time.

"**D**on't be that guy." We've all heard those words before, but that hasn't stopped many of us from being that guy. Many of us have been that guy even after making conversation about not being that guy while sober-minded. That's exactly the guy that I used to be and for as long as I can remember, it was that way. I would drink and drink and drink until I had no control over my behavior whatsoever. Sarcasm, irrational speech and actions, and many times, anger, most often became my belligerent state of mind.

An embarrassment to my family and friends on many occasions, my behavior was the undoing of many relationships. For years, it wasn't abnormal for me to make inappropriate remarks or gestures to other men's spouses whether they were my friend or not. Sadly enough, at many times these spoken-for women were interested. Don't think I'm bragging for one second, because I am not bragging in the least bit. My faulty behaviors of the past are nothing to brag about. On the contrary, those old behaviors made me a wretched, despicable, evil man. To act out in the manner in which I used to do was to be a low-down, dirty, invasive, intruding, worldly, sorry individual. For a long time, I felt so much regret for these actions: I'm not going to sugar-coat it at all.

What I came to realize was that, in order to fully change for the better, I had to honestly and whole-heartedly repent and seek forgiveness from GOD. Not only that, but I had to forgive myself before I was ready to move on. I used to let guilt and regret eat away at me for so long and it only led to depression. After various PTSD-related incidents in my life, everything would be miserable for a while, and then things would pass. Maybe I would find a new crowd of so-called friends to hang out with who didn't know my flaws and prior follies, but even when I found these new "drinking associates," it was only a matter of time before I, yet again, ruined more relationships. My life was a vicious cycle.

It wasn't until I was ready to change my way of life and be the Christian I am called to be that I was ready to heal. If there is any one theme to my story, it is that no one can fully recover without GOD. This is the only way I was able to get close to a normal life, which I am working to improve on a daily basis.

The key to successful recovery is prayer and a relationship with GOD. The word "relationship" tends to be thrown around loosely, when in fact, a relationship is an important connection between two beings. There is nothing strange about having an actual, factual, working, living relationship with GOD the Father and His Son, JESUS CHRIST. I know this, because I have a personal relationship with GOD. I'm not referring to the wishful, but noncommittal attitude of those who can't accept or fully understand complete truths about GOD. No, it is completely different when you come to the point in your life when you allow GOD to personally fill you with His HOLY SPIRIT.

It is an amazing feeling. It is an emotional experience. The most amazing experience I have personally ever experienced happened in my home. It might sound crazy to a nonbeliever, but there is nothing crazy about it. It was truly beautiful. One night, I had just finished reading my Bible. My wife was sleeping next to me and I was watching television. The show I was watching was very interesting. It was about JESUS and how He rose from the dead three days after being crucified. The show explained the various times in which JESUS appeared to His disciples after His resurrection. It was very touching and educational and left me in a sense of agreement, as far as how I had believed the events may have taken place.

After the show was over, I turned the television off, prayed and went to sleep. At some point in the night, I began dreaming of the events I had watched on TV similarly, but not exact to how I had seen them. In the dream, I was with the disciples and I could see JESUS every time they saw Him after the resurrection. I knew it was a dream, but it felt so real. Just before the dream ended, something resembling a stone tablet came out of nowhere and hit me in the face as I was looking at JESUS on the shore from the boat on the sea and instantly I woke up crying. It did not hurt and I was not crying because I was in pain. Rather, I was crying because I had been filled with the HOLY SPIRIT and I felt a joy like I'd never felt before in my life and I knew at that moment how real GOD truly was. He had revealed it to me and I was so happy, I laid there in my bed smiling and crying tears of joy for what seemed like an hour. In the midst of my crying, I prayed and gave thanks to GOD for the blessing He'd given me and for JESUS. Then I went to sleep and slept more peacefully then I ever had before. That night was the most amazing thing I had ever experienced and for the first time, I truly understood the power of the HOLY SPIRIT.

Luke 21:34
"Be careful, or your hearts will be weighed down with carousing, drunkenness and the anxieties of life, and that day will close on you suddenly like a trap.

Luke 1:15
for he will be great in the sight of the Lord. He is never to take wine or other fermented drink, and he will be filled with the Holy Spirit even before he is born.

Lord, I thank You and praise You, Father. Thank You for Your Son, JESUS and Your HOLY SPIRIT, the Comforter. I love you, Father. I pray in JESUS' name. Amen

The GIGS Diagram below is a model of how instant gratification followed by guilt follows sin. It is a vicious cycle brought on by a multitude of reasons, whether any given individual realizes what is going on within them or not. After a person experiences a traumatic event, this person often feels depressed and empty inside, as well as other negative emotions, such as anxiety and others. This can last for the majority, if not all of their daily life. Because of these down-in-the-dumps, bad feelings, these individuals strive to feel good inside by whatever means they can and the easiest ways to achieve this is by instant gratification: for example, sex, drugs and alcohol, which often leads to guilt. As in my case for years, guilt is often felt due to some sort of let-down, whether it is morally and/ or legally.

The down and depressed individual often allows him or herself to create more trouble in his or her life by allowing the guilt to eat away at them. The troubled individual expresses him or herself in the form of negative thoughts, speech and actions, which is sinful and thus recycles the entire process. The only way to properly come out of this situation is to seek help in the form of therapy by various means, depending on how severe the case is or just by simply opening up to loved ones and listening to advice.

The most important thing anyone can do is get down on their knees and pray and do personal business with God. You can also get in touch with a trusted pastor or elder or Christian family member or friend and receive guidance on living a life as Christ intends. Pray and read the living Word found in the Holy Bible and seek salvation by repenting and being forgiven. Get involved in productive activities. Focus on the rewards of giving and don't worry about being given to. Love everyone, but first love yourself. A house cannot stand if the foundation is weak, so build your house on the rock that is Jesus Christ.

GIGS Diagram

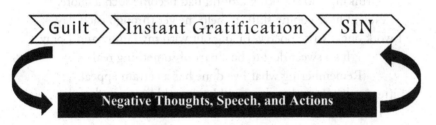

Bitter Sweet Surrender

Surrender such as this is oh-so-bitter-sweet. Surrender to sobriety is the
very best treat.
More sweet than bitter with the choice that I made,
I get to keep my family and quit the games that I played.
Bitter in the sense that my friends are no longer here—
I guess I'm not as fun, when I'm not drinking beer.
And that's ok, I enjoy my family today.
I have my wife, our son and our daughters and its better this way.
We're closer now than we've ever been before.
Drinking and sneaking around had become such a chore.
Now, I have coping skills to help me get through each day.
I work out, I write poetry, I hang out with my family and I pray.
It's a sweet deal to be a part of something real.
Remembering what I've done has a certain appeal.
Bitter in the sense that there will be no cold beer on a hot day . . .
For me, one drink leads to a drunk. I only know one way.
So for today and all that follow, I surrender to GOD'S will.
I choose to live a fulfilled life. I don't want or need cheap thrills.
There was a sweet sensation, a new sense of freedom when I changed my
way of life.
Bitter in the sense that there won't be many events or weddings. I'd
rather have my wife.
I've put her through so many tough times throughout the years.
All because I wanted my cake and to eat it too, right along with the
booze and beers.
I stayed out for so many late nights that turned into day-time fights.
I always used to put my faith in the bottle, which I held so tight.
Now, I'm going to spend the rest of my days somehow trying to make it
all right.

Cy Mulholland

I once heard someone say, "What if we woke up one morning and only had what we thanked GOD for yesterday?" That got me to thinking, "Am I grateful enough for the blessings I have received? Do I show that I am appreciative, or do I take advantage of it all?" I came to the realization that I am guilty of not showing enough appreciation for the things GOD has done for me and I want to make it a point to do this as I should.

There are a lot of things many people don't realize when it comes to prayer and praise. There is a lot many don't understand about blessings and giving thanks. Regarding prayer, I realize now that I don't have to feel greedy as I used to, when asking for certain things and I know that GOD tells us to bring our case before Him when it comes to praying for things. He tells us that He will hear us out and decide. This doesn't necessarily mean He will act as quickly or in the exact manner that we would like Him to, but He will hear us. In the HOLY BIBLE, John tells us:

1 John 5:14-15
This is the confidence we have in approaching God: that if we ask anything according to his will, he hears us. 15 And if we know that he hears us—whatever we ask—we know that we have what we asked of him.

Prayer works and GOD's judgment is just in all things. When GOD makes a decision in our lives, it is important that we agree with it. He is indeed all-knowing and all-powerful and of course, He loves us and will only makes decisions that are best for us and glorify Him. When in prayer, it is much of the time ok to ask for things that many—and I for one—used to not ask, due to the fact that I felt I was being greedy. I know now that when I ask in JESUS' name and believe it can be done, then it will be done. Man should not put GOD to the test, but my wife and I can speak first-hand about the Truth that God does give merciful answers to prayer.

We have prayed for many things together and many have been answered. We pray for many things in a wide variety of aspects. For each one of our three children, while in the womb, we prayed for health and it was given to us. I understand that not everyone is this fortunate, but GOD has His reasoning for everything and nothing touches us that has not first passed through GOD's hands.

I remember when my wife was pregnant with our third of three children and second daughter, and my wife and I prayed for her to be born a healthy baby. My wife is not a fan of red hair, but it was a possibility that we could have a child with red hair, since my Mom has hair that color. However, our first two children were born with blonde hair and brown eyes. During her third pregnancy, my wife prayed that GOD would grant us a healthy baby, even if it meant our daughter would have red hair. She did this because one of her friends had recently given birth to a severely-disabled baby girl. Oddly enough, my wife gave birth to a beautiful blue eyed, red-headed little girl. John goes on to say:

1 John 5:19-20
We know that we are children of God, and that the whole world is under the control of the evil one. 20 We know also that the Son of God has come and has given us understanding, so that we may know him who is true. And we are in him who is true by being in his Son Jesus Christ. He is the true God and eternal life.

My wife and I have prayed for many things: deployed soldiers, those who are sick or suffering in any way. But most importantly, we have prayed for nonbelievers and for those doubting GOD, that they may have faith and come to GOD with all their heart and soul, trusting in the LORD that His will be done. I have seen prayer answered so many times, that I know His influence in our lives is an undeniable Truth. I remember the times I have fallen short and not committed my whole heart to the LORD; every single time I have done this, as far back as I can remember, things have happened to remind me that I am doing wrong.

Such is the case with everyone, whether they believe it or not. In one particular situation I remember my wife's vehicle began to run poorly, shortly after I had revisited my shortcomings. When the engine got to a certain amount of revolutions per minute (RPM), the vehicle would begin to shake and the check engine light would come on. This took place for days and I received the message loud and clear, so I soon got my act together. My wife would pray that the LORD would fix the vehicle on a daily basis and she believed whole-heartedly that it would be done. At that time, I was at a low point in my faith and still hadn't quite acquired the knowledge that I have now. Due to the fact that I was not filled with the HOLY SPIRIT, I figured that I was going to have to come out of my pocket a great deal to get the engine problem fixed.

One morning, when my wife went out to start her car and load the kids up so she could run some errands, she realized her car was no longer shaking and there was no check engine light, even though this problem had been consistent for weeks. We kept watch on it whenever we would drive her car around and the problem never returned. Once we realized that GOD had stepped in and intervened by fixing the car, we prayed and gave thanks to Him. It was an amazing feeling. Of course, a nonbeliever would argue that this situation was merely a coincidence, but the power of the almighty GOD cannot be denied. It is written in the HOLY BIBLE:

James 1:2-8
Consider it pure joy, my brothers and sisters, whenever you face trials of many kinds, 3 because you know that the testing of your faith produces perseverance. 4 Let perseverance finish its work so that you may be mature and complete, not lacking anything. 5 If any of you lacks wisdom, you should ask God, who gives generously to all without finding fault, and it will be given to you. 6 But when you ask, you must believe and not doubt, because the one who doubts is like a wave of the sea, blown and tossed by the wind. 7 That person should not expect to receive anything from the Lord. 8 Such a person is double-minded and unstable in all they do.

I will continue to be grateful and give thanks for all that I am blessed with and I will strive to be better tomorrow than I was yesterday. I will pray with confidence while I ask that not my will but the LORD's will be done. I will accept and agree with His decisions. I will pray for wisdom and it will be given to me and because of this Truth, I will possess the ability to love more and have stronger faith in the one true GOD of all creation. Because of this, I will be a better man and a better servant. Because of this, I will be a better father and a better husband.

Lord, thank You for Your many blessings and I pray, Father, that anyone reading this will seek out all of Your Truths contained in the HOLY BIBLE. I pray in JESUS' name. Amen

Avoid the Nouns

When in recovery, it's important to avoid certain nouns.
Avoid people, places, things and sounds.
You know the ones that can take you back to that place.
I don't want to catch a glimpse—not even a trace.
I'm talking about those dang triggers:
Events, sights, smells and figures.
There are those things that stick to your subconscious like glue.
You may be oblivious; you may be without a clue.
You best believe your mind, your inner being: it knew.
Relapse begins before you drink. It's true.
It took me a lifetime to realize not to depend on myself.
Reach out and touch someone for the sake of your health.
Strength in numbers is the addict's wealth.
I no longer set myself up for failure by going it alone.
I've learned there's no such thing as a ten-thousand-pound phone.
I no longer isolate and let my mind roam.
I get out of my room; I get out of my home.
My glass is half full and that is no bull.
No more drunken fool or being a complete tool.
No more friends till the end because I like to spend.
When you don't help the beer flow, those so-called's don't want to go.
And that is ok: I have the nouns I need today.
The people that I share my places and things with, they love me anyway.

Cy Mulholland

oday was a good day and most days are. It feels so good to be sober today. I went to my son's first soccer game of the year and they won. The weather was perfect. Not too hot and just the right amount of cloud cover. My wife, my kids and I had a great time. Now, most of our days are enjoyable this way, but I remember when I used to put less important things before my family.

I used to do things such as get drunk at home by myself or at another drunk's home. I remember many times in the past when I agreed to family functions, but when it came time to participate, suddenly drinking became more important. It used to be a regular occurrence that I would start an argument with my wife, just to make an excuse not to spend time with the family. Then I was out the door, with or without a plan, and there was no telling when I was coming back or what I was doing while I was gone.

I would stay out till three or four in the morning before I finally made it home, and there my wife would be sitting on the couch, waiting up for me. I was always up to no good, being out that late. I hung out with fellow soldiers, most of who were not married and had no kids. It was always a situation destined for destruction. Even if I didn't cheat on my wife, I was always flirting and making an effort to do just that. Even when I did spend time with my family, it wasn't quality time. I still wore my mask everywhere we went and by that, I mean I still had a drink in my hand, even when I was spending time with the family. The person I was when I was drunk was not the person I really was or was meant to be. It was like putting on a mask. I was hiding the real me and I was hiding my problems.

Such is the case with any addict. We try to escape our reality or find a new one. Even if that's not how we feel about it, we are simply trying to find something that makes us feel better, because something else is making us feel so bad. Once again, this is why I began having sex at the age of twelve. The question is, was it a coincidence that at this same young age, I began drinking and smoking marijuana? The answer is, absolutely not. I was too young to understand what I was feeling inside. I only knew that losing my big brother made me feel so bad on a daily basis that I had to find something to make me feel better.

The truth is that I didn't realize that fact at the time, but after evaluating my situation years later as an adult and being educated through various resources, I came to realize that what I had acquired, due to my brother's suicide, was PTSD. As I have mentioned before, my symptoms were only amplified by deploying to Iraq for three combat tours. PTSD is a serious problem and to this day it remains to be a seriously misunderstood problem. Though we know much more about this disorder—in large part due to the most recent war—there are still many people who are uneducated about PTSD. Almost everyone knows someone suffering from PTSD. We all know someone who has served in the military, police force, fire department, or as an EMT. Many of us know someone who has been raped, abused, nearly killed or murdered, or a combination of these things and/or someone who has witnessed a traumatic event.

These are the reasons many people drink, do drugs, and act out. Any outsider looking in knows this, but doesn't have the capability to understand, unless they educate themselves about the complicated disorder that PTSD truly is. This isn't to say that everyone needs to know and understand PTSD in depth, but when an individual is a friend or family member to someone suffering with this disorder, it would definitely be beneficial for that person to have a greater knowledge of what their loved one is going through.

A common problem with individuals who are suffering from PTSD is that they don't find help before it is too late and they either overdose or intentionally take their own lives, because they feel they had no other option. Much of the time, the one suffering feels too mentally beat down to reach out for help. Often, those suffering are hurting so deeply that they do not care enough to reach out for help. It is in cases such as these that a close friend or relative with knowledge about PTSD would have the ability to help their loved one, before it's too late.

Fortunately for me, I have a loving wife who never gave up on me and constantly applied pressure for me to get help. And thankfully, when I did get myself into situations that could have been potentially dangerous and life threatening, I always managed to get arrested or find my way home safely. I am indeed grateful for the times I have been arrested and hospitalized, because those situations, although negative, assisted in my recovery. Sometimes, we have to fall flat on our face before we can get back up.

2 Corinthians 6:14
Do not be yoked together with unbelievers. For what do righteousness and wickedness have in common? Or what fellowship can light have with darkness?

Lord, thank You for allowing me the time and resources to understand my purpose in life. I pray in JESUS' name. Amen

Hopes & Fears

I have hopes and fears. I've had them for years.
My hopes are my dreams. My fears are of beers.
My dreams drive me forward. My fears lead to tears.
My fears are of many things. I hope they subside.
I fear I may hold too much negativity inside.
I hope to not do that, I hope to stay up. I fear I may spill after he fills my cup.
Hopefully, I believe and fear only one.
I find hope in fearing the Father and following the Son.
Together, They take away my fears, even though They are One.
I fear the decisions I could make, but I hope my journey's just begun.
I hope I achieve my goals, but I fear I may fall short.
I hope I keep a clear head and not let fear distort.
LORD knows, I can't afford another bad report.
I hope to control my fears the best that I possibly can.
I know if I use the skills I've learned, I'll be a better man.
There is much less fear than there is hope.
I'm not struggling to climb; I'm sliding down the slope.
I no longer fear the pill, the gun, or the rope.
Recovery is selfish, but we're all feeling the effect.
With the focus on me and then the others, I have maximum time to reflect.
This tends to keep me out of trouble. I'm not so often suspect.
I can allow myself to be the man I'm supposed to be.
This is what we expect.

For a little while, I had been hanging out with this guy from time to time. It was after I had already come to that point in my life where I knew I had arrived. I came to a point in my life when I finally knew what my purpose was and that I no longer wanted to drink. It was a feeling of peace. It was an awakening. My eyes were opened wide, I understood for the first time what was truly important in life and I realized where the answers were to all of my questions. The answers are in Jesus.

As I had mentioned, I was hanging out with this guy who I had met at IOP, which is Intensive Out-Patient for alcoholics. I had him over for dinner to eat with my family and a couple times to work-out with me in my garage, where my gym equipment is. I knew he and his wife were having some problems and were talking about divorce, so I would listen to him and be the person he could vent to. A couple weeks went by, and he mentioned that he and his wife had made some progress and that they would soon be spending a weekend together. I was happy for him and told him to let me know how it went. Well, it turned out that things didn't go so well. That weekend, he found out that she had an affair and now they were certain to get a divorce, after twenty years of marriage.

This bad news sent him over the edge, and he went on a drinking binge that landed him back in the hospital. I only found out, because he called me from the Behavioral Health Hospital, requesting that I bring him some cigarettes. After that, I didn't hear from him for a couple of weeks.

Finally, I saw him at the WTU (Warrior Transition Unit), which was where we were both stationed at the time. WTU is a unit where soldiers can go to recover from an illness or an injury. When I saw him, we made small talk for a few minutes and he asked me to call him so that we could work-out sometime. I called him a few times, but one of us always had something going on. I then saw him once again at the unit, when I was signing back in for duty after I had been on leave for a week. He was very drunk and tried to hold a conversation with me, but it wasn't working so well.

He was speaking sarcastically and he was belligerent. I told him to be safe and that I hoped he would get sober. When I went to walk away, he tried to get me to stop and continue the conversation, but I told him, "I have to go. My family is outside in the car." He then said, "Man, family isn't important. Family can wait." I in turn told him, "No buddy, my family is important to me and I won't make them wait. Goodbye." I could tell by the look on his face that he knew our friendship was over. I had tried to help him before and told him to call me anytime if he ever needed to talk to someone when he was struggling. It had to be that way, because in my heart I believed that, with his present attitude, he would never change. I wish him the best and I know there are many like him in the world. There are many that are not capable of change, until they choose it, and because I value my sobriety, my well-being and the well-being of my family, I will not allow myself to associate with those that are not willing to change their lives for the better. I will pray for them.

Psalm 27:1
The LORD is my light and my salvation—
whom shall I fear?
The LORD is the stronghold of my life—
of whom shall I be afraid?

Lord, I pray that You would bless the one I have written about, because You know him. Give him the strength to change and to find You, I pray Lord. I pray in JESUS' name. Amen

CHAPTER FOUR

MIND FIELD

—————

Burden from impacts felt by various means are concealed
in the subconscious mind.

I'm a Loose Trigger

"I'm a loose trigger": those were your words.
I was just a child: you were a man.
I didn't deserve this . . . neither did you.
You were my hero. You are my hero no longer.
You made me weak by not being stronger.
You were my big brother, the one I looked up to.
What did I do? What example is this?
You promised you would come with me when I left that morning.
When I returned, you were gone and so began the mourning.
As far back as I can remember, there was a smile on your face.
Few times was there any other emotion there.
I remember thinking you could do no wrong.
I was so happy when you were around. No fear, no doubt.
I love you, but you took the easy way out.
I was so lost and I'm still trying to find myself.
You changed my life forever.
I've since found a best friend that will never leave me.
She loves me unconditionally.
I forgive you brother, but I fear for you.
We will never see each other again.
You should have asked for help.
You became a statistic, a figure.
All because you were a loose trigger.

The highway patrolman had just pulled us over and told us to go home. The mood in the car was tense. My parents were confused and talking back and forth about what could be the matter. My dad was upset. What seemed like forever was actually a short ride home. We pulled up outside of our house and my parents went inside, while the three of us kids stayed in the car.

After a while, my brother-in-law came outside, got into the car and we drove to the grocery store. He said we were going to get donuts, but would not tell us what was going on. When we were done at the store, we returned to the house and we accompanied my brother-in-law up to the door. I was the first to walk in, followed by my little brother and sister. I remember seeing frowns on everybody's faces and my mom and dad had been crying. I asked what was going on and that's when my dad said, "Rod's dead".

My big brother had killed himself in our dining room and to this day nobody knows why he did it. If someone does know, they have never told me. Thinking back, I remember him giving away some of his belongings . . . Belongings that he liked very much, but neither I nor anyone else thought anything of it at the time. What I do know is that my big brother took himself out of our lives.

He was more than a big brother. He was my hero. He was the one I looked up to more than anyone else in the world and he was gone in an instant. He forever changed my life and that wasn't fair, but I still love him and I always will. I know I will never see him again and I have long since faced that reality.

I sometimes wonder what could have been if he had stuck around. What would my life have been like? I probably would have done better in school and put more emphasis on all things in life that are more important than partying. I probably would have been happy. Then I think about the other side of the spectrum. I think about the fact that I probably wouldn't have ever met my wife and had our children. Then again, I never would have known that.

There are so many what-ifs, but these are the things I think about. He chose to leave because he was hurting. Something was causing him mental anguish. I will most likely never know what it was, but it changed my life forever. I was never the same. I never got good grades the way I had before. I was never genuinely happy like before. The fact is, I had PTSD long before I ever went to combat. The war just created more traumas.

Before my brother pulled the trigger, he said, "I'm a loose trigger."

1 Corinthians 6:19-20
Do you not know that your bodies are temples of the Holy Spirit, who is in you, whom you have received from God? You are not your own; 20 you were bought at a price. Therefore honor God with your bodies.

Lord, thank You for life and the strength and courage to overcome its challenges. I pray in JESUS' name. Amen

PTSD

PTSD and what it means to me;
I learn more about PTSD all the time.
I learn where it comes from and its effects on my mind.
These Post Traumatic Stress Demons are so unkind.
The only ones who understand have been where I've been.
Will I ever live a normal life, or will I be this way till the end?
I was only a kid when he Put This Sibling in Danger.
He took himself out of my life, like some kind of stranger.
It was selfish, unfair and so very mean.
My best friend went away and left me nowhere to lean.
My life was changed forever when I Put Those Strange Drugs in my
system.
My loved ones tried to stop me, but I would not listen.
I thought I was hard and Put Time into Selling Drugs.
To get out of trouble, I wore a wire on supposed friends that were thugs.
I was a scared young kid who really had no choice:
A scared young man that listened to his own voice.
A little while later, I decided to Put This Stupid Deranged life in check.
I decided to join the Army. I thought, "What the heck?"
After all, I was going down in a Podunk town.
No more acting like a clown, time to put the needle down.
Put Down the Syringe, Dummy and get your life together.
Nothing around you is changing except for the weather.
So I stayed home, stayed clean, watched TV, got in shape.
Occasionally, I watched family videos on tape.
Soon, it was time to ship off to the Army.
I had big hopes of saying good-bye to the old me.
They Put This boy in a Swift Deploying unit called 3ID.
Then it was off to Bosnia, but it didn't matter to me.
My new, loving wife had my back, you see.
I Pulled Those Strange Duties, like guarding mass grave sites.
Then I returned home to my brand new baby boy and my wife.

Cy Mulholland

Deploying became the norm, but when I came back she was always there.
It's amazing she doesn't have a head full of grey hair.
I trained in Georgia, California, Louisiana and Kuwait,
Not knowing that war would soon be my fate.
They Packed These Sardines Deep in that Air Force can.
Then it was off to Iraq, not Afghanistan.
When I was a young man, you could've never told me this was part of GOD'S plan.
But His will not mine be done and I understand.
We third ID invaded in '03.
I went back in 2005 and 2007;
That many trips across the pond would get anyone anxious for heaven.
It's for a Purpose That Soldiers Do the things we do.
I don't expect you to understand or even agree with the path we choose.
We go and do what someone has to do and so you won't have to.
These things I've experienced have changed my life, but they will not define me.
There's always hope and I find ways to cope:
PTSD will not be my rope.

J ust because I have this disorder doesn't mean that it has to be my undoing. It doesn't have to be an excuse and it doesn't have to tear my family apart. All good things are possible through JESUS. The truth of the matter is that an individual has to be willing to seek help. There are some things we just can't deal with on our own.

I was once told by an old-timer in a treatment facility that if he had a toothache he wouldn't go to a car mechanic to get it fixed. I took that to be sound advice, meaning that, whatever issues we have, it's important to go to the subject matter experts for help. I personally know that trying to go about recovery on one's own will not work, and if it does, it's going to be a more painful journey than it has to be.

More than anything, it is important to seek a personal relationship with JESUS CHRIST. He loves us so much and He is the only way to salvation. He is the source of my strength and if you get into the word and you pray, He will answer. I know, because I have been answered and I feel His presence.

It is vitally important to be pro-active in recovery, whether one is dealing with drugs, or alcohol, or PTSD, or sex, or emotions, or anything else. Whatever the case may be, it is so important to get involved with something. There is a world of help out there and I only write these things from my personal experiences. If an individual is a family man or woman, it is absolutely selfish of us not to get help. It's worth it and there is a feeling like no other when you break those bonds that have been holding you down for so long. There is a feeling of, "I have arrived."

James 1:12
Blessed is the man who remains steadfast under trial, for when he has stood the test he will receive the crown of life, which God has promised to those who love him.

Lord, let me not forget the journey I have taken to get to where I am today and help me, Lord, to stay on the path I am on. I pray in JESUS' name. Amen

No More Steam

My self-esteem is as low as it can go,
Though this is not exactly what I show.
My mind always races; I don't know where to go.
I'm full of myself for no reason at all.
Always walking around like I'm ten feet tall;
I carry myself as if bullets can do me no harm.
That should be a red flag, it should be an alarm.
What goes around, comes around;
It always catches up to me.
Oftentimes, people can see right through me.
I'm notorious for always putting up a front.
Inside me, this is not the life-style I want.
I'm running out of steam: there is no self-esteem.
Do any of you out there know what I mean?
I tell myself I'm strong and that few times I'm wrong.
Sometimes, I am the life of the party.
Other times, I make it hard to get along.
In my mind most women find me attractive.
This leads to me being overly sexually active.
I hurt people because I hurt, but I'd give them my shirt.
All my life, I've been a flirt.
All my life, I've gone after the skirt.
Pain, pain, go away. You've taken my steam for another day.

The road to recovery is filled with highs and lows. Some days are good and some days are bad. Some days, I feel motivated and on top of the world and other days, I slip and fall and roll down that very same hill. That's one thing that I can say I'm continuously working on in recovery, because let's face it, recovery is a never-ending effort. I find myself these days catching many situations before they become problems that could be avoided.

When we let ourselves get down and depressed and are feeling nothing but lows, that is when we go out and search for a way to make ourselves feel better and more times than not, as alcoholics and addicts, we look in the wrong direction. One of my biggest problems has always been the fact that I found it so hard to pick up the phone and call someone when I was struggling with an issue. I wouldn't even tell my own wife, who was in the very same house with me. I would skip that entire helpful tool of reaching out to someone and go straight for the drink or the cheat for instant gratification; instant gratification that was there and then gone in the blink of an eye. Then, due to the guilt and the shame, I would always feel worse than before. More times than not, if I went to drink, I would end up in some kind of legal predicament and if I went out to womanize, I would always feel guilt and shame over it.

That senseless acting-out got me in nothing but trouble, anyway. Take it from me, it's not worth it. It is my advice that if an individual is having a bad day, he or she should talk to someone and if that person feels like they can't talk to their significant other about some things, then he or she should have a support system in place that provides the ability to talk to someone about any of his or her potential issues.

That may sound really simple. That's because it is. It's just a matter of deciding how important your sobriety is to you and how pro-active you want to be in your recovery. Once an individual picks up that ten-thousand-pound-phone, as the saying goes, and realizes that it doesn't actually weigh that much, chances are they will feel better about things. I'm just stating what works for me and I've talked to a few other people who have said the same. Everything is easier with help. I make it a point to not allow myself to feel like I did the day I wrote the previous poem.

Romans 5:3-5
More than that, we rejoice in our sufferings, knowing that suffering produces endurance, 4and endurance produces

character, and character produces hope, 5and hope does not put us to shame, because God's love has been poured into our hearts through the Holy Spirit who has been given to us.

Lord, help me to help my brothers and sister when they are in need, just as I have been helped when I was in need. Let me not dwell in sorrow and self-pity, because these things are not intended for me. I pray in JESUS' name. Amen

I've Done More With Less

I must confess, I've done more with less.
I've done more of nothing than most of the rest.
At times, I've been challenged and few times, I've passed the test.
It's easy to see I'm far from the best.
At times, my efforts were very strong.
Sometimes, my efforts lasted very long.
Failure, it seems, is what I'm to be.
I'm a slave in my own mind, when I should be free.
I was born in the south and raised in the west.
As you could've guessed, I thought I was the best.
The fact of the matter is, I'm no better than the rest.
I've climbed tall mountains and fell back down.
I've been the class clown, but really just a clown.
Now, I don't hear a sound, 'cause there's no one around.
Everything seemed to teeter when I was supposed to be a leader.
With tunnel-vision and traffic tickets, in this world, I'm merely a speeder.
My woman, my wife, my best friend in life has had to put up with many toils and strife.
The bitter sweetness of beers and the chill of fears bring tears.
I should've been focused on bringing good cheers.
I've done more harm with not much.
I am so often out of touch.
It's too bad I never come through in the clutch.
I know it is ample to set the example;
The hopes and dreams of my children I will not trample.
I have to provide direction, more than a sample.
I've done more damage than building with no tool.
I think I'm so cool when I act like a fool.
I often act as if I'm the rule.
I've done more with less. I must confess—
More harm in less time, done bad instead of good.
I never seem to do the things I should.

I lied and she cried. Her eyes were opened wide.
Considering the damage I've done, I deserve to have died.
Many times I've been blessed, but they weren't appreciated.
I am not worthy of the One by Whom I was created.
I'm going to do more with less.
I'm still livin' because I was forgiven.
It is my faith by which I am driven.
There's always hope. That is how I cope.
I refuse to live my life as a dope.
So, here's to my kids. Don't do what I did.
I did more with less, every time I backslid.

Admitting my problems was a valuable tool I learned in the not-so-distant past. For the majority of my life, I never would have admitted that I was an alcoholic and I never knew what PTSD was till just a few years ago. Therefore, I was clueless to the fact that I was an alcoholic due to my PTSD. All I knew was that from the time I was twelve-years-old, I had made mistake after mistake after mistake. Looking back it all makes sense, and as I've written before, my best friend and big brother committed suicide when I was just eleven-years-old. What I've come to learn from the "experts" is that when someone experiences a traumatic event and goes untreated for a long period of time, it messes with the chemistry in that person's brain. The communication between the individual's lower brain and upper brain gets interrupted.

Due to the amount of stress I experienced when I was a child after my brother took his own life, I did not fully mature in some ways. When he died, I was sad, lonely, and depressed, so I did whatever I had to do in order to make the pain go away. In order to feel better, I kept on acting-out through alcohol, drugs and sex, but it was always only a temporary fix. I was actively involved in all three of those behaviors at the age of twelve and I never looked back. I felt I had nowhere else to turn. I felt like I couldn't depend on anyone, because the one person I looked up to the most had checked out. That was my thought-process as a child. I know now that everyone in my family was hurting the same way I was.

In my early adulthood, for the most part, things were no better. When I wasn't working, I was partying and when I was working, the only thing I was thinking about was partying, because for a little while it helped the pain go away. Three tours to the war in Iraq only amplified my PTSD symptoms. It wasn't until I learned and understood what was going on within me that I decided to change my ways and fully turn my life over to the will of GOD. It's important to me to be a good example to my children and a supportive husband to my wife. Now more than ever, I understand the importance of positively influencing and shaping my children's outlook and future. It's my duty as a parent to share with them the gospel of JESUS CHRIST and to teach them morals and the values of life.

1 Chronicles 16:11
Seek the LORD and his strength;
seek his presence continually!

Lord, help me to take what I've learned from my mistakes and teach my children not to repeat them. Lord, watch over my family and bless them and protect them. I pray in JESUS' name. Amen

Avoid & Isolate

Well, this is just great. Do I avoid or isolate?
It's funny that I know better, yet try to choose my own fate.
It's not that I've ever eaten from a silver plate—
It's that if I don't avoid people, places and things, I become irate.
Avoid and isolate, different, but one and the same.
If I perform both of these tricks, I'm the one to blame.
That's the way I like it. Seems that's how it must be.
I find peace by not dealing with society.
If it's better for everyone, shouldn't this be how it's done?
Truth is, it's not best for my wife, our daughters and our son.
Sometimes when I write these words, I sound so dumb.
The war has been taxing and I feel so numb.
I know I'm human, merely a man, but I should be strong.
I've been this way for so long. What the hell is wrong?
I hear the advice and it sounds real nice. I remain at fault, because I
never think twice.
More often than not, I'm naughty, not nice,
All because my mind feels like it's locked in a vice.
You know what they say, "An excuse is like a grenade."
One day, I may fall on one and my life will quickly fade.
Only playing, I just said that, but now sleep for writing I must trade.
I am so tired and my mind feels frayed.
Tomorrow it will take concentration, but I'm going to avoid isolation.
My eyelids are too heavy, due to this sleepy sensation. Good Night.

It has been my experience that avoidance and isolation are a means of temporary relief from an ongoing problem. When I would quit drinking, I would stop hanging out with all those supposed friends I used to drink with. That led to avoiding everyone and isolating myself to my bedroom. I would come home from work at the end of a long day and go straight upstairs and take a shower, but after I was done with that I didn't join the family downstairs. No, instead I remained in my bedroom sleeping or watching television. I would do this for hours, as my wife would yell upstairs every so often, asking me if I was going to come downstairs and spend some time with the family. I would respond with, "In a little while." She knew that meant I was not coming down then and that I probably would not come down at all. Occasionally, any one of my three children would come upstairs and try to get me to come out for some kind of family interaction. I always told them the same thing, "Maybe in a little while." They weren't dumb either. They knew that meant I was not going to budge from napping in my bed or watching sports, the discovery channel, or the history channel on my television.

When my family was able to get me out of the house, it always ended up being a miserable experience because I wasn't able to tolerate interacting with society. When we would go to the grocery store, I wouldn't last more than twenty minutes before I was freaking out and walking out to the car to isolate until the rest of the family had completed the remainder of their shopping. When we would go to restaurants, I always had to sit at a table that allowed my back to be to the wall, so that I could have my eyes on everyone around me and so that I could scan for all of the available exits in case something were to happen: whatever that might have been. This is how my mind worked.

I say "worked" because I have learned to cope better with the PTSD symptoms that I acquired from combat, even though they are still present. It is a continuous effort when dealing with recovery from PTSD. I've learned that it takes time to get the mind out of that "fight or flight" mode we keep ourselves in while in the combat zone. When we spend a year and often times longer in a hyper-vigilant state of mind, the lower brain loses communication with the upper brain and that's what causes us to remain in that "fight or flight" mode, as outlined by Colonel Hoge.

2 Timothy 2:12
If we endure, we will also reign with him; if we deny him, he also will deny us;

Lord, let me not forget that You have blessed me with a wonderful family and let me give them the time and direction they deserve from me. I pray in JESUS' name. Amen

No More Time

No more time, but the clock moves on.
Why can't I? What the hell is wrong?
It appears as if the time that was here is long since gone.
The digital clock seemed to keep it frozen in space.
Give it a few seconds and soon another number will take its place.
Where did it go? I do not know.
I have very few things that I can show.
I have some memories to remind me that it was here.
Where is it now? It is nowhere near.
Staring at the clock, so much time is wasted.
I chew up time before it's even tasted.
Some pieces of time I wish could be erased.
I'm running out of time as if I'm being chased.
I suppose it's time for me to get on the right path.
The bad times are starting to catch up with me at last.
I'm in the present and in the future. The bad times are coming from the past.
I need to fish for more, so a time-line I will cast.
If that fails, I know not what to do. I will have wasted your time and
wasted my time, too.
You must get out, before there's no more time.
To waste it on me would be a crime or a shame and I'm to blame.
There's not a clock in the world that you can tame.
What is time? I find it odd. There's no more time, so I'll make my peace
with GOD.

t does no good to sit and dwell in the past, but I have my share of stories about time wasted. Today, I live in the present and make plans for the future, but I keep the past in the back of my mind so as to not repeat it. I am grateful that somehow, someway, I was able to realize that my problems—my issues that had been troubling me for years, resulting from traumatic events—would never cease to affect me and my loved ones, without help.

I remember one night I had been drinking very heavily throughout the day and I wanted to continue drinking throughout the night, but my wife had taken the keys from me. No matter what I said or did, she would not give them to me. I was yelling at the top of my lungs and cussing up a storm. Finally, when she had had enough and I wasn't paying attention, she went out the back door and loaded the kids into her Chevy Trailblazer. I realized what was going on by the time she was backing out of the driveway, and because we lived at the end of a dead-end street, there was only one way to go. Before she could pull off, I was in front of her vehicle so that she could not drive away. I was still yelling and carrying on and scaring the kids, because she still refused to give me the keys to my truck. I proceeded to climb on top of her car and looked at her through the windshield and pleaded for her to give me my keys before she left. She would not budge, even after I walked on the very top of her SUV for a moment while the kids were crying inside. She was yelling at me to stop—it was a very chaotic event. After a little while, I jumped down beside the car next to her window and that was just enough for her to be able to speed away.

The next morning she came back to check on me, only to find a house that appeared to be turned upside down. I had tipped over all the furniture. I had thrown the majority of the dishes and other items, breaking many of them. It looked as if a tornado had swept through our home. And then there was me, passed out on the floor. I couldn't recall most of the events from the prior evening, because I had blacked out. (Blacking out due to drinking in excess was a regular occurrence for me.) Evidently, I had torn the house apart looking for my keys, which my wife had taken with her when she left. I must have searched everywhere I could think of until I passed out and the keys weren't even there the whole time. What a silly and foolish drunk I was. I wasted so much valuable time, but I waste time no longer.

Cy Mulholland

2 Thessalonians 3:13
As for you, brothers, do not grow weary in doing good.

Lord, thank You for allowing me the time to see what truly matters in this life and the ability to come back to You. Thank You for love and the family You have blessed me with. I pray in JESUS' name. Amen

Operation Wal-Mart

There I was, behind enemy lines. Location, Wal-Mart.
I had my squad with me, armed with a single shopping cart.
Usually I prefer a solo mission, but command shot me down.
Her guidance was to take my team; there would be too many walmartians around.
We deployed that day from Kentucky and shortly thereafter it was time to SP Fort Knox and head down Route 31W.
Along the way, I briefed the enemy situation to my crew.
It was me and the LT in our Hummer H3.
And in the back were our trusty three.
SGT Mulholland, SPC Mulholland, and PVT Mulholland, too.
We'd been on missions like this before, way more than a few.
As we past PL Big M Chevy, we knew we were getting close.
I looked back and noticed PVT Mulholland doing her pre-combat ritual of picking her nose.
We pulled onto Objective parking lot and dismounted.
We moved out in a column; all my people were counted.
Soon, we breached the sliding glass doors.
I noticed there were two-legged mines on the floor.
We began negotiating the course and so began Phase One.
We didn't know the dangers that lay ahead, but we knew the battle must be won.
We had to clear the objective of groceries and that is never fun.
I thought it might be a good idea to assault the toy department.
I knew there we could find a slingshot and marbles if we found the right compartment.
My wife, I mean the LT said, "NO", and onto the grocery aisles we went.
We'd been there for about twenty minutes and I was totally spent.
I looked at my troops, I looked at my wife and I told her, "I just can't."
So with an about face, I left that place.
I aborted my mission without haste.
I went to the car to isolate.
I had to walk away, because I didn't feel so great.

Cy Mulholland

I can't be around people and I don't know why.
It's like I don't even want to try.
I needed a drink; I needed some kind of high.
So much times is wasted, it just passes me by.
I hate living like this and I don't want to die.
Why do I still rhyme with the letter I?
I guess I will stop and so it's good bye.

I often write about isolation and the way it affects me, because it has been a problem throughout the years for me and my family. It used to create distance in my relationships with my wife and my kids. As previously mentioned, I would shut myself up alone in my room, watching television or just lying in bed with nothing but my thoughts, which made me want to drink so that the thoughts would supposedly dissipate. That was never the case. When I drank to cope with the stress from the memories and nightmares of the things I experienced in combat, it only made things worse. Many times, I ended up in jail, which led to fines and court costs and on a couple occasions, my poor judgment landed me in the hospital.

Isolation is a master hinderer and can be a killer. I know because of my experiences, and so many soldiers take their lives because they feel they absolutely cannot cope and there is no other way to make the pain go away. Suicide rates in the military are at record highs. I was never open to the idea of killing myself, simply because my faith in GOD forbids it and I believe it is an unforgivable sin. Also, I could never do that to the people that love me, especially my wife and kids. Simply put, isolation is no good for anyone. It's a lose/lose situation.

Here are a few facts and statistics about post-traumatic stress disorder, those who suffer from the condition and the consequences of unresolved PTSD.

- *More than five million Americans suffer from PTSD annually.*
- *Estimates suggest that one in 13 U.S. citizens will develop post-traumatic stress disorder at some point during the course of their lives.*
- *One in three rape victims will develop PTSD.*
- *Though reasons remain unclear, 10 percent of women will receive diagnoses of PTSD, while only five percent of men are diagnosed with the disorder.*
- *Three out of 10 individuals who have spent civilian or military time in a war zone will develop PTSD.*
- *PTSD has been heavily associated with alcohol abuse, with more than half of sufferers becoming alcohol dependent.*
- *Nicotine dependency among individuals with PTSD occurs at twice the rate of the general population, with 45 percent of those with the anxiety disorder regularly smoking cigarettes.*

- *Individuals suffering from PTSD engage in abuse of illegal and prescription drugs at a rate of 35 percent—nearly three times the rate of drug abuse in the general population.*
- *Among veterans, those who come under fire experience higher rates of PTSD development. In fact, those with a single exposure develop PTSD at the general-population rate of 4.5 percent, while those with two firefights had an incidence rate of over nine percent. Thirteen percent of those who came under fire three to five times developed PTSD, while one in five soldiers with more than five exposures to firefight developed PTSD.*
- *Enlisted soldiers experience PTSD at a rate that is double that of officers.*
- *Soldiers in the Marines and Army have been found to be four times more likely to develop PTSD then individuals serving in the Air Force or Navy.*

Galatians 6:9
And let us not grow weary of doing good, for in due season we will reap, if we do not give up.

Lord, thank You for showing me how to love and the power of loving. I pray in JESUS' name. Amen

The Chute to My Ladder

I'm trying to find the chute to my ladder.
However, my thoughts always seem to scatter,
constantly mixing around in my mind like batter.
Only bad memories, spiraling into the depths of my brain, matter.
I climb and climb in search of a way to get down.
The water keeps rising and I'm afraid to drown.
One can only go so high before they come crashing to the ground.
What do I do? It's not only about me.
Besides my wife, I must care for our three.
In order to do that, I must find a way,
I must find a release: for a chute, I will pray.
I must find a way out, leave this night for the day.
This never-ending ladder seems to have no end in sight.
The ladder keeps me amped-up and on edge, as if I'm still in the fight.
I claim to be a good doer, but I still wrong the right
My family is falling off the ladder, because I'm a selfish man.
Will I continue to climb or reach out my hand?
My wife has always been there for me, but I must find a chute on my own.
Or could I be wrong? Maybe I can't do this alone.
I've tried to call out for help, but there is no ring-tone.
I'm steadily climbing this ladder: someone throw me a bone.
What am I thinking? Everyone's trying to help me.
It is I that won't let myself be free.
The rungs on this ladder are getting so tight.
I need to find a chute soon . . . hopefully before tonight.

Cy Mulholland

t took me long time to realize that there was so much help out there that I didn't know about. Today, I'm well aware of the resources that are available to me. I know for me it's important to stay actively involved in church. I am so thankful for JESUS and the One that sent Him for the sacrifice and forgiveness. My spiritual connection with GOD is the most important thing in my life. It gets me through each day by helping me cope with the memories, the nightmares, and flashbacks. I'm so grateful for my wife Carleeh. At times, when I am drifting or zoning out, she brings me back.

I know that it is important to seek help for my issues, through subject matter experts. Therefore, when it comes to things such as my alcoholism, I go to the experts that deal with alcohol issues for help. I'm currently enrolled in the Army's substance abuse program and occasionally I meet with friends who are active in sobriety. I meet with friends every Tuesday night that I can, because they are active in sobriety and I can relate to all of them. I learn something new every day and I always walk away from fellowship with some useful knowledge or something helpful from a story I may have heard. I see a therapist as well as a psychiatric doctor once a week for my PTSD. I take medication and use coping skills such as writing poetry and working out to get through each day, but first and foremost is my relationship with GOD.

Revelation 3:11
I am coming soon. Hold fast what you have, so that no one may seize your crown.

Lord, grant me the motivation to do something to help someone else in need. I pray in JESUS' name. Amen

The Voice of Reason

Is it honest or does it lie?
Few times does it sound good when it's looking me in the eye.
Actually, it annoys the hell out of me,
And I cannot figure out exactly why.
I want to do my own thing. Your advice feels like a bee sting.
For me, there is no season for the reason.
No matter what you tell me, I will hear nothing.
I may listen, but I will not adhere.
Are you done yet? Because I'm out of here.
Go ahead, try and talk me out of my next mistake.
I thought I felt something, but you are nowhere near.
Somewhere deep inside, I know I need you.
We were close, but I said we are through.
You always come back like you're on the attack.
I'm supposed to let you in and I know it to be true.
Go away reason, or stay at home. Right now, I need to be alone.
Don't try to call me; don't pick up the phone.
I will not answer: I never have.
It's self-centered time and I'm in the zone.
I'll be out there in the trees, just my thoughts and I.
I know you love me, reason, but please try not to cry.
It could be worse: I could end up in a hearse.
Too many wrong decisions and I know I could die.

E verything we need to know in order to be successful in this life is in the Holy Bible. We are only human, but that is not an excuse. I know that redemption is not a free pass to live however I want. I have a choice when it comes to my decisions. The fact of the matter is, the deck was stacked against us from the beginning. Soon after the world began, sin entered a perfect world through the influences of the devil and mankind's pride. In that moment, this world began to die and so did its inhabitants.

There is a lot I don't understand in this world, but I learn something new every day. I have come to have a much greater knowledge of temptation than I used to. I've paid attention to the trickery by which I have been deceived and have learned better how to combat it. I listen to those with far greater wisdom than my own. I listen to GOD-gifted and anointed men such as Pastor Curtis, a near and dear friend of mine whom GOD has used very powerfully in my life. For that, I give full thanks to GOD Almighty.

We are only human, and sin will never be fully withdrawn from our lives until time no longer exists: Until the evil one has been cast into eternal ruin and can influence us no longer. We will make mistakes, but by the grace of GOD and faith in JESUS CHRIST, who paid for the very sins that we commit, we are forgiven. Our Father knows that we are incapable of living a perfect life in this world, where temptation from Satan is so powerful. The evil one didn't get to where he is today by not having some kind of power. Granted, GOD allows him to have these capabilities and for us that is hard to understand, but it is not for us to understand. We will never understand the awesomeness and amazing power and logic and wisdom of GOD. We could not understand it. I know the one thing that I need to understand is that GOD is my creator and He created me so that He could have fellowship and a loving relationship with me. I am His.

He loves us so much that He sent His Son to pay the full price for all of mankind's sin. He gave us the law that He knew we were incapable of upholding, in order to show us our dependence on His help. He then told us He was going to send the Savior in advance and He then sent His Son to do everything He said that He would do when He explained it through the prophets. It was a lesson. We cannot do it without him. We will fall short. We will make mistakes. We will sin. Our Father in Heaven asks that we strive to do our best and that we acknowledge His Son as the risen Savior and King who conquered death, because death has no bonds on the

Almighty and All-Powerful GOD. He does not give us a free pass to sin, simply because we are forgiven. If we falter and choose to willfully remain in sin, He will remind us why we should not do so. He loves us more than we could ever possibly imagine.

With love comes discipline. That is why He saved us from our own weaknesses and the influence of the evil, deceitful, condemned devil. He loves us too much to not offer us the grace to come to Him in Heaven. We simply must make the choice to accept His grace. By having faith and believing in CHRIST JESUS, we are saved. Amen

1 Peter 5:8
Be sober-minded; be watchful. Your adversary the devil prowls around like a roaring lion, seeking someone to devour.

Lord, I praise Your Holy Name. Thank you, JESUS, for saving me and thank You for loving me, my Holy Father GOD. Lord, I thank You for Your grace and forgiveness. I love You, Father. I pray in JESUS' name. Amen

Cymptoms

My name is Cy and it is pronounced sigh.
Oftentimes people ask me if it is short for something and why.
No, Cy is my name and I'll get to my point.
I'm going to write you another poem and I won't disappoint.
There are symptoms to just about every disease.
Please bear with me if you would please.
I have Cymptoms for my alcoholism and PTSD. I'm learning to cope,
but it has taken time, you see.
Not only I, but my family too. They've had to put up with my
Cymptoms for more years than a few.
More than a few years, one of my Cymptoms is tears.
Another one of my Cymptoms is the drinking of beers.
Beers and other booze, whichever I choose; every time I drink is a time
that I lose.
Other Cymptoms include, but are not limited to: yelling in a very
loud voice;
The throwing of household goods of my choice;
Then there's the punching and kicking of holes in the walls—
I didn't drink till I drowned, but I had many falls;
More times than not, I would drink and drive.
I'm so glad I didn't kill anybody. It's a wonder I'm alive.
Some rare Cymptoms I experienced included jumping on a moving car.
The Cymptom of being untouchable never got me very far.
This disorder is painful. This disease is insane.
I had to learn to recover. I had to learn to restrain.
If I hadn't sought a normal life, there would've been nothing to gain.

My family and I went down to a place called Saunders Springs. It is a pretty little place where the kids can play in the water and we can go hiking on the several trails that are there. It is very peaceful and often I like to sit down and watch the water while I think and pray.

Yesterday while we were there, one of my wife's friends, a lady we go to Church with, stopped by to visit. Her husband is currently deployed to Afghanistan and is about half-way done with his tour there. GOD-willing, he and the men and women from his unit will make it home safely. At one point while we were all conversing, I asked her how her husband was doing and how he was in his faith, because she had been talking to him about GOD and he had some uncertainties. She went on to tell us that he no longer refers to himself as a Christian, where he once had. It reminded me of myself a few years ago and the toll PTSD took on me.

What makes us lose heart and faith in our GOD so quickly in hard times? It seems that so often we doubt GOD or give up on Him altogether when we need Him most, when in fact GOD is with us every step of the way. When distance is created between GOD and ourselves, it is always because we walk away from Him.

For me, the situation was slightly different than the gentlemen previously written about, because I never lost faith or hope while I was deployed to Iraq. I began to doubt upon returning to the United States, because I couldn't understand why GOD would allow so many bad things in the world to happen. I couldn't make sense of GOD allowing my friends to be killed in combat: this was due in a large part to the fact that I was immature in my spirituality, which I have since grown in immensely.

However, at the time, I had lost heart and walked away from GOD and walked straight into the arms of the bottle. Drinking, and later womanizing, became my way of coping with all the painful memories, along with the fear and doubt that there might not be a GOD. What I didn't realize at the time, but I am well aware of now, is that I was listening to the deceptions of Satan.

It is so important for us all to remember that there are two sides to every situation, especially when it comes to spirituality, or 'spiritual warfare,' as it often referred to. The evil one would have us all believe that there is no GOD, and if we buy into these lies, then we give him power: power over our lives and possibly the way we spend our eternity. That's a lot to take in and when statements such as this are made to certain individuals, it is too much for them to understand: which is, once again, a deception from the devil himself.

I often speak and write about the fact that there is no grey area when it comes to faith and spirituality and I stand firm in that. This doesn't mean that we are either righteous or sinner: it means that in cases such as this, one is either of GOD or one is of the sinful world. We are sinners regardless of what we believe, because the devil does have very powerful influences in this dying world. It's what we do in our faith and daily lives to combat his evil schemes that is important and that is why it is referred to as spiritual warfare. We are all going to make mistakes, but we cling to JESUS the Savior when we catch ourselves in sin and repent and strive not to repeat these wrong doings. This does not give us a free pass to indulge in life's sinful pleasures and preplan to ask for forgiveness. That is not just. Willfully living in sin without ever committing to honest repentance and accepting the Lord's saving grace with your whole heart is to die in sin.

I do know that nothing is hidden from the Father or the Son. When it comes down to it, we have to be strong in our faith, or we will lose it. When we walk away from GOD, we are allowing ourselves to be deceived by the devil, whether we realize it or not. We walk out from under the light that is GOD's grace and we step into the shadows. I don't ever mean to seem harsh, but it is irrelevant whether a person believes in GOD or not. He does exist and He is the Creator of us and all things; Without His love and His grace, there will be no salvation. Without CHRIST JESUS there is no life: only death.

John 14:6
Jesus answered, "I am the way and the truth and the life. No one comes to the Father except through me.

I have experienced my rock-bottom and it was not a pretty sight. I believed in GOD and I walked away from GOD, but He never left me. He loves us too much to ever give up on us. It is my hope and prayer that someone reading this and who is in that same situation that I was will come to an understanding of God. If anyone is having a hard time understanding why GOD let's things play out the way they do, or is questioning whether GOD exists or not, I would challenge that person to hold on and have faith.

God has a plan. He has a plan for me, people like me, and everyone else in this world and He did truthfully send His only Son to die on the cross in order that the price of our sins would be paid in full. He loves us. We are His children and one day we will leave this place and feel the impact of sin and deception in our lives no longer. The things we don't understand in this world will be revealed to us and our Lord will greet us with open arms and He will tell us, "Welcome home, faithful and trusting servant."

Lord, thank You for opening my eyes when they were heavy and my vision was blurred by the deception of the world and thank you, Lord, for providing the rock for me to build my house upon. I pray in JESUS' name. Amen

Normal People

I see normal people. They are everywhere.
They seem to walk through life without a care.
I see normal people. They appear to be alive . . .
Unlike the soldier who feels dead inside.
It looks as though they are light on their feet.
The soldier is weighted down: he's stuck in concrete.
Nothing is the same; it didn't used to be this way.
Tomorrow will be today, but nowhere near yesterday.
There are four letters on the lock binding the chains around his feet.
These chains of knowledge and weakness provide a feeling that is
bitter-sweet.
Some try to give the soldier a hand, but normal people don't have to
understand.
Most won't try, but some do help when they formulate the proper plan.
The soldier has a partial envy and seeks a normal stand,
Though he wouldn't trade anything for his boots filled with desert sand.
Normal people have it made: innocence and a normal life.
And I agree, that's the way it should be.
Someone cut loose his load with a great, big, normal knife.
To be a normal man with a normal life is indeed each soldiers' goal.
These abnormal circumstances have finally taken their toll.
To live that way would mean to be free.
What is normal to you is not normal to me.
The letters on the lock spell PTSD.

Thanks days, I feel normal and what a great feeling that is. The truth is, I don't remember ever feeling this way before in my life. I feel worry-free, kind of like a child, but with a new maturity and a slight wisdom that I've never had before. I finally discovered how to get back to a normal life. It was a long, hard road to get here, because there are so many things than can cloud a person's mind once they have experienced trauma. Looking back, it seems kind of silly, but on the other hand I remember the important fact that I am only human. I keep in perspective the fact that we live in a dying world, where everything is stacked against us: By everything, I mean sin and death and its millions of different, complicated faces.

I will get into that more on a later time and page. What I know now—and it does seem kind of simple—is that I can have peace and be stress-free, so long as I am striving to do the right thing. As long as I am making every effort to do the "Right Thing," then there is no reason for me to stress. Even when the world is throwing everything at me and it could seem that there is no way out, I can be patient. When there are times of financial stress or someone else's bad day is spilling over onto me, I can still have peace because I have Jesus.

If there is one message that I am able to get across throughout the entirety of this book, it is just that JESUS saves. He is the source of everything that is good, kind, loving, faithful, peaceful, sharing, hopeful, giving and stress-free. He is where I have found this amazing peace that I longed for all my life. The moment a person realizes that everything good and just comes from Him and that every negative feeling, thought, or action you have ever experienced comes from the evil one and your own weakness, that individual discovers that he or she has power over sin by His grace.

It is really that simple, but for some of us, it is not so easy to get there, because we are so lost in the chaos of our own negativity or pity. I had to learn how to properly mourn and respect the fact that everyone dies and everyone must prepare themselves ahead of time for that and what is after. Many people have obstacles such as this, that they are either trying to get past or have given up on and have surrendered themselves to their temptations. I hope and pray that they find JESUS. As for me, my brothers and sisters, I have arrived.

Hebrews 10:36
For you have need of endurance, so that when you have done the will of God you may receive what is promised.

Lord, thank You for counting me among Your children and allowing me the time to come back to You. I know there will be challenges to come. I know adversity is on the way, but with You Lord, my Savior, I am not lost. I pray in JESUS' name. Amen

Knowledge and Weakness

So often, I take things for granted.
Often, I choose to do the opposite:
The opposite of that which I know is right.
I choose to do the wrong, simply in spite.
Somehow, I tell myself that I'm ok,
But if I died today, there is no way.
I am a foolish man and that's easy to say.
Knowing right from wrong, I still turn away.
I have the knowledge, but I'm weak. My life is one, long, losing streak.
Never changing and living every day like I'm guaranteed next week.
Ever rearranging my morals and boldly I speak.
It's easy to sound knowledgeable and tell others what's good,
But it's all for nothing if I'm not living as I should.
It's a weakness to know better and do as I please.
There will be no excuses in the end, when I fall to my knees.
The Jew and the Gentile, they both agree.
We will all be judged and there will be no plea.
I can't be of this world; I want to live when I die.
While pondering so much disappointment, sometimes I cry;
And then back at it again like I don't even try.
Knowledge and weakness is a bad combination.
I must swallow my pride and use recognition.
If I don't change my ways, there will be no compensation.

S o often throughout the years, I have taken so many things for granted. I've taken my GOD and my Lord and Savior Jesus Christ for granted. Though I am not worthy of His forgiveness, though I receive it, I still take it for granted. What a loving Father He is. I will never fully understand the awesomeness of His power and how He could forgive me, time after time, after all of the mistakes I have made throughout my lifetime.

He gives more than forgiveness. He has blessed me with a beautiful loving wife, Carleeh and three amazing children. I have a ten-year-old son named Cainen, an eight-year-old daughter named Cennady, and a two-year-old daughter named Celeste. I am so grateful for the four of them and even though I know how blessed I am to have a wonderful family, I still took them for granted. I let the pain and misery of my PTSD drive me straight into the arms of alcohol. Instead of being at home with my family, I went out with supposed friends who were really nothing more than drinking associates. I would stay gone all day and out all night and come home when the sun was coming up. I would go to the beach, out to local bars and out to clubs.

All the while, my wife was at home wondering where I was and what I was doing. I was up to no good. I would drink till I was oblivious to anything that was going on around me. I would black out and get into fights and make passes at other women. I didn't even take into consideration whether they were married or not and I sure didn't mind that I was.

At the end of every night of partying and being up to no good, I would come home and there was my wife, sitting up on the living room couch, waiting up for me and wanting answers, which of course were replaced by lies from me. My out-of-control behavior led to me cheating on my wife several times throughout the years. She eventually found out and left me for a little while. That little while ended up being just another drinking binge for me. Eventually, we worked it out and she and the kids came home. However, it was made very clear that I was to get help and get well and I agreed.

Ephesians 6:18
Praying at all times in the Spirit, with all prayer and supplication. To that end keep alert with all perseverance, making supplication for all the saints,

Lord, give me the wisdom to recognize temptation when it occurs and the strength to turn away from it. Thank You for my family and good health. I pray in JESUS' name. Amen

Get Well Soon

Stay pro-active in your recovery. You know what to do.
Get well soon, self. It's been a hell of a ride.
I'm afraid the beating has left you injured inside.
You've been hard on yourself for so long now.
It's amazing that you're still here, but I don't know how.
What's important is that you've finally decided to change.
Not every soldier is capable of that, after going down-range.
I know you've seen and done things that were indeed strange.
Some have to make sacrifices to bring forth change.
I was happy to see that you put down the drink.
You were up to your neck in booze, but you didn't sink.
Remember that you have to put your sobriety first.
Find healthy ways to cope and overcome the thirst.
I know at times the anxiety makes you feel like your head could burst.
It is vitally important to realize things could be much worse.
Everyone has problems. You are not alone. Do not isolate yourself in
your own home.
You have a family that loves you very much. Keep them close to you and
don't lose touch.
You've been through a lot. PTSD is not easy.
Continue getting help for the combat stress. Don't worry about
who sees me.
I know you lost your brother long ago and you don't understand.
Just try to remember that GOD does have a plan.
Well, I wish you the best and I'll be praying for you.

Cy Mulholland

For those who are suffering with Post Traumatic Stress Disorder, it is very important to come to terms with the fact that the average person in society does not understand what we are going through and it would be unrealistic for us to expect that from them. It took me a long time to discover that fact, but I am grateful that I did come to an understanding. For instance, an individual who has been struck by an Explosively Formed Projectile (EFP) while on a combat mission and watched half of his crew die in front of him cannot understand what a rape victim has experienced, whereas the rape victim cannot understand what the combat veteran has experienced.

The point is that we all have our problems. This is how the world works and as long as we keep these things in perspective, we will all be better off because of it. One of the problems in today's society is the growing amount of people developing their own reason for being angry and owning it. Anger projected outwardly until it affects others is irrational. It is natural to be angry at times, but there is no reason whatsoever for any one individual to let his or her anger affect anyone else. To this day, I haven't met anyone too old to take a time-out.

Too often, our loved ones are affected by anger that has nothing to do with them. It is especially sad when children feel the brunt of their parent's anger: something I was guilty of for a long time. Until I was able to forgive myself, I was very regretful for many of the actions that I allowed my children to witness: many times in the form a drunken rage.

Many of us—to include myself—have been guilty of projecting anger toward random strangers. I can't count how many times I have road-raged or snapped at some innocent bystander who I felt was looking at me the wrong way at a grocery store. Likewise, I have felt the impact of others' anger and aggression that had absolutely nothing to do with me. Now, after dealing with many of these situations throughout my struggle with PTSD, I try to remember that I don't know where others have come from and what they have been through.

In my lifetime, my struggle has been my brother's suicide when I was a young child and my three combat deployments to Iraq. For others, their struggle may be due to the fact that one of their parents abandoned them at some point in their life. Yet for others, it may be that their parents were always there, but abusive in one form or the other. GOD takes no sin lightly and He definitely doesn't take harming a child in any way lightly. There is no way to know where a stranger's anger comes from and because of this, it is important for us not to pass judgments on each other. It all comes down to respect: Respecting others as we would want to be respected, just as we are called to love and treat others as we want to be loved and treated.

Hebrews 12: 1-2
Therefore, since we are surrounded by so great a cloud of witnesses, let us also lay aside every weight, and sin which clings so closely, and let us run with endurance the race that is set before us, looking to Jesus, the founder and perfecter of our faith, who for the joy that was set before him endured the cross, despising the shame, and is seated at the right hand of the throne of God.

Unfortunately there are those in this world that could care less about my two cents worth of advice or anyone else's. There are those who claim that they are incapable of loving or being loved. There are many in society who act as if the world owes them something, because they have been wronged, not knowing or remembering that CHRIST suffered a great deal more than they have had to endure and He did so without ever sinning. Some people, it seems, are just too angry for change and they would tell someone like me, who has learned from his mistakes, to take his own medicine, not knowing that now I do. I will pray for those out there still walking and talking with a hardened heart and mad at the world, in hope that somehow, some way, a spark will be ignited within those cold hearts and become a light that will burn bright for the GOD of love and kindness.

Hebrews 12: 3-15
Consider him who endured from sinners such hostility against himself, so that you may not grow weary or fainthearted. In your struggle against sin you have not yet resisted to the point of shedding your blood. And have you forgotten the exhortation that addresses you as sons?

"My son, do not regard lightly the discipline of the Lord, nor be weary when reproved by him. For the Lord disciplines the one he loves, and chastises every son whom he receives."

Cy Mulholland

It is for discipline that you have to endure. God is treating you as sons. For what son is there whom his father does not discipline? If you are left without discipline, in which all have participated, then you are illegitimate children and not sons. Besides this, we have had earthly fathers who disciplined us and we respected them. Shall we not much more be subject to the Father of spirits and live? For they disciplined us for a short time as it seemed best to them, but he disciplines us for our good, that we may share his holiness. For the moment all discipline seems painful rather than pleasant, but later it yields the peaceful fruit of righteousness to those who have been trained by it.

Therefore lift your drooping hands and strengthen your weak knees, and make straight paths for your feet, so that what is lame may not be put out of joint but rather be healed. Strive for peace with everyone, and for the holiness without which no one will see the Lord. See to it that no one fails to obtain the grace of God; that no "root of bitterness" springs up and causes trouble, and by it many become defiled;

Lord, I pray for those out there who are lonely and hurting. I pray for those out there who are angry and neglected. Father, I pray for all those who are lost and in need of guidance, love and a helping hand, that they may have it. In JESUS' name I pray. Amen.

CHAPTER FIVE

SUPPRESSED FIRES

Anger and aggression that cause discontent, confrontation,
violence, and fits of rage must be extinguished,
in order to live a normal life.

The City Speaks

The city speaks. The city never sleeps.
The city is bright. The city is a sight.
The American dream, the American way.
Everything changed on the ninth month, the eleventh day.
The city is alive. The city heard the whistle.
On that day, through the air, flew two human-guided missiles.
The city never thought. The city did not expect
That one day, those towers would no longer be erect.
The city felt the sting. The city heard the ring.
On that day, a new war changed its very being.
The city holds the people. The city is the people.
But they who struck the city are those who are not equal.
The nation heard the screams, our brothers and sisters cry.
We heard the sounds from the city, except from those that died.
This world is a place of good and evil.
A place of slave and free.
Our home is a free nation. Slaves, we will never be.
The city still speaks. The city will never sleep.
The city is still bright and our country will stand and fight.
We still have dreams. It's the American way.
In the end, this entire world will burn and it's you that's going to pay.
But for now, the city lives and our nation lives on.
We will always proudly stand and sing our anthem song.
And we will never stop the fight until we right the wrong.

remember how our nation came together when we were struck in such a violent and horrific manner on 9/11. I remember the immense feeling of anger and sadness, when so much innocent blood was spilled. I remember the indescribable feeling of not being able to make sense of the possibility of the United States of America being attacked in such a way as this. I couldn't then and I still can't understand to this day how a people could have such hatred in their heart that they make it acceptable to kill noncombatants. The events which occurred on 9/11—in combination with my three tours in combat—have contributed a great deal to my symptoms with PTSD.

As I mentioned, I remember our nation coming together. There was a feeling of unity that hadn't been felt in years and I remember wondering why it took something like this to achieve it. I thought this feeling was here to stay, but little did I know that in just a few short years, that feeling would begin to dissipate. It seemed as though many of the people that came together and held each other and cried with each other forgot, only a few years later, how much they needed each other.

I am grateful that we do come together in our hardest times. One thing this grand country of ours will never do is lay down when faced with adversity. We have a good habit of standing up for freedom and most of the time we stand for that which is right. The same should be said of service members about themselves. It's hard to do, but it is a huge achievement when one finally realizes the importance of standing up to painful memories and self-trainings in the ways of resiliency and perseverance.

We stand for freedom all over the world: Not just our own. We make sacrifices for those that can't always stand up for themselves and we always have. I'm grateful that I'm a citizen of a country like ours.

However, I wish we could remember the full intent of our forefathers for our country. I wish we could remember the morals and values we were founded on. I wish we could remember that our country is a nation under the one true GOD, the GOD of the Bible. I wish we were all on the same page where the value of life is concerned: I can't believe that there are more than fifty million children that never had a shot at life, in our country alone.

But wishing doesn't fix anything, so I will continue to pray and hope. Moreover, I will hope and pray that those struggling with PTSD will recover and endure.

Cy Mulholland

Matthew 24:13
But the one who endures to the end will be saved.

Lord, help us as a people to remember the value of the life that You give. Help us to remember the importance of standing together through the good times and the bad. Father, help us to remember the morals which You have given us to live by and the principles this country is based on. In JESUS' name I pray. Amen

There I Was

There I was, no shit, you've heard it time and again.
Tell me where you were the day the towers fell, my friend.
I was on the tank range, Red Cloud Hotel, stacked behind several crews.
When I finished my run, I returned to the base line.
That's when I heard the news.
They sat us down in the bleachers there.
They shared with us the latest scare.
As the Captain spoke, all I could do was stare.
I knew this meant war, but I didn't care.
As the day grew longer, so did the death toll.
So many dead Americans . . . I was ready to roll.
I wanted revenge, I wanted to regain control.
As I watched the TV, I saw one jump after another.
I watched the towers fall, the first and then the other.
When I saw these things, a single tear fell from my eye.
Then the sadness was replaced by anger and I forgot how to cry.
I wanted a chance to kill the enemy, even if it meant that I might die.
There I was; where were you? I know you were hurting like I was, too.
I know it changed me. How did it affect you?
I was happy to see our country reunite.
I feel comfort in knowing we stand up for what is right.
We didn't start this, but we will finish the fight.

Cy Mulholland

t is very comforting to live in a country where there are so many brave men and women. I choose to believe that the majority of Americans are good people that help make this country a better place, too. We all have our share of problems, but I believe that most people out there aren't trying to collect handouts, but are trying to better themselves. It is my opinion that it is perfectly fine to receive help, as long as one remains pro-active and doesn't take advantage of people or organizations. I receive a lot of help for the issues I have because of time spent in combat, but I'm not taking advantage of anyone. I have set goals for myself. I have a plan and every intention of following through with that plan. My cup is half full. That's the way I have to be.

It's too easy to get down in the dumps and depressed and I have spent a large portion of my life that way. I refuse to live that way anymore. Today, I see the positive in everything and I keep everything in perspective. Whatever has happened has already happened. I can't change it and a lot of the time I may not be able to make it better. That doesn't mean I have to feel down about it. That will get me nowhere fast.

One of the hardest things for me to deal with has always been the loss of loved ones, whether it is family, friends, or brothers in arms. That has always been the number one cause of my depression, ever since my brother's suicide. I know it will be hard for me to lose the ones I love in the future, whoever they may be, and I have no idea how I will handle it, but I know that my head is on straighter than it has been in a while.

I want to give another special thanks to all of the men and women that defend our nation, right here on our own turf. Thanks to the Firefighters, Policemen, Coast Guard, Homeland Security and the many others for your service. Thanks to all of the family members that support them. It takes all of us to protect what we have here. GOD bless those brave Firefighters and all others who gave their lives in New York City, trying to save lives on 9/11. That is the American spirit. That is the American way.

2 Timothy 4:18
The Lord will rescue me from every evil deed and bring me safely into his heavenly kingdom. To him be the glory forever and ever. Amen.

Lord, bless and comfort all of the family members that have lost loved ones in the defense of freedom, both here and abroad. I pray in JESUS' name. Amen

Never Again

Looking through my sight, I see you.
My rounds take flight and your blood does too.
Before I pull the trigger, "On the way", is my battle cry.
Screams of agony and pain are your only reply.
I traverse and scan and ponder your last thought.
"It's not something I wanted, but it's what I was taught."
I think to myself, "It didn't have to be this way. This is insane."
But I know that we didn't start this war.
It was a radical and evil deception that flew those four planes.
You struck first and spilled innocent blood.
So, with a prayer to the one true GOD began a red, white, and blue flood.
It came in many forms: ships, planes, and tanks with the goal of putting
an end to your cowardly pranks.
We attacked with concentration, with troops from all over our nation.
We came with many Warriors, Black Knights and Desert Rogues.
We came with thunder and lightning and Screaming Eagles to
destroy our foes.
We came with steel rain and sent our message loud and clear.
We may fight till the end of time on your land, but never again will you
strike us here.

Cy Mulholland

ike most Americans I will never forget where I was the day the twin towers fell. I was stationed at Fort Stewart, Georgia. I had been there since the summer of 1999. That day, my company and I were on Red Cloud Hotel, a tank gunnery range where we were firing tank table seven. (That is more or less a practice run for tank table eight, which is the actual qualification table.) Tank gunnery is how tankers train on their crew duties in order to prepare for war. It is more or less a giant shooting range for tanks.

Anyway, there we were. I had just finished my table seven day run when I noticed all of the tanks in our company pulling onto the base line, which was abnormal because most of the time we were continuously trying to push crews down range, one after the other. The 1st Sergeant had us all sit on the bleachers right there on the base line between the tower and the bore site line.

There, the company commander informed us all that our country had come under attack and that planes had struck the twin towers in New York City. He informed us that it was unknown who was responsible for the attack, but that we should begin preparing ourselves mentally for the possibility of going to war. You could have heard a pin drop. We could only imagine how bad it actually was, until a few days later when we were back at home and we could watch the footage ourselves on television.

I couldn't believe it the first time I saw the one tower burning and then the second plane hit. I was enraged every time an innocent American leaped to their death from the burning buildings. I watched the replays as one tower fell and then the other and I cried. I wanted so badly for the ones responsible to pay for what they had done. At the time, I had no idea what the future had in store for me, but as it would come to pass the 3rd Infantry Division—of which I was a part—would play a huge role in the War on Terrorism. I deployed three times to Iraq in defense of our great country and, though my days in combat are over, I am eternally grateful for all those who have and still do stand for what's right in defense of the American people.

Romans 12:2
Do not be conformed to this world, but be transformed by the renewal of your mind, that by testing you may discern what is the will of God, what is good and acceptable and perfect.

Lord, bless all of the brave men and women who make sacrifices in the name of freedom, both in our country and abroad. I pray in JESUS' name. Amen

You don't understand

You don't understand and you never will.
You've never been in my boots. They're too big to fill.
I don't mean to sound cocky, but what I say is real.
I'm grateful for those of you that say "thanks" and stop to shake my hand.
I know it's hard, but I appreciate the fact that you try to understand.
At least there are some out there that don't hate us and that's grand.
Some out there can't handle the truth. They don't understand what it
takes to get the job done.
Maybe it's because you've never lost a daughter or you never lost a son,
Or maybe you used to support us, until you lost someone.
Please remember the cost of freedom is high.
To sustain our freedom, some must die.
I can't help that you're still asking why.
You don't have to understand, but I'm asking you to try.
I've been to the fight three different times and many times nearly
lost my life,
And three times I was fortunate to return home to my wife.
Soldiers like me and families have to live with the loss.
We never forget those who paid the ultimate cost.
They paid the price for us all to live.
Maybe you will realize that and maybe you will forgive.
Tomorrow and the day I lost a brother in arms share the same date.
I survived the war. Now where lays my fate?
I woke up today; I have a fresh start.
I don't know if it's enough to lift a heavy heart.

Cy Mulholland

So many times, I've flown home for R&R leave from Iraq. Once, I flew home for leave from Bosnia. It was such a good feeling to be going home after a few months of not seeing my family. It's a feeling that is almost indescribable. I was so excited every time. I had butterflies in my stomach and a smile that wouldn't quit. I always hoped that time would go by so slow while I was home, but it never did. I always had so much fun and time flies when I'm having fun.

For me, there was always a stop in Atlanta before moving on to Savannah where my wife would pick me up. I remember getting off the plane there and taking care of all the Army's formalities as quickly as I could. I remember walking through the terminals and watching, as most people just carried on as they would any other day, which was fine. But the kids in the airport always seemed to take interest in the uniform and that was cool.

Occasionally, a stranger would walk up to me and shake my hand and welcome me home. Greetings like that always felt good. Most people didn't take notice, but there are those few that take the time to show their appreciation.

Unfortunately, I wasn't only excited to be home to see my wife and our children. I couldn't wait to have that first drink and all the others that would follow it. As soon as I was complete with the administrative things we had to do for the Army, I was off to get a drink. I knew of a certain VIP lounge that offered free drinks to service men and women. So there I was, enjoying my free drinks and getting a pretty good buzz going until it was time to go to the gate and board the plane to Savannah. It was a short flight, only about a half hour. My wife was always there to pick me up.

It was a very happy moment, greeting each other with kisses, hugs, smiles and laughter, but my wife could always smell the alcohol on me. Every time, she would say, "You couldn't wait, could you?" She didn't get upset because she was so excited to see me, but I knew she always hoped I would greet her at the gate sober, so that it would just be me and my real emotions coming out, untainted by alcohol. I was never patient enough for that, though. If I could change many things about the past, I would, but I'm not going to "should" on myself today.

Revelation 21:7
The one who conquers will have this heritage, and I will be his God and he will be my son.

Lord, thank You for my sobriety today and may You bless me with many more days like this one. Please give me the strength and courage to meet You all of the way. I pray in JESUS' name. Amen

Well Done

Well done, Seal Team Six. You made the right pick.
Thank GOD we have freedom fighters such as you.
Dedicated to GOD and country, you never stop till it's through.
Thank you from my heart for all that you have done.
Your freedom-filled hearts never stop till you've won.
I've been to the fight and I know times are tough.
You go above and beyond, no matter how rough.
You special ops, you elite, you really bring the heat.
You killed that evil tyrant, you ensured no retreat.
You took no prisoners, you got the job done.
In the end, it will be our team that has won.
From soldier to SEAL, I can imagine how good that must feel.
I will never know exactly who you are.
What I know is that you will go the distance, no matter how far.
You are the heroes, the unsung and you don't ask for much.
You accept this life that keeps you so out of touch.
Thank you, brothers and continue the fight.
I am grateful to you that I can sleep at night.
Thank you, all of you who bleed red, white, and blue.
We patriots at home welcome and love you.
You are in my thoughts and prayers. You are the best.
Do what you have to do and come home, GOD BLESS.

I wrote "Well Done" as a way of expressing my personal appreciation to the men that were responsible for taking down one of the most evil men to ever walk the earth. I knew they would most likely never see it, but it made me feel good to put something down on paper. At the time, I didn't realize that I would later be writing a book such as this, containing my thoughts and feelings. After I decided to write this book however, I thought it might be a possibility that somewhere down the road, maybe one of the members from SEAL TEAM SIX would happen to see my poem to them.

When I first heard about this team and how they are the most elite force our military has, I became an instant fan, even though I am in the military myself. They are the best of the best, not some actors on a movie screen. No, these are the men movies are made after. The cool thing is that they don't do it for fame. They do it because they are American Warriors and from the day they were born, they were destined to be a part of a team that is mirrored by no other in the world. I'm not taking anything away from the rest of us Soldiers, Marines, Sailors, and Airmen, but for now I am talking about Seal Team Six.

We are all called to perform certain duties and it takes all of us to accomplish the mission, but they are the all-stars. The very best go places that no one else can and do things that no one else will, but even the best fall in combat. The other day, I was watching the news and the headline read something about a chopper being shot down in Afghanistan and more than thirty warriors had been killed, including twenty or so men from Seal Team Six. I was instantly saddened, as I am any time I hear news of an American warrior losing his or her life. However, the way I reacted was much different than my typical reaction.

Like losing people I love and care about, it has also been very hard for me to lose those I have served with. Not only that, but I struggle with hearing news of any service men or women losing their lives in combat. It used to be that every time I heard news such as this, I would run directly to the bottle to help numb the pain and sooth my PTSD symptoms. At least, that's what I thought I was accomplishing.

You might ask, "Why were you so broken up about it? You didn't even know them." It doesn't matter if I knew any given fallen warrior or not. There is a certain bond amongst us and our families that is indescribable and impossible to comprehend, unless you have served or loved someone who has served. The difference for me is that today, I do not run to the drink to cope with the loss. Instead, I mourn the loss and I pray for their families. I no longer try and hide the pain. I honor those that have given the ultimate sacrifice. For the rest of my days, I will appreciate my family and the blessings that have been given to us. I will not waste time, because my brothers in arms who have fallen have no more time to waste.

Revelation 3:21
The one who conquers, I will grant him to sit with me on my throne, as I also conquered and sat down with my Father on his throne.

Lord, bless and comfort the families of the many fallen. And may the children who have lost parents in the name of freedom overcome the challenges that lie ahead of them. I pray in JESUS' name. Amen

Celebration is Motivation

There was celebration all over our nation;
The way we went about it led to their temptation.
Right now, they are massing in great concentration.
The louder we cheered amplified their frustration.
We want them to hear us: our pride is our foundation.
They will attempt it again, after much contemplation.
Killing their leader was intense motivation.
"We're going to kill number two," is the message we send.
Your own people give us the answers; their principles, we bend.
A little water here and there—our motivation, we lend.
The price to kill you cowards is worth it in the end.
So, saddle up that camel and to your purpose tend.
Killing you radical bastards has become our favorite trend,
And we will try to rid the world of you until the very end.
We want you to burn, we want you to hurt. No one will hear your cries.
If it were up to me, I'd dip you all in hot oil and make a batch of
extremist fries.
You think I'm playing and yes it's funny. I smile every time one of you dies.
The entire free world wants to be rid of you, there are no whats or whys.
We need to sanction your trades and sanction your evil lives.
We need to cut every single one of your crooked ties.
The freedom loving world is sick of every one of your deceitful lies.
And I can't wait for your final words and your final good byes.

This War on Terror is a war that has no end. The United States of America is a freedom-loving country that will never cease to stand up for what is right and just. I am proud that I was one who stood up and fought in the name of freedom. I used to wonder if it was worth it for our country to fight for the rights of the entire oppressed world, but today, I say it most definitely is. We, as Americans, and being the most powerful nation on the face of the earth, have a duty to the rest of mankind to help and spread the message of hope and freedom. This is what I believe. It may not be what someone else believes, but I see a world that is only going to get worse and if it is possible to save brothers and sisters in need, then we should. It would be selfish not to.

It's not just about us. It's about mankind. If we are doing the right thing, then we are letting the Lord's light shine through us and expressing the love and compassion that He would have us express. I have stood in defense of the freedom-loving world. I stood with my brothers on the battle field and defeated a force of evil. Today, I will do something somewhere to help somebody and the world will be that much better because of it. We should all try and give and not worry about being given to.

James 4:6
But he gives more grace. Therefore it says, "God opposes the proud, but gives grace to the humble."

Lord, bless the Soldiers, Marines, Airmen, Sailors, Coast Guard, Policemen, Firefighters, CIA, FBI, Homeland Security and the countless others that have and continue to make a stand in the name of freedom. Lord, comfort their families. I pray in JESUS' name. Amen

Good Riddance

It's been a while since I've seen this level of celebration.
People filled the streets all over the nation.
They shouted "U.S.A." and "Bin Laden is dead,"
A little bit of joy for the families of those that bled.
Once again, the country came together and many agree,
It was better to take him dead, not alive, and bury him at sea.
It's been a long fight, but we're still going strong.
It's been more than a decade and that's way too long.
I wish we could bring it to a close and bring my brothers and sisters home.
The end of this conflict is still unknown.
As you've read before, my glass is half full.
We are responsible for his death and that is just cool.
The war will go on, this war has no end.
I've been to the fight, I tell you the truth, my friend.
So let's get it out of our system and prepare for the next battle.
There are more terrorists in this world than there are cattle.
Celebrate America, rejoice, it's your choice.
I'm happy, but silent. I won't yet raise my voice.
I know he's gone and this is good news.
What do we do now? What will our leaders choose?
It's a war that won't end, but it's one we won't lose.
I remember where I was when Hussein met his end.
We are forced to sustain this pattern forever, my friend.

Cy Mulholland

I wrote "Good Riddance" while I was undergoing in-patient treatment. Like the vast majority of Americans, I was absolutely thrilled that the world had been rid of Osama Bin Laden, who was a mass murderer of innocent, freedom-loving people all over the world. He received what was long overdue. As a soldier that has served three tours in the War on Terror, I was relieved that he was gone. I knew at the time that the battle was far from over, but it was another step in the right direction.

I was still participating in my stay in the Brook Hospital in Louisville, Kentucky and I had just laid down to go to sleep, when the nurse that was on duty that night came into my room and said, "They killed Bin Laden. It's on the news right now." Of course, I jumped out of bed and slipped on my shower shoes and darted down to the day room to see what was going on. Sure enough, the headline read something along the lines of Bin Laden being killed by American forces. I was relieved.

Hebrews 10:23
Let us hold fast the confession of our hope without wavering, for he who promised is faithful.

Lord, bless all of the freedom-fighters around the globe that stand for what's right in defense of our nation and for a flag that proudly stands under GOD. I pray in JESUS' name. Amen

Random

Random are the thoughts in my mind, like a movie reel.
They are not of peace; they are of the kill.
High-stress moments when my mind races.
I drift far away to foreign places.
A place of sewage-soaked city streets.
A place where everyone feels defeat.
In my mind, a sense of concern, and a strange smell.
I find chaos suddenly and everything goes to hell.
Or does it find me? Yes, more times than not.
I remember the days when I made bodies rot.
Now it's luck of the draw and did you see what I saw.
The methods to our madness have more than one flaw.
Restrictions on triggers elevate many figures.
Conflicts aren't decided by who it is that is bigger.
Used to be for a short time there was an abundance to engage.
A corpse cut in half and sottered at the waist was so much more than rage.
Aggression became timid and hands became tied.
City streets at a moderate pace is one wild ride.
I appreciate the fact that we fought the good fight.
And also that I know now that I was justified in GOD's sight.
I'd be lying if I said it wasn't more funner as a lead tank gunner.
I killed my share to include more than one runner.
With large rounds from a big gun, I made lots of pieces.
The important thing though, is that my angers are now peaces.

Cy Mulholland

P astor Curtis, a close friend of mine and a brother in Christ, is a huge help in my spiritual growth and recovery. He spoke recently about anger and as always is the case, he delivered a powerful message. He is truly anointed by GOD and is one of the most effective speakers I have ever had the pleasure of hearing. He has had a huge, positive impact on my life and I am grateful to GOD for that.

After receiving the message, I began thinking about anger, because for the majority of my life it was the majority of my life. I realize that there are many people in this country who are hurting and angry for various reasons just as I was, but what causes us to be trapped in that frame of mind for so long, and for many, a lifetime? The obvious answer, of course, is always Satan, but we cannot forget the fact that we have free will. It's true that anyone can and will be attacked by the evil one, because he is a powerful force, but it seems to me in some cases that living in anger is considered somewhat faddish and cool.

One can walk around at the mall or even the grocery store or sometimes even at church and see individuals displaying their advertisements of anger directly on the shirts they are wearing. Just recently, I saw a shirt that read "Sin City," not at all an uncommon title for many things, including Las Vegas and the movie. Indeed, the world finds it "cool" to not only be angry, but to live in sin. This is what happens when the evil one deceives.

He is crafty and he applies enough influence to just the right degree in order to influence not only the nonbeliever, but many times believers as well, so that we allow ourselves to see and accept the satisfaction and instant gratification of sin. One might ask, "Why would anyone want to be angry?" and the answer once you put it in perspective is clear. With anger comes the coping mechanism. The coping mechanism varies for everyone, but oftentimes (as in my case) it is alcohol. Stating from personal experience, alcohol was a gateway for me to "alleviate" the anger I felt, as well as use other substances and even sex outside my marriage. It is a matter of fact, I used to create problems at home so that I had a reason to run out and do whatever I wanted.

Now granted, PTSD was the underlying issue, which brings me to my next point. We allow ourselves to cope with PTSD as we see fit. It is the perfect opportunity for the evil one to display his influence. The sad thing is that the nonbeliever doesn't even realize what is going on when this is taking place, which is why it is vitally important for efforts to be made to reach these suffering individuals. Especially in the military, PTSD combined with Satan's influence and the soul's misuse of free-will, is THE primary cause for so much drug use, alcohol abuse and suicide, among other things. There is a lot of help available to us all who struggle with this disorder and a message is being broadcast: however, it is not being delivered in the proper manner and that is not going to change within society. The majority of the world's population puts minimal to zero faith in the healing power of GOD. I realize the Lord puts people, places and things in our path to assist us in our daily lives, but it is when we acknowledge, repent, give thanks and have faith in the Almighty GOD that blessings come to us abundantly.

Therefore, it is the duty of all Christians, particularly Christians who have and are successfully managing the war with recovery, to spread a message of healing to others: the cure for PTSD is JESUS CHRIST. He is the surefire way, He is the life-line that we can all grab onto in order to be pulled out of this dark deception: this belief that we must live a life of pain and suffering.

To the nonbeliever: no one just wakes up one day and decides "I go to church and I am happy now." It doesn't work that way. The message I want to get across to all nonbelievers who are suffering with PTSD is that when we receive this relief, it is not just words. It is Jesus: it is something that one feels within him or herself. The HOLY SPIRIT is felt and I know this because just as I am typing these words now, I feel the HOLY SPIRIT in me. I feel peace, love, joy, happiness and I know within the depths of my heart and soul and mind that I don't need a drink. All I need is love. That is all we need. GOD is love and His love is found in the Word and the Word was with Him even before time began. He is the Creator of all things and the source of peace and everlasting life. Amen.

Instant gratification followed by guilt follows sin. There are various feelings that follow instant gratification. These feelings can be doubt, fear and loneliness, as well as anger (which I commonly refer to). Most commonly, there is a combination of these feelings. However, dwelling on and encouraging such thoughts, speech and actions is sinful. Christians, as well as nonbelievers, go through points where there are feelings that seem impossible to pull out of. However, any knowledgeable Christian should know that, though there are hard times and lapses in judgment, this truth remains: we can be forgiven. An individual must repent of his or her sins and invite JESUS to come into his or her life. Then there is new life. Burdens are lifted and the fear, doubt, loneliness and anger are gone. One becomes a member of a new family and an acceptance like no other is realized. Love replaces all that was wrong in one's life. Someone reading might ask, "How is that possible?" and I reemphasize, it has to be believed to be realized: It requires repentance and is strengthened by the Word. Just imagine how good it must feel to have peace and forgiveness for all of your sins.

Mark 16:16
Whoever believes and is baptized will be saved, but whoever does not believe will be condemned.

The problem—and I know, because I spent the majority of my life there—is that many have this outlook: for example, "The beer taste so good and makes me feel so good that nothing could ever replace that. Studying the Bible and going to church is never going to make me feel as good as getting drunk." This is deception from the evil one to your mind, body and spirit. Often, and even when temptation is placed in front of me, I think back to when I was a drunk. I remember the pain that drove me to drinking and I remember the pain that was amplified by the drinking. I remember the pain that was amplified by the cheating, drugging and gambling, among other things that were brought on by deception to my addictive personality. These were combined with a weakness towards temptation, brought on by a lack of awareness: Awareness to the fact that I was being deceived when I thought these things were my own good ideas. I remember feeling a multitude of emotions and getting drunk, followed by a hangover. I remember getting drunk and arrested and going to court and then being even more angry with the world than before and starting the entire vicious cycle all over again. If those still suffering could see that I used to be much like they are now and know the peace that I have now, I know they would give JESUS a chance to work in their lives. They would accept the opportunity to no longer be angry, to no longer argue and fight and be the cause of commotion.

James 1:19-21
My dear brothers and sisters, take note of this: Everyone should be quick to listen, slow to speak and slow to become angry, 20 because human anger does not produce the righteousness that God desires. Therefore, get rid of all moral filth and the

evil that is so prevalent and humbly accept the word planted in you, which can save you.

1 Corinthians 13:4-7
Love is patient, love is kind. It does not envy, it does not boast, it is not proud. 5 It does not dishonor others, it is not self-seeking, it is not easily angered, it keeps no record of wrongs. 6 Love does not delight in evil but rejoices with the truth. 7 It always protects, always trusts, always hopes, always perseveres.

Ephesians 4:26
"In your anger do not sin": Do not let the sun go down while you are still angry,

Ecclesiastes 7:9
Do not be quickly provoked in your spirit, for anger resides in the lap of fools.

Proverbs 29:22
An angry person stirs up conflict, and a hot-tempered person commits many sins

I have ears to hear so I listened and I heard. It is my hope and prayer that those who are still fighting the war within will do the same and have victory in JESUS. Amen

Lord, let me be an instrument of Yours so that I may spread a message of Your healing and more will be saved. I pray this in JESUS' name. Amen

Powerless

You won many battles, but I've won my war.
I finally have the strength and courage to settle the score.
Combat and loss are the cause of my PTSD.
However, you no longer have any control over me.
I fought you on the battlefield and in city streets.
I beat you there and came home to defeat.
Losing my own battle on account of you,
I refused to be counted among the surrendering few.
Powerless over my thoughts and actions no longer,
Letting go of painful burdens, now I feel stronger.
To feel the loss at home is to give you victory over me.
By taking control of my life, you are powerless over me.
So here I am, so close to a normal life.
I have my kids, my freedom, and I have my wife.
You have your desert and you have your illusion.
I have peace. You have chaos and confusion.
No doubt you will never, ever learn.
I will fly away and you're going to burn.
When it comes down to it, I let myself go.
You are powerless; you have no victory to show.
I feel at ease. I'm happy and smiling.
For my faith and my family, I'll never stop trying.
I am loved and not angry; my life is low-stress.
Never again because of you will I be powerless.

solation is no good for anyone, but is common for those of us who struggle with PTSD. It is a common topic I like to discuss because of its severity and the damage it causes. Isolation is commonly viewed— by those who know what they are doing to themselves—as an escape. However, it is not an escape: it is a trap. It is a trap that we set for ourselves in our very own minds.

By escaping the outside world and its stressors, we find ourselves locked away in the dungeon of our own minds. Isolation is not only self-destructive, but it eats away at various relationships as well: most importantly, our relationship with GOD.

The Lord tells in his Word that two are better than one, by saying that where believers are gathered in His name, He is there also. For years, I didn't realize why I created distance between myself and those who love me. One of the main reasons I drank was so that I could be around others, including my family. Alcohol acted as a feel-good mediator, until the point when I drank too much and then it became a gateway for past experiences and memories to come flooding out in negative speech and actions. In order to avoid impacting others with my negativity, I isolated myself from those who love me and from the outside world. This decision only made things worse for me and for my relationships.

According to Ronald B. Adler and Russell F. Proctor II in the text book Looking Out Looking In, 13th Edition, medical researchers have identified a wide range of health threats that can result from a lack of close relationships. For instance:

A lack of social relationships jeopardizes coronary health to a degree that rivals cigarette smoking, high blood pressure, blood lipids, obesity and lack of physical activity.

Socially-isolated people are four times more susceptible to the common cold than are those who have active social networks.

Social isolates are two to three times more likely to die prematurely than are those with strong social ties. The type of relationship doesn't seem to matter: Marriage, friendship, religious ties and community ties all seem to increase longevity.

The likelihood of death increases when a close relative dies. In one Welsh village, citizens who had lost a close relative died within one year at a rate more than five times greater than the rate of those who had not lost a relative.

Cy Mulholland

By contrast, a life that includes positive relationships, created through communication, leads to better health. As little as ten minutes per day of socializing improves memory and boosts intellectual function. Communicators who are willing to acknowledge their possible limitation have lower blood pressure than those who are more defensive. Stress hormones decline the more often people hear expressions of affection from loves ones.

I feel fortunate to still have my marriage. There were so many times when my wife could've packed up and left me because of the lack of attention I gave her, among other things. According to society, she would have been justified in doing so, but she loved me enough to stay, in hopes that I would come around and be the man she married. GOD answered her prayers and I am a better man and we have a stronger marriage because of it. Because I give her the attention she wants and needs, we are able to work together effectively as a team, which is how a marriage is supposed to work.

Also, by not isolating, I am able to attend church and family functions. I am able to use the crawl, walk, run method to better allow me to go into places such as restaurants and grocery stores. By using this method, I can set realistic goals for how long I can reasonably expect to remain comfortable in a public location, beginning with a ten-fifteen minutes "crawl phase" and moving on from there, gradually increasing the amount of time I am able to comfortably spend in any given environment. Thirty minutes may be my "walk phase" and one hour might be my "run phase." No time frame is wrong or right: Different individuals, depending on where they stand in their recovery with PTSD, will be able to tolerate different amounts of interaction. It is ok and expected for the individual to want to sit with his or her back to the wall, scan the room for exits and survey his or her surroundings. These are other areas that we strive to improve in time, with the ultimate goal of possessing the ability to interact with society as our normal selves on a regular basis. It is most definitely not a race and it requires a lot of patience, not only of the sufferer, but also of family members and friends.

Post-Traumatic Stress Disorder is the cause of much pain and discomfort for individuals and relationships, but with love all things are possible. GOD is love and GOD lives in us, if we allow Him into our hearts. My advice to anyone reading this is that if your heart has been hardened, give GOD a chance to heal the wounds and begin to avoid self-medication and isolation.

Ecclesiastes 4:9-10
Two are better than one,
because they have a good return for their labor:
If either of them falls down,
one can help the other up.
But pity anyone who falls
and has no one to help them up.

Lord, thank You for peace, faith, hope and most of all love, and for allowing me to share Your message with others. Let my days glorify You, Lord. I pray in JESUS' name. Amen

The runners

So many memories from that city, I'll never forget.
For so long, I beat myself up over things I used to regret.
Was there some way I could have prevented what went wrong?
This is the question I asked myself for so long.
Out on mission, searching for a target one day,
Optimistic from recent success, I was feeling ok.
Turning down a side road, the target was acquired.
Putting another one away was all I desired.
They began to run and I dismounted and ran after.
This was the trend of what would be my final combat chapter.
I was weighted down by gear, so they were much faster.
They ran into a house where screams transformed from laughter.
Jumping from rooftop to rooftop, it was no use.
I ran back down the stairs to the street, hoping not to lose.
The two runners jumped down at the end of the street.
I could not catch them before they made their retreat.
A shot rang out as I got back in my truck.
It seems an unfortunate soul was out of luck.
We drove to and dismounted at the end of the block.
The runners got away, because they punched an innocent man's clock.
There in the middle of the street, careless and dead.
Was a brain-matter scattered old man in a pool of red.
The last thing that went through his mind was a burning hot piece of lead.
Where I could have lost my life, the old man did instead.

The majority of service members who experience traumatic events have too many concerns to allow them to seek help for their mental struggles. That is not to say that a service member has to be directly impacted by an attack or be within visibility of dead and severely injured bodies in order to be traumatized. It is a proven fact that even service members who rarely stepped foot off the patrol base but were in close proximity to mortar and rocket attacks have been effected by PTSD. The point I want to make is that most of these individuals refuse to get the help they need, for various reasons. I used to be one of these misfortunates. Below are some of the reasons many do not seek help.

Difficulty accepting that they have a mental health problem;
Uncertainty about what help is available;
Concerns about stigma;
Mistrust of health professionals; and
A belief that 'I should be able to handle this alone.'

According to Lisa C. DeLuca of suite101.com, as many as 1/3 of soldiers returning from Iraq and Afghanistan will have troubling psychiatric symptoms or Post-Traumatic Stress Disorder: an unprecedented number of Iraq and Afghanistan combat war veterans are seeking PTSD therapy, but many others suffer in silence.

Combat soldiers are highly skilled at "toughing it out," whatever the problem is. They are trained not to reveal anything that may be perceived as a "weakness." The word weakness is in quotes because PTSD, anxiety and depression in soldiers is not, in fact, a personal weakness. Combat war veterans sometimes judge themselves as being weak because the condition makes them feel weak. Just because a person feels weak does not mean that he or she is weak.

For the Iraq war veteran, it seems like "toughing it out" will offer a sense of control and a feeling of strength to combat the uncomfortable feeling of weakness. Soldiers may be used to solving most or all problems this way. The ability to tough it out is a skill that is absolutely necessary when it comes to a combat situation. When skills like toughing it out are utilized for good repeatedly in life and death situations, setting them aside can be extraordinarily difficult. Soldiers are reluctant to give up skills that work and that have made it possible for them to come home alive from war.

Soldiers should consider that while toughing it out is an essential skill in war and in many other situations, it is not the most helpful approach to dealing with mental health. At certain times during recovery from PTSD, anxiety and depression, it can be helpful to employ these skills, but it is not helpful if the skills prevent the soldier from seeking advice and help from a competent mental health professional who can help the soldier develop an effective treatment plan.

The sad truth about stigma is that it is true when it comes to PTSD in the military. Seeking help is looked on as a weakness and it does affect careers negatively. In many occurrences where service members reach a breaking point—as was the case with me—they are punished instead of receiving the help they need. Oftentimes, leaders use their ability to cope as an irrational example and reason why the soldier, marine, airman, or sailor should possess the same capacity and tolerance to cope with trauma.

The fact of the matter is, higher-ranking NCOs (Non Commissioned Officers) and Officers do not share the same duties, nor do they typically experience trauma to the same degree as the younger service members on the "front lines" in combat environments. It's hard to believe that while suicide-rates in the military continue to climb, there are still high-ranking leaders who continue to punish and inflict pressure and harm on those suffering, instead of getting the service members the proper help and treatment they need. Such was the case with me.

I was working on Fort Knox in the 2-16th Calvary Squadron in early 2011. I had been struggling with PTSD for the majority of my life and was finally beginning to receive the help I had needed for so long. After my mental struggle reached a boiling point and my drinking alcohol to cope with my PTSD symptoms had gotten out of control, I spent 30 days in the Lincoln Trail Behavioral Health Hospital. My stay in this hospital was very beneficial and I was beginning to develop some very useful coping skills to assist me in my struggle with PTSD. I remember being excited to leave and get home to my family, when the day came for me to be discharged. However, I had no idea what my Squadron Commander had in store for me. As soon as I returned to my unit back on Fort Knox, I was read an Article 15, which in the military is a form of punishment. A few days following that, I was stripped of my Staff Sergeant rank, which I had held for more than six years. I couldn't make sense of why the Army would send me to get help for problems that were out of my control—problems that had been acquired while serving my country in combat, and indeed a brain injury—just to turn around and make life even harder on me and my family, who also had to bear the brunt of Army life and multiple deployments for years.

A few months later, I once again found myself in financial debt due to the decrease in pay and back in the mental hospital because of my inability to cope. This is the very reason why so many service members are reluctant to seek help for combat stress and PTSD. Where and when will the line be drawn between what's good for the unit and what's good for the individual service member? When will leaders in the military come to the realization that the unit can carry on while the few who are struggling get the help they desperately need? When will leaders in the military realize the importance and severity of PTSD?

Months later, I was offered the opportunity to get my rank back after leaving 2-16 CAV and transferring to the Warrior Transition Battalion, but because the Lord had already blessed my family with financial stability through other means, I turned it down.

1 Peter 3:8-9
Finally, all of you, be like-minded, be sympathetic, love one another, be compassionate and humble. 9 Do not repay evil with evil or insult with insult. On the contrary, repay evil with blessing, because to this you were called so that you may inherit a blessing.

Lord, I pray that the leaders of this military will act out of love on behalf of the men and women whom they lead. I pray in JESUS' name. Amen

CHAPTER SIX

OUTLOOK OPTIMISTIC

—•—

Breaking the chains of anger, fear and doubt and reaching out is the ability to walk out of the shadows and into the light.

THE HELPER

I never expected to meet the helper when I walked through the doors of
this strange shelter.
Truth is, I didn't know what to expect, but I knew I had to get my life in
check.
We talk in groups, more than a few.
Most can't understand what we've been through.
The helper, he cares. Twenty or so listen with stares;
This man who has been there, he knows what I mean.
He helps me get away from the war-machine.
Over and over again, we pour our hearts out.
For a time, the pain slips away: no fear or doubt.
The helper shows us how to cope with the pain.
He's a great example of how to stay sane.
Because he helps us, in turn it helps him.
Together, we all escape a life of sin.
With this pencil and my heart as a stencil, I utilize the helper as a
differential.
I take my thoughts and memories and write them down.
For me, it's a way my innocence is found.
What a great idea! Who would have thought?
This lesson I learned, this tool I was taught.
I realize now my life is still great. The war was a glitch.
No one in this room will ever forget Rich.

I am forever grateful, first of all to GOD for His awesome love and how He works in my life. I will forever be grateful for His wisdom and methods of helping His children. I am amazed how He uses people, places and things in my life to get what He wants out of me and that He never gives up on me.

GOD is love and I love His channel of communication, His gift of prayer, which has played a crucial role in my recovery. I am grateful to friends and family who never gave up on me and to strangers who answered the call to help others in need. I am so blessed.

GOD is amazing in so many ways. I find it truly awesome how He is continuously placing people in my path who assist me in my growth not only in recovery, but in my relationship with JESUS as well. He does this for all who put honest faith in Him. Most of the time, the good Lord strategically places people in my path in a manner so that both I and the person in question benefit from each other.

Such is the case with Rich. By helping others, he too is helped. He is able to share his experiences and listen to the experiences of others. I learned a great deal from Rich and he played a monumental role in my recovery, not only by introducing me to my greatest coping skill, but also by helping me to realize that I am not alone in my war with recovery.

I remember Rich telling me and the others in the combat stress group at the Lincoln Trail Behavioral Health Hospital a story of a time in Vietnam when his helicopter was shot down. Most of the soldiers who were in the chopper with him died in the crash, but Rich laid there in the jungle with the majority of his body broken and unable to move, alive. He stared at the sky for hours, in and out of consciousness and in severe pain. At one point, he woke up to enemy soldiers searching him and the bodies around him for anything that could be of use to them. They took his boots off of his feet, as well as other things. Rich remained as still as he could, pretending to be dead. When the enemy soldiers finished with their loot, they left and Rich again passed out. The next time he awoke, it was night and I remember him saying he felt a sense of peace as he gazed at the stars in the sky. After some time, he again faded away and woke up with bright lights shining in his face. He was safe in the hospital and his days of fighting in the Vietnam War were now over, but his struggles with the war within had only begun. Rich would go on to spend the next twenty plus years of his life as a drunk and a drug-addict, until he received the help he needed. Now, Rich pays it forward by helping today's warriors learn to cope with painful memories experienced in combat by positive means, as opposed to drinking and drug-use. I will be forever grateful to Rich and more importantly to GOD for allowing me to meet Rich and learn from him the importance of coping with PTSD.

Warriors have been struggling with the effects of combat from the time combat became a part of this world. Now, thanks to GOD in Heaven putting people, places and things in my life to encourage healing, the warrior within me has peace in JESUS CHRIST.

Colossians 1:10
So as to walk in a manner worthy of the Lord, fully pleasing to him, bearing fruit in every good work and increasing in the knowledge of God.

Lord, thank You for Your love and grace. I pray in JESUS' name. Amen

Broken Record

Your record sounds like mine: it's broken all the time.
My actions repeat themselves. I have a pattern;
Round and round, like the moons around Saturn.
Will I ever learn, or will I only burn?
Will I remain lost, or their respect shall I earn?
I am so easily addicted, so self-confusing.
Throughout my vicious cycle, it's more than alcohol I'm using.
I must put a stop to it or my family I'll be losing.
Yes, it's true; I'm cruising for a bruising.
So from this point on, it's my welfare I am choosing.
I'm going to poke myself in my lustful eye.
I'm going to stop the bleeding, before I die.
No longer will I continuously make her cry.
I'm going to do my best and not live in sin.
I'm going to pick my battles carefully; choose the ones I can win.
No more competing in the competition of my wish.
I know it to be unwise to try and out-drink the fish.
I can't allow myself to partake of the drinks that blur me.
They make me feel worse; they do nothing for me.
I'm not going to write things and say things and not follow through.
I'm going to do exactly what I said I'm going to do.
I'm not going to lie: what I tell you is true.

Cy Mulholland

t is amazing to me how forgetful I am. It seems like no matter what my plan is or how many goals I set for myself, I forget how serious and hopeful I once was about accomplishing any given goal or plan. However, this is not always the case.

Yes, sometimes I do honestly forget, but most of the time when I set goals for myself, I get complacent or I do not maintain my motivation with concentration. This was particularly true in the past. These days, I do my best to stay focused.

Don't get me wrong, I have always taken care of my priorities, paying bills and providing for my family. The problem I had was not taking care of myself in things like staying out of debt, eating right, reading my Bible on a daily basis, going back to school and the most obvious: avoiding alcohol. The silly thing about this is that I always made these things out to be so much harder than they are. They are actually very simple tasks and when I set my goals and achieve them, I feel so much better mentally, physically and spiritually.

These days, I make it a point to remain disciplined and follow through with the things I say I'm going to do. I allow my words to become actions. Though I am not perfect and I still do (and always will) make mistakes now and then, I strive to do the right thing, not only for my family, but also for myself. I know now that if I don't take care of myself, there is no way I will ever be able to take care of anyone else. It is like when you're in an airplane and they tell you if anything goes wrong to adjust your oxygen mask before you help anyone else with theirs. You can't help them if you can't breathe.

John 15:7
⁷If you abide in me, and my words abide in you, ask whatever you wish, and it will be done for you.

Lord, thank You for clearing my mind and opening my eyes and quieting the noise of the world so that I can focus on Your purpose for me. I love You and I thank You. I pray in JESUS' name. Amen

Four Walls

There are four walls in my room. There are four walls in my head.
Four walls can be vicious; they'd rather see me dead.
I know four walls are white, but I only see red.
Four walls are quick to point out that I made my own bed.
I appreciate the fact that four walls have a door.
In order to get through it, I must put my feet on the floor.
I know it's the right thing to do: I feel it in my core.
Isolation is too easy; it's only me I do it for.
While time exists, it's time to settle the score.
Enough already! I didn't do this to myself.
It's time I stood up and restored my health.
I'm going to spread my wings and no longer fly stealth.
Goodbye, four walls! I follow your lead no longer.
I'm listening to the wind beneath my wings: I feel stronger.
If it were actually a word I would tell you, you are wronger.
I'm opening my eyes now to see that the walls are white.
And it's for me, my family and my soul in which I fight.
I'm leaving four walls; I don't care if you fall.
I'll never hold you up again. Not ever, not at all.
I'm opening the door now, so four walls, close your eyes.
When you open them, I won't be here; it should come as no surprise.
I'm standing outside, no walls and no longer in my own head.
I no longer feel cold. I feel the sun on my skin instead.

 Cy Mulholland

After each tour in Iraq, I would get progressively worse with my alcoholism and PTSD. Though I had no idea what was going on at the time, part of my PTSD symptoms was isolation. After the first two tours it was bad, but when I came home from Iraq in 2008, there was an even more distinct difference in me. But like I said, I personally was unaware of the change within myself. How could I see it? I mean, I always heard the stories of Vietnam vets coming back different than they were before they left, but I didn't think such a thing could ever happen to me.

It did. After I quit drinking, I quit doing a lot of things, like spending time with my family or focusing on my work. By far, the worst mistake I made while isolating was neglecting my family. One of the most important recommendations I could ever make to someone in recovery is to not shut your family out. Let them be a part of recovery in a positive manner. It is vitally important to love and to be loved. Isolation equals no social functioning, which is detrimental to the physical, mental, emotional and spiritual health of the isolated individual. Our families need us and we need them. By working together with friends and family, recovery is not only much more possible, but successful.

Mark 13:13
And you will be hated by all for my name's sake. But the one who endures to the end will be saved.

Lord, thank You for strengthening me and encouraging me to look and move past the obstacles placed in my way by the world. I pray in JESUS' name. Amen

Chosen

I want to be more like those who were chosen.
I don't want to stand here, lost and frozen.
I want to be one who will stand for what is right.
I want to fight the good fight and in the end take flight.
I want to love and be loved; Give, but not given to.
I want to be less like me and more like You.
I want to sacrifice something and have some meaning.
Not for the glory of my own, but for the One on the throne.
I don't need to be known, but by Him alone.
I want to do what's right for only His sight.
I want to leave wrong behind and not do things in spite.
For some I stand at ease, but for Him I pray on my knees.
He is the only one I want to please.
I must remain humble so that I do not stumble.
I know that this world will steadily crumble,
And for those that have chosen to remain in this world, frozen:
They all will learn that this place must burn.
And though our Father loves us, our Father is stern.
There's a light on the other side of the road that I crossed.
Now I stand in the light and I pick up my cross.
He loves me. He chose me. I will never be lost.
The waves rock the boat, but I will never be tossed. Amen

Cy Mulholland

We are not perfect beings. In the beginning, we took a perfectly good earth and killed it, but that's a topic for another conversation. I slip and fall on my face from time to time, even though I have knowledge of GOD'S will for me. What's important is that today I don't plan to sin willfully and when I do make a mistake, I seek forgiveness and a way to make it right.

Ecclesiastes 9:11
Again I saw that under the sun the race is not to the swift, nor the battle to the strong, nor bread to the wise, nor riches to the intelligent, nor favor to those with knowledge, but time and chance happen to them all.

Lord, please forgive me of all my sins. Help me not repeat the wrong I have done. Father in Heaven, put things in my path that remind me of the importance of being the Christian man I am called to be and let others see Your light shining through me. I pray in JESUS' name. Amen

Half Full

There's plenty of half empty in this world of many.
Most wouldn't share a penny. Not one, not any.
One could go crazy, be unmotivated, and lazy.
One could escape, drink and drug and be hazy.
Some use optimism as criticism and pour it all out.
Others criticize and don't optimize and scream and shout.
We live in a dying world without a doubt.
You tool, is it half full? Stop acting like a fool.
You act as if you never went to school.
What is it that drives you to be so cruel?
The full want peace and the empty want pieces.
The crooks want us all to sign off on government leases.
So what is it, half full or half empty?
One has vacant pockets. The other has plenty.
That would be fine. That would be ok,
Except the one you chose is only worried about his pay.
You may not understand, but read between the lines.
We are no longer taxed, we only pay fines.
Greed is a killer and money bag filler.
Try to look past it all and see what's waiting for you.
There's peace on the other side. I know it to be true.
Help someone you know and help a stranger too.
Help as many as you can. At least help a few.
We need to be kind in a world that's so cruel,
And live our lives like a glass that's half full.

GOD is love, as it is plainly stated in the Bible. It seems to me, though, that we as a people forget this more and more all the time. We forget that our Father in Heaven is the source of faith, hope, and love and that the most important thing that He wants us to do is to love Him and one another.

There seems to be a spirit of anger sweeping over the world today. So many people are only worried about themselves and I'm sorry to say that at times, one of those people has been me. How is that possible, when I have a wife and three kids? Yet that is the way I carried myself for the majority of my marriage. Most of the time, I was only concerned about my own greed, my own feelings and only what made me feel better. It came to the point where I realized that I could either get down and depressed and wallow in the guilt and regret I felt, or I could stand up and make a change in my life and create a better life for my family.

I chose the latter. I quit drinking, for what I hope is the final time. I say "hope," not in a discouraging way, but because in my sobriety I've realized it's wise to take it one day at a time. I'm not a fortune-teller and I definitely don't have a crystal ball to know for sure that I will never drink again. But I know that, as long as I wake up every morning and tell myself I'm a nondrinker, followed by prayer and meditation, I set my day up for success.

It's amazing, the amount of quality family time a person can spend with his or her loved ones when he or she is no longer concerned with drinking or drugging or the party. I have come to realize the fun I have without drinking is far better than the supposed fun I had while partying. There is no hugging the toilet and throwing my guts up, or waking up in the morning with a migraine headache. That sounds like fun, right? I definitely do not miss that kind of fun, nor does my family miss me having that supposed kind of fun.

Another thing I've learned in this choice is that kids are smarter than we give them credit for. Both my ten-year-old son and my eight-year-old daughter have told me more than once, separate from each other, "I'm so glad you don't drink anymore, Daddy." Those words hit me right in the heart. It felt good to hear and was hard to hear at the same time. It made me remember the impact that my alcoholism had on these innocent little children of mine.

Revelation 3:12
The one who conquers, I will make him a pillar in the temple of my God. Never shall he go out of it, and I will write on him

the name of my God, and the name of the city of my God, the new Jerusalem, which comes down from my God out of heaven, and my own new name.

Lord, give me the wisdom to remember what truly matters in this world. Let me remember to love and to teach love to my children in the name of JESUS. I pray in JESUS' name. Amen

The Unce

For whatever reason, I have the urge to write about the Unce.
It's kind of silly, but I'm going to do it more than once.
This is important: resilience, because it brings forth brilliance.
It comes from inside sources like courage, values, beliefs, and confidence.
Let your appearance reflect perseverance.
This goes hand in hand with competence, which leads to excellence.
Keep in mind, everything should be done in moderation, not over-indulgence.
Don't be the one using connivance and causing disturbance.
In the end, this will only lead to a grievance.
Stick with persistence when lending assistance.
Use vigilance and conveyance to transfer your skills to diligence.
If you haven't, you will learn that this takes consistence.
More than anything, remember the only way comes from the One with omnipotence.
Forget this, and you'll end up with not even a pittance.
To forget that would simply be an impudence.
To forget that would mean for you no inheritance.
What I'm saying is pray and read the word. Do it in abundance.
Then you will see that you will find His acceptance.
You want to be ready before you meet the hearse or the ambulance.
I hope this makes sense. I hope you don't feel like a dunce.
Remember these words: don't forget about the Unce.

L ord, let me remember for the rest of my days the importance of having the heart and faith of a child. Allow me to gain back a portion of the innocence that I have lost throughout the years and always, Lord, Your will be done. I pray in JESUS' name. Amen

HOMELESS VETERANS

The U.S. Department of Veterans Affairs (VA) states the nation's homeless veterans are predominantly male, with roughly five percent being female. The majority of them are single, come from urban areas, and suffer from mental illness, alcohol and/or substance abuse, or co-occurring disorders. About one-third of the adult homeless population are veterans. America's homeless veterans have served in World War II, the Korean War, Cold War, Vietnam War, Grenada, Panama, Lebanon, Afghanistan and Iraq (OEF/OIF), and the military's anti-drug cultivation efforts in South America. Nearly half of homeless veterans served during the Vietnam era. Two-thirds served our country for at least three years, and one-third were stationed in a war zone.

Roughly 56 percent of all homeless veterans are African American or Hispanic, despite only accounting for 12.8 percent and 15.4 percent of the U.S. population respectively. About 1.5 million other veterans, meanwhile, are considered at-risk of homelessness due to poverty, lack of support networks, and dismal living conditions in overcrowded or substandard housing. Although flawless counts are impossible to come by—the transient nature of homeless populations presents a major difficulty—VA estimates that 107,000 veterans are homeless on any given night. Over the course of a year, approximately twice that many experience homelessness. Only eight percent of the general population can claim veteran status, but nearly one-fifth of the homeless population are veterans. In addition to the complex set of factors influencing all homelessness—extreme shortage of affordable housing, livable income and access to health care—a large number of displaced and at-risk veterans live with lingering effects of post-traumatic stress disorder (PTSD) and substance abuse, which are compounded by a lack of family and social support networks.

A top priority for homeless veterans is secure, safe, clean housing that offers a supportive environment free of drugs and alcohol. VA's specialized homeless programs served more than 92,000 veterans in 2009, which is highly commendable. This still leaves well over 100,000 more veterans, however, who experience homelessness annually and must seek assistance from local government agencies and community and faith-based service organizations. In its November 2007 "Vital Mission" report, the National Alliance to End Homelessness estimated that up to about half a million veterans have characteristics that put them in danger of homelessness. These veterans may require supportive services outside the scope of most VA homeless programs. Veterans need a coordinated effort that provides secure housing, nutritional meals, basic physical health care, substance abuse care and aftercare, mental health counseling, personal development and empowerment. Additionally, veterans need job assessment, training and placement assistance. The most effective programs for homeless and at-risk veterans are community-based, nonprofit, "veterans helping veterans" groups. Programs that seem to work best feature transitional housing with the camaraderie of living in structured, substance-free environments with fellow veterans who are succeeding at bettering themselves; Government money, while important, is currently limited, and available services are often at capacity. It is critical, therefore, that community groups reach out to help provide the support, resources and opportunities most Americans take for granted: housing, employment and health care. Veterans who participate in collaborative programs are afforded more services and have higher chances of becoming tax-paying, productive citizens again.

How can we help?

Determine the need in your community. Visit with homeless veteran providers. Contact your mayor's office for a list of providers, or search the NCHV Database.

Involve others. If you are not already part of an organization, align yourself with a few other people who are interested in attacking this issue.

Participate in local homeless coalitions. Chances are, there is one in your community. If not, this could be the time to bring people together around this critical need.

Make a donation to your local homeless veteran provider.

Contact your elected officials. Discuss what is being done in your community for homeless veterans.

Philippians 4:8
Finally, brothers, whatever is true, whatever is honorable, whatever is just, whatever is pure, whatever is lovely, whatever is commendable, if there is any excellence, if there is anything worthy of praise, think about these things.

Philippians 1:6
And I am sure of this, that he who began a good work in you will bring it to completion at the day of Jesus Christ.

Lord, I pray that hearts will be opened and love will be spread and many will be helped in Your name. I pray in JESUS' name. Amen

The Beach

The beaches of Jamaica are my happy place, my place of Zen.

It's the most beautiful place I've ever been.

My wife and I went there together. We enjoyed the food and the weather.

It was the time of our life; we'd never felt better.

The cool breeze and the feel of warm sand on our feet and the king-size bed in our four-star suite.

It was the honeymoon that we'd waited for far too long.

Everything was so right. It was as if nothing could go wrong.

I had just made it back from the fight once again.

When I close my eyes, I still feel the sun on my skin.

I can hear my wife's voice while I'm standing on the balcony.

My thought is paradise as I look across the sea.

Her voice pulls me inside, she wants another baby. I feel the same, there is no if, but, or maybe.

In the crystal clear water, we hold each other tight.

I look into her eyes and press my lips to hers. She is the most beautiful sight.

This is the greatest feeling in the world; I want it to last for eternity.

In this moment with this woman is the only place I want to be.

Here, they provide everything for us; they treat us like royalty.

Although I am on the beach no longer, I close my eyes and it makes me stronger.

When times get tough, I can instantly go back there.

I can escape the war; go to that place without a care.

The beach, the water, the sand, hand-in-hand.

The suite, the balcony, the bed, it's in my head.

This is the place where I want to be, in that moment with her hair all around me.

One very therapeutic tool that I use on a regular basis is meditation. It is a great way to clear your mind and relax. There are two ways I do this. The first and most important form of meditation I practice is something I take from the Holy Bible and use in my daily life. The Bible says "Peace, Be Still." This means that GOD calls us to have peace and be still and know that He is GOD. That is exactly what I do. When no one is around and I know for a fact that I won't be disturbed, I go to my dimly lit or dark room, where there is no noise. I lay down on my bed and I remain perfectly still and clear my mind of any negativity. I take a few deep breaths and believe with everything in my being that I am releasing any tension I may have been experiencing, as I exhale. Once I am completely relaxed and focused, I am free to be directed by GOD where ever He would have my mind go. This process helps me make a lot of difficult decisions and it helps me plan for the future, by preparing myself to make better decisions than I had in the past. Along with prayer, it is one way I maintain a spiritual connection with GOD.

The other form of meditation I utilize is very effective, but not quite as important as the previous method. This method is something I also use to relax myself. Much of the time, however, I use this method to help me calm down and bring myself into a better mood. I learned this helpful tool in anger management. Similar to the previous method, I may sit or lay down anywhere I may possibly be at any given time and close my eyes. From that point I will take a few deep breaths once again, breathing in fresh air and ridding myself of the old stale air as I exhale, releasing the negativity every time I breathe out. Some of the time, I will also imagine a calm soothing color being breathed in through my nostrils, such as blue or green. And when I exhale I may imagine a hotter and more negative "bad energy color" such as yellow, orange, or red. Once this is complete and I am very relaxed, I may feel as if I'm floating or sinking down into my cushioned seat or bed. When I feel comfortable moving on, I will vividly go to my happy place.

This may sound cheesy, but it works for me. I'm not saying it will work for everyone, but if done properly, it can have positive benefits. I go to my happy place, which I described in the previous poem. With my imagination I recall what I was feeling, seeing, smelling, hearing and possibly even tasting. Each person's happy place can be where ever the individual wants it to be, so long as it allows that person to relax and be at peace.

Personally, meditation allows me to enjoy a more peaceful and productive daily life with a far more rational thought process. It allows me to feel better physically, mentally, and spiritually and I highly recommend that everyone give it a try and at least find out if it's for them or not.

2 Peter 3:18
But grow in the grace and knowledge of our Lord and Savior Jesus Christ. To him be the glory both now and to the day of eternity. Amen.

2 Peter 1:10
Therefore, brothers, be all the more diligent to make your calling and election sure, for if you practice these qualities you will never fall.

Lord, thank You for the spiritual insight that no problem on this earth is worth stressing over, because I know that I may call on You, Father. I pray in JESUS' name. Amen

Adversity is Coming

Today was a good day, like nothing could go wrong.
This is when I have to be careful, because I know it won't be long.
Adversity is coming. It happens every time.
Everything will be going great and suddenly will stop on a dime.
Sunshine and laughter are dashed away by bad news.
Thoughts of drinking could enter the mind and everyone could lose,
Or I can plan ahead and utilize the maintenance that is preventative.
I'll do what it takes to protect my sobriety and the people with whom I live.
Today was a good day, but adversity is on the way.
It's only a matter of time, so for good decisions I will pray.
Someone may be rude or I would get an unexpected bill in the mail.
No problem is worth the cost. This train cannot be derailed.
The evil one will try and trap me with his snare,
And I will adapt and overcome his tactics, because I care.
Adversity is coming, but it doesn't matter to me.
The only things that matter are my GOD, my family and sobriety.
Life is going to happen and it's going to happen on its terms.
I want to say I led a good life before I'm eaten by the worms.
Today was a good day and tonight is a good night.
My family is safe and my wife and I didn't fight,
Due in large part to me making things right.
I quit the drink. I left the darkness for the light.
Things are going well. There's not a single problem in sight.
I know adversity is coming, but my future is still bright.

It's amazing how a professional athlete who has so much talent and has proven him or herself in front of millions of fans can suddenly appear to have lost all or most of the talent possessed, in the middle of the athlete's prime. At times, they never regain any momentum, leaving their fans in complete dismay as to what happened to their hero.

It blows my mind to hear of a famous multi-millionaire go bankrupt or to court and even to prison, over ethics violations and fraud. I'm not throwing stones, but if we pay attention we start to see a pattern. The same things could be said of just about anyone who has experienced folly and I'm pretty sure, though on a different scale, we have all partaken in some kind of action or misconduct that we should not have.

The majority of us have watched television recordings of police officers beating innocent people during routine stops more than once and in various locations. Politicians get removed from office because they are held to high standards and seem incapable of fulfilling their obligations. High-school teachers have on more than one occasion had inappropriate relationships with students. The list goes on and on.

The farther we walk away from the will of GOD, the more painful our lives become, because it is then easier for the evil one to afflict us. GOD does not punish us, as some believe. Rather, the fault is our own for creating separation between ourselves and GOD by willfully engaging in sin.

The same can be said about many service men and women and their various short-comings and misconduct that have been brought to the attention of the American public. Many of these behaviors are due to the effects of traumatic experiences during combat. The U.S. Army has now put in place Officers and Non Commissioned Officers (NCOs) who specialize in Master Resiliency Training, which helps Soldiers, family members and Army civilians with Comprehensive Fitness. This focuses on the five dimensions of strength: emotional, social, spiritual, family and physical.

I for one appreciate the fact that the Military is putting more focus on areas regarding Combat Stress and PTSD. The most important element to all of this, which many people do not realize, is the spiritual aspect. Spiritual resilience is the key to all success, but it is not defined by government power-point slideshows and it cannot at any time be conducted as check-the-block training, the way so many things are in the military.

It is more than just one section in a line of various strengths that we all refer to. Our faith in GOD is the single most important thing we have in our lives and it is the key to happiness in every aspect of our lives. Whether it is emotional, social, family or physical, our spiritual connection with GOD through JESUS CHRIST is what makes peace and stability possible. The soldier that I once was—immature, both emotionally and spiritually—had to go through hard times before learning what it actually was to have a real connection through the HOLY SPIRIT. It wasn't until I had suffered enough that I realized I was never going to survive this life on my own. Knowing that, I came to realize that by not accepting JESUS as my Savior and turning my life over to the will of GOD, I would not have life after death. Only after hitting my biggest bump in the road of life and hitting what I refer to as my rock-bottom (because rock-bottom is different for everyone) did I whole-heartedly seek the will of GOD in my life. It was then that change was possible and my spiritual resilience was established. I can only hope and pray that, for anyone struggling with any problem in his or her life, he or she will seek first the will of GOD at all times.

Isaiah 41:10
So do not fear, for I am with you;
do not be dismayed, for I am your God.
I will strengthen you and help you;
I will uphold you with my righteous right hand.

Lord, it is my hope and prayer that those who are struggling and are lost will find their way to You by first seeking the light. I pray in JESUS' name. Amen

Recharge

Sometimes we have to rejuvenate:
Turn from what's wrong before it's too late.
The decision-making process is no time to hesitate.
Prioritize and don't add too much to your plate.
Take charge and with your whole mind be at large.
With your hopes and dreams, take charge.
Barge into success. Inventory your story.
Remember the most important story and all of its glory.
Live with love and give and don't worry.
Let life be what it is and let light flow like slurry.
Remember what real value is and your vision won't be blurry.
Add spark to someone else's day with a bear-hug that's fury.
Helping out will help you on the inside.
Let go of foolish pride. Let the troubles backslide.
Be high on life. Spread your wings and glide.
These are the thoughts by which I abide.
Strengthen the family: do not divide.
Remember GOD'S love is very tall and very wide.
There are days when I catch myself living in sin.
Those are the days I reflect and take my own medicine.
With a lot of love to strengthen me from above,
I remember who I am and what I'm made of.
Please pass this message on, but don't take it from the Searge.
Every now and then, we all need to recharge.

t seems that everyone has pet peeves. We all have something that bothers us. It doesn't matter who we are: we all have at least one thing that just gets on our nerves. After all, that is one of the foundations of sin and not a single human walking the earth is perfect . . . though some may think they are. I for one am far from perfect and I would have to admit that one of my pet peeves is the statement, "That's not fair".

It was more or less imbedded in me from childhood. When I would make that comment as a child, my Dad used to reply, "Life isn't fair." It became something to live by. If I maintain that perspective, I always remember that there are those out there that have a much worse life than I do.

I forgot this principal I was raised by for several years, during the lowest points in my struggle with PTSD. After much treatment and a spiritual reconnection with GOD, I remembered that valuable lesson that my dad taught me. Now, of course, I teach my children the very same thing . . . though they don't like to hear it.

Life oftentimes does not seem fair and this is generally due to a lack of understanding. It is a lack of ability to look outside ourselves and realize that there actually is an entire world population that exists and that the world does not revolve around us alone. For years, my speech and actions would have led anyone to believe this was my outlook and for the most part it was, because my traumatized mind was so clouded I couldn't see that everyone else mattered just as much as I did. I had to come to the realization that, while it would be nice to receive something for my sacrifice, the Army didn't actually owe me anything.

When it comes down to it, I owe myself to open my eyes, ears and most importantly my heart, to the voice of GOD. That is exactly what I eventually did and I am very grateful that GOD is so loving and patient. So many people believe strongly that they are owed something by someone or a group of someones, so much so that they overlook what is more important; the fact that they have the ability to help someone else. It's hard to argue the fact that there is something very gratifying about helping others in need. Oftentimes, we don't realize that one act of kindness can start a chain reaction of kind acts, resulting in the world being a slightly better place. The opposite side of that is too often people don't realize that a negative act has the very same power to start a chain reaction of angry and harmful actions. Unfortunately, the world consists more of the latter.

I often make statements within the walls of my own home that resemble something along the lines of parents having the ability to discipline their children without the use of an angry tone of voice. After all, much of what children learn and how their personalities are shaped is hereditary. Something we all should keep in mind is the manner in which we are disciplined by our Heavenly Father and we are all indeed disciplined by Him, whether we believe it or not. For those of us that believe this fact, can we not all agree that He disciplines us without raising His voice and speaking hatefully? It's true. GOD is love and therefore nothing from GOD is hateful. We have the ability to do the same thing with our children and we must not forget the fact that our children are also and more so GOD's children.

In the same fashion a boss doesn't have to yell at his employee, except to alert him that something is falling or to execute something in a hurry, but even in these situations we could pause and exercise patience in the same manner that we would want someone to be patient with us. I don't know anyone who prefers to be yelled at hatefully and I don't know of any situations that have benefited from outwardly-expressed negativity that could not have gained more from positive energy. When it comes down to it, we can all practice and learn the ability to take a moment to breathe and think rationally about any situation. Don't get me wrong. We are to discipline our children and even spank our children when it is warranted, but it should be done in a loving manner and the punishment or discipline should always fit the wrong doing or misbehavior.

James 1:4
And let steadfastness have its full effect, that you may be perfect and complete, lacking in nothing.

Lord, let me think of more than myself and help someone in need today. I pray in JESUS' name. Amen

Responsible for Responding to the Response

I'm learning to be responsible for my response.
The way I respond affects another's response.
If I'm responding negatively, then how will they respond?
To respond in such a way would be irresponsible.
Irresponsibility is no good for anybody.
Depending on how you respond to irresponsibility will determine the response you get.
How will you respond to reading a poem solely about response?
Maybe you feel it was irresponsible of me to write a poem this way.
I feel responsible for your response to these words today.
On a serious note, I am responsible for the way I respond to a response.
If one responds badly to my response, then that is irresponsible of her or him.
In a case like that, the chances of someone responding positively are mighty slim.
Taking responsibility for being responsible and responding to the response is key.
You are not responsible for the writing of this poem.
That responsibility falls on me, but like me, you are probably responding with, "What the heck does this mean?"

Cy Mulholland

One of the most important things I had to learn while figuring out how to cope with PTSD was how to respond to those things that would set me off, due to my short fuse. For the longest time, my thinking was that it was perfectly normal to blow up on people and many times to try to fight people. My anger did indeed get me into several fights and arguments with people. I thought that was just a part of life and that people should see things my way, as if I had some kind of infinite wisdom that they were unaware of. Wow, who did I think I was, right?

Looking back at the old me, that is exactly what I think: "Who did I think I was?" I was self-centered and as far back as I could remember, I had a problem with authority. I was very rebellious as a kid and those behaviors continued on into my adulthood. Rejecting authority is a prominent characteristic of PTSD.

Also, looking back, I came to realize that it was shortly after my big brother had killed himself that I became so rebellious. By the age of twelve, I was sexually active, I was drinking and drugging and I rebelled against any form of authority. And I thought all these behaviors were normal. That is definitely not a healthy combination. I'm lucky I made it to adulthood at all.

I remember being a teenager driving around in my 1990 Nissan pickup truck with a forty-ounce beer or some other form of alcohol sitting in my lap, on a regular basis. Chances were I had a bag of marijuana or some other drug in my pocket as well. I did these things because I was rebellious and felt that I was untouchable. And if someone got in my way, I would sure let someone know about it. I would get into fights and a lot of the time I'd get my butt kicked.

I didn't respond well to anything. I didn't respond well to authority and I definitely didn't respond well to adversity. I thought I had everything figured out. I knew nothing about humility. Today, I'm aware of my flaws and I have humility. I learn from my mistakes and I have humbled myself in the sight of the Lord.

Hebrews 10:35
Therefore do not throw away your confidence, which has a great reward.

Lord, help me to take the things I have learned through reading Your word and remain humble as You would have me to. I pray in JESUS' name. Amen

Sober talk

Let's talk some sober talk.
It's all about walking the walk:
I mean as opposed to living as a drunk,
Waking up every morning, smelling like a brewery or a skunk,
Depending on how eventful the past evening had been.
I have some pretty wild stories I could tell you, my friend.
I've been there time after time and over again.
Many times, I came close to my story's end,
And then promised my wife I wouldn't do it anymore.
Telling those lies became quite a chore.
It's hard work keeping everyone happy, while living in sin.
I had to focus on my wife, my kids and my addiction.
Much of the time I was a deceiver, making my wife a believer.
And eventually, we were all a pain and misery receiver.
So many times, I made her cry and I couldn't tell her why.
It wasn't too late. I had to try before I die.
The key to getting sober and staying that way is plain:
You have to stop doing the same things and expecting a different result:
that's insane.
I had to reach out for help and not do it on my own.
I only met failure when I went at it alone.
Alcoholism is a disease and a demon at the same time.
JESUS is my way, my truth, my life and my rock on which I climb.
Don't take it from me, but take it from the clock.
You can have the time of your life with a little sober talk.

Cy Mulholland

Not only are substances such as alcohol and other drugs a bad way to cope, but they are plain and simply bad for us. There is no nutritional value, unless one is elderly and one's doctor tells he or she it would be a good idea to have a glass of wine every evening to help with certain things related to one's health . . . and that's still an unviable option for the alcoholic. Good practice for those in recovery is to do the opposite of what they are accustomed to doing. Instead of tearing ourselves down by abusing a substance that only makes things worse, we have the option to focus on our health, thus building ourselves up. Eating and drinking healthy foods, as opposed to getting drunk or high all the time, allows us to feel energized instead of hung-over and can be exciting and motivating.

My wife and I were in the store the other day, when we noticed a salesman standing on a make-shift stage behind a counter with a microphone headset on. I could see from a distance there was a blender in front of him with various foods. The blender was running nonstop and it immediately caught my wife's attention. She told me she was going to see what it was all about and I stayed behind to look at running shoes. After she had been over there a while with various other customers watching the demonstration that was taking place, I moseyed on over to see what was going on.

As I walked up to meet my wife and greeted her with a hug and a kiss, I noticed the blender was still running and I thought to myself, "How has that thing's little motor not burned out yet"? As I began listening to what the demonstrator was saying, my wife, Carleeh, began explaining to me that this item was no regular blender at all. It was a Vitamix. She went on to explain that her parents used to own one when they owned and operated a coffee/ice cream shop years ago. She mentioned how it was so easy to make great tasting smoothies, along with various other meals, such as different kinds of soups. After hearing this, she had captured my interest, so I continued listening to the salesman talk about the various benefits of owning this device.

When the blender stopped, he evenly dispersed the contents into four rows of paper cups. I picked a cup up and noticed that it was warm. The device had not only mixed the ingredients, but heated them as well. It was a delicious tortilla soup. He then went on to prepare lemonade. I was amazed when I saw him cut a lemon in half and throw the entire thing in the blender. He then proceeded to add a bunch of grapes, stem and all, with some ice and organic sugar. I watched as the machine buzzed for a few moments; then it stopped and he once again poured the beverage into fresh cups and we all had a taste.

The consensus was unanimous. It was one of the best-tasting lemonade beverages I had ever tasted. There were no chunks of stem or lemon. It was smooth, refreshing and delicious. The highlight of this device is that it breaks food down very finely so that more of the beneficial vitamins and minerals can be absorbed by the body. My wife voiced her desire to own one and I agreed, so I put it on layaway. It will indeed be a worthy investment.

Now I'm not a spokesman for the company which created this device: however, it got me to thinking how important it is to eat healthy, so that we may be healthy and productive.

In the same light, we need spiritual food in order to remain spiritually healthy and spiritually productive. I've mentioned before that spiritual well-being is the key to all other aspects of our lives and it is absolutely true. There are no ifs, buts, or maybes. If a person allows him or herself to remain spiritually sound, then the chances of that person being successful in other aspects of life are indeed higher. God can heal anything. He indeed can, has and will. A good way to start off the day is with prayer and reading the Bible, if even one chapter. I often walk around my house singing whatever praise happens to be stuck in my head at the time. I give thanks to the Lord and I am not shy when it comes to asking the Lord for things that would be useful in my life and others' lives. I ask that His will be done in all things.

I keep in mind at all times that when asking the Lord for blessings in all aspects, such as the healing of others, protection over my family, nonbelievers to come to GOD, safety for deployed militants and their families, financial stability, direction, and various other things, the importance of GOD being glorified in all this comes first. If it does not give glory to GOD, then it is not worthy of His blessing. And that which is not of GOD is of the world. The following scriptures are written in the HOLY BIBLE:

Joshua 24:15
But if serving the LORD seems undesirable to you, then choose for yourselves this day whom you will serve, whether the gods your ancestors served beyond the Euphrates, or the

gods of the Amorites, in whose land you are living. But as for me and my household, we will serve the LORD."

2 Thessalonians 1:11-12
With this in mind, we constantly pray for you, that our God may make you worthy of his calling, and that by his power he may bring to fruition your every desire for goodness and your every deed prompted by faith. 12 We pray this so that the name of our Lord Jesus may be glorified in you, and you in him, according to the grace of our God and the Lord Jesus Christ.

Lord, grant me spiritual food to nourish my soul so that my body and mind can do Your will. Always LORD, I pray that Your will be done and that in all things You will be glorified. I pray in JESUS' name. Amen

CHAPTER SEVEN

OBJECTIVE SAINT

New life and love is found in JESUS CHRIST.

Who was I?

I was the innocent child with family all around.

I was innocence lost after that fatal sound.

I was a drug-addicted kid.

I was an alcoholic at twelve years old, 'cause that is what I did.

I was a teenager that all but gave up on school.

I was the one who hung out with the wrong crowd, because I thought I was cool.

I was the one who couldn't play the sports I loved because I wouldn't make the grade.

I was a sex-addicted teen who only cared about getting laid.

I was the student that graduated on time by the skin of my teeth.

I was the problem-child who caused my parents too much grief.

I was the addict alcoholic who is lucky to be alive.

I was the receiver of a wakeup call that helped me find the drive.

I was the scared young private getting smoked in basic training.

I was the young man that realized a new way of life is what I was gaining.

I was a journey cross country not knowing what to expect.

I was a proud soldier with core values like loyalty, duty and respect.

I was the life of the party who thought I could do no wrong.

I was the one who found trouble and it didn't take long.

I was the one that went through women like I changed my underwear.

I was the one without boundaries, still living without a care.

I was the one GOD smiled on, the day I met Carleeh.

I was the man that made my smartest decision: to get married and start a family.

I was the soldier who deployed time and time again for my least favorite uncle.

I was he whose life was changed forever by the war.

I was the man that would never be the same as before.

I was the carrier of so much pain and burden.

I was emotionless, though inside I was hurting.

I was one that decided to get help.

I was he that realized I couldn't do it by myself.

I was sick from alcoholism and PTSD.
I was struggling and now I've finally been set free.
I was guilty, but now He has forgiven me.
It doesn't matter who I was, but who I am today.
I am clean, I am sober, I am forgiven, I am driven, and that, my friend,
is the only way.   .

was sitting in my Humanities class, daydreaming, as I chose to do most of the time, due to my opinions concerning the ideas taught in the class. I had seen something on the Discovery channel during Shark Week that had amazed me. Being the nerd that I am, I couldn't get it out of my mind.

Bear with me. During one of the shows, they showed a killer whale attack and eat a great white shark. This blew me away, because I had always thought that great white sharks were the meanest, most deadly animals in the ocean. I guess you could say I thought they were the kings of the ocean. I have never been a fan of sharks, especially great whites, so I was glad to see that video.

It appeared that the killer whale swam up from under the shark and struck it on the belly, knocking the shark unconscious. The killer whale then proceeded to devour the shark. I remember thinking how cool that was.

I later went on to look up more videos online and I found a killer whale, who was nicknamed by researchers and known for eating great white sharks. This time, the orca bit into the shark with its initial strike, killing it and once again, eating it.

The things I had seen that day got me to thinking how, in a way, this situation was much like GOD in His dealings with Satan: GOD of course being the killer whale and Satan being the shark-turned-dinner. In my mind, in this scenario, the ocean is like the world with its multitude of life-forms. Like Satan, the shark moves through the entire world, stirring up trouble and feeding on the weak, tired, stressed and slow inhabitants, thus causing chaos and turmoil. I smiled to myself, as I thought about the Truth of GOD's power and glory striking Satan down to the pits of hell for all eternity. I have a broad imagination. Just then, I heard my teacher say, "Write that down. It's important," and on that note, I came back to the classroom.

He was speaking of some worldly fellow from long ago and his beliefs on humanity. He spoke of these various archetypes, which are supposedly complexes of experiences that come upon us like fate. He went on and on with what sounded to me like complete gibberish. A partial classroom of nonbelievers sat there and carried on with the foolish conversation, but I took no part in it. I once got involved in a conversation in that class, voicing the Truths that I'm aware of as a Christian and the entire class became a chaotic uproar. After that, I sat and observed and immediately mentally shot down every man-made idea they spoke.

It is those situations by which it is easy to see just how much influence Satan has in the world. The evil one's influence on man tells us that we have figured everything out on our own with only the things we can physically see. Therefore, there is no need for GOD. How blind, arrogant and prideful can a man or woman be? I suppose every bit as prideful and full of him or herself as Satan was and still is today.

The worldly, overly-educated man tells us that who we are comes from our subconscious mind and that we are pre-destined to be who we are. We are told through the humanistic approach that there was no real reason for the Rabbis to decide on the books of the Old Testament: that there was no divine intervention. The world tells us that GOD has limits and this is exactly what the evil one wants us to believe. By casting his lies and having power over others, faith is lost and the realness and power of GOD is taken into question by those who don't realize that there are two sides to everything.

When an individual chooses to listen to another man and is deceived by the lies of the world, that individual has made the choice to listen to Satan rather than GOD, whether they are aware of what is happening or not. Thus, they have been bitten by the shark: but fear not, for the power of the one true King of Heaven and earth is coming to strike down the evil and deceitful shark on our behalf.

Another point I would like to make is that, while it is very healthy and helpful for we who are in recovery to go back to school or continue on with our higher education, it is equally important to keep in mind that we will be exposed to worldly views by means of humanities and science, as well as other classes. As Christians, it is important to stand strong on the rock of salvation and not be persuaded by the evil one or his followers. Stand in the light and when moving from one point to another, walk around the shadows. By this, I mean remain focused on the LORD our GOD and all He is. Remember that He is the one true GOD of all creation and with Him, we cannot lose.

He is the way, the truth, and the life. GOD is love and we are called to love in all that we do. We are called to love even those who mean to deceive us, but do not be unequally yoked. "Unequally yoked" means that you should not become involved with those who refuse GOD the Father, His Son JESUS CHRIST and the HOLY SPIRIT.

Cy Mulholland

1 Corinthians 6:9-11
Or do you not know that wrongdoers will not inherit the kingdom of God? Do not be deceived: Neither the sexually immoral nor idolaters nor adulterers nor men who have sex with men 10 nor thieves nor the greedy nor drunkards nor slanderers nor swindlers will inherit the kingdom of God. 11 And that is what some of you were. But you were washed, you were sanctified, you were justified in the name of the Lord Jesus Christ and by the Spirit of our God.

Lord, let me stand firm in the Word and not be deceived by the world. I pray in JESUS' name. Amen

STARTING OVER

Now is the time to begin a new chapter.
It's time for me to take control of what I can, hereafter.
It's a new beginning with far less sinning.
The hearts and minds of my family, I'll be winning.
No longer will I waste time, but spend time.
I will focus on my wife and kids all the time.
I will face my fears and not taste the beers,
And I know at times, I have to release the tears.
I won't sip the bottle and live my life at full throttle.
I'm going to slow things down, so I can see what's around.
These past few years have come and gone like a sound.
It's time to start over, time to transform.
No more for this army will I ever conform.
Never again will I put on this uniform.
Time to start over, Washington: here we come.
For the first time in years, I no longer feel numb.
Man, reenlistment sure was dumb.
But now is not a time to live in the past.
These soldiering days are over at last.
The army, the war, and my brothers, you see, will always be a part of me.
But it's time to start over, time to let go.
It's time to go back to the people I know.

One thing I can tell you for sure is that today I am a nondrinker. What I know is that I don't want drinking to be a part of my life. It's not the example I want to set for my children. I don't want the problems it helps create in my marriage. I want to live a life in good health. I want to eat right and exercise. I want to be the best father and husband I can be. I don't want to get complacent and I am not over-confident. I am motivated and I am dedicated.

I still make mistakes, but they are not amplified by alcohol. And to this day I still learn from them. I still learn from my wife and my kids and my Heavenly Father every day. I never want to stop learning, because I know that's when I will stop growing. I must hold myself to a high standard and that means being the best man and Christian that I possibly can be. I've put my family through enough already: I hate to say it, but it is definitely true.

I'm going to spend the rest of my life being the family man I know I'm supposed to be.

2 Corinthians 1:21-22
[21]Now it is God who makes both us and you stand firm in Christ. He anointed us, [22]set his seal of ownership on us, and put his Spirit in our hearts as a deposit, guaranteeing what is to come.

Lord, grant me the strength to remember who I am and to call on You through prayer, always. I pray in JESUS' name. Amen

BETTER MAN

I want to be a good man. That's my plan.
I want to have morals and values in the palm of my hand.
No longer will I blame Satan for the problems in this nation.
I will focus on GOD with great concentration.
With opened eyes, I will utilize the free will I now see.
I will take care of me, my wife and our three.
Like a shepherd tends his flock, I will lead my family.
And I will follow my shepherd, the one who is Holy.
Just today, I received some good advice.
It was about my anger and not being nice.
Before I react, I need to think twice.
Some tell me I can be a heck of a guy.
When I'm not angry, I'm just Cy.
I've found that I can cope with a pen and a pad.
When I write down my thoughts, I no longer feel sad.
So that's what I'll do. I'll write them down and share with you.
Then maybe I'll realize that I'm a good man, but I can be a better man.

As I've mentioned before, for the majority of my childhood I fell short of my full potential. It took me a while to figure out why. I knew why I felt bad, but I never knew quite why my grades went down and never came back up. I didn't care enough to try and understand why drugs and alcohol became such a large part of my life. I couldn't explain why it was that I was so angry all the time.

And why did I isolate myself at such a young age? Why was I always getting into fights for one reason or another? Why was it that I had such a negative outlook on life? Unfortunately, those feelings and behaviors carried over into my adult life and it wasn't until recent years, with help from the "experts," that I was able to pin-point everything back to when I was eleven years old.

My big brother, my hero, my best friend, killed himself. He was twenty-one years old and I was in the fifth grade. I remember waking up that morning and getting ready to go out of town for a wrestling tournament. My big brother was nowhere in the house and I remember feeling concerned, 'cause he was supposed to go with us to my event. I knew he had been out with his friends that night, so I figured he probably was not going to make it and I was bummed out.

Just before we were ready to head out the door, he came in. Shortly after, he realized his fiancé had stayed the night at our house, not knowing where he was. He got upset that she had done this and decided not to go with us to the tournament. We left without him.

My dad, my mom, my little brother, my little sister and I were driving down I-80 for a little while when a highway patrolman pulled us over. He informed us that we needed to turn around and head home. We knew something had to be wrong.

It is important to remember that PTSD can impact us throughout our lives on various occasions. As I stated in my case, I first experienced trauma as a child before I even had any idea what Post Traumatic Stress Disorder was. As an adult, before I ever gave myself time to heal or recover from what I had already experienced, I went off to war, where my symptoms became progressively worse with each of my three combat tours.

I put so much emphasis on this, because it is vitally important to deal with each and every traumatic experience separately and combined by different means of therapy and medication and spiritual growth. The most important of these is a spiritual connection with GOD, our Father in Heaven.

Jeremiah 32:40
I will make with them an everlasting covenant, that I will not turn away from doing good to them. And I will put the fear of me in their hearts, that they may not turn from me.

Lord, help me to remember daily that we all are given free will and the opportunity to come to You for a new life. I pray in JESUS' name. Amen

What Happens Next

What happens next is up to me.
I get to choose who I want to be.
Will I take the path to nowhere, or will I be free?
Does the past repeat itself? I guess we will see.
What happens next, where will I go?
Will I live a normal life? Only time will show.
Can I find myself or remain lost? I do not know.
Am I learning to cope? Am I learning to grow?
Will dreams finally sprout from these seeds that I sow?
What happens next? Will I let those that love me down?
Can I finally wise up, before I end up in the ground?
Should I permanently stop trying to hide myself in this town?
I need to stop looking down and plant my feet on the ground.
I need to do as they say and turn this frown upside down.
What happens next is up to me.
I have to make like an Asian and establish some chi.
I must break loose from these bonds and set my soul free.
Stop isolating myself to my room, internet, booze and TV.
It is vitally important to be that man I should be.
I say time and again, what matters are my wife and our three.
What happens next doesn't only affect me.
Want to see what's next? Keep reading this book.
If you are curious, flip through these pages and look.

We all have problems. We all have issues. Some of us are alcoholics, some of us are drug addicts, some are sex addicts and some of us have experienced things that have forever changed our lives. Some of us have even been shot, blown up and lost a limb or two, or eyesight because of it. However, we are still here and we still have a pulse.

> **It's no different for anyone who's had a setback and is struggling to recover. You have to keep your spirits up to keep moving on fighting back toward a normal life.**
> **—Bryan Anderson, No Turning Back**

So what's next? What path do we choose? There are only two options in this life. There is no grey area. It is one or the other. Good or bad, light or darkness. Will we live a life of discipline and obedience, or of self-pity and wrong doing? What happens next is up to any individual that would make the decision to live free rather than to be a prisoner of his or her own mind.

That was the very decision I had to make and I'm happy to say that I made the right decision. Because I made the right decision, I am sober. I'm the man I'm supposed to be, that I have been called to be. No, I'm not perfect and I never will be, but I will wake up every morning with a smile on my face and thank GOD for another day—every single day, clean and sober. I will, for the rest of my days, remain pro-active in my recovery and I will always be involved with some kind of group and my family. I will avoid isolation, so that I don't get lost in my own head.

These are the things I think about all the time. Another thing that is very important to remember is not to get overly confident, because that leads to complacency. I know, because I made that very mistake on more than one occasion.

At one point in time, I had quit drinking and I had just about made it to my one-year mark. I was very motivated; however I wasn't involved in any kind of program. I was white-knuckling, going it alone. I had no support system and when I hadn't had a drink in exactly eleven months and three weeks, I went out and drank again.

I let my family down, but more importantly, I let myself down. I threw away so much progress, but all was not lost. See for me, that relapse was what got me actively involved in recovery. It just so happens that I made enough bad decisions that someone else recognized I had a problem and here I am today. I'm happy, I'm sober and I'm grateful. We have to ask ourselves, "What happens next?"

Hebrews 6:1
Therefore let us leave the elementary doctrine of Christ and go on to maturity, not laying again a foundation of repentance from dead works and of faith toward God,

Hebrews 2:1
Therefore we must pay much closer attention to what we have heard, lest we drift away from it.

Lord, thank you for all your many blessings and allowing me the opportunity to be counted among your children. I pray in JESUS' name. Amen

The Afters

What happens after my treatment is complete?
Will I be successful, or will I repeat?
Repeat is a trend that I must mend. To repeat again would mean the end.
I must uphold my standards: I cannot bend.
What happens after I leave the Army?
Have I made the right decisions: does my wife agree?
Will I be able to support the ones I love?
Maybe it's a chance to show what I'm made of.
I can't allow us to go down. I must rise above.
What happens after my punishment is read?
Will I stay motivated or be discouraged instead?
It is crucial that I be the man I'm supposed to be.
My family, they rely and depend on me
I refuse to be enslaved by stress: I am free.
What happens after we move to our new home?
I know that for once, my wife won't feel alone.
We will be close to her family and that will be nice.
The original plan was to go to my home, but that wouldn't suffice.
We have to plan our future. We needed to think twice.
What is it that happens after this life?
Of this I am confident: There is no more pain and strife.
It is my destination, my place of rest. It is the reward after passing the test.
I hope to be there with Carleeh, Cainen, Cennady, and Celeste.

often refer to achieving higher education as a very useful coping and growing skill and indeed it is. Along with writing poetry and focusing on my mental, emotional, physical and most of all spiritual well-being, bettering my education has proven very beneficial. Not only does it prepare me to be successful in the world's job force, where most of the cards are stacked against us: it also exercises my mind.

I never fully applied myself as a kid, as I've mentioned before and I really do have a good time with my college education now. I particularly enjoy math, which is funny, because I could not stand math as a kid. I could not focus on it long enough to put any of the numbers and letters together to where it actually made sense to me, but now I have a great time with it. It's like a puzzle of numbers and letters—being that I'm in pre-algebra—to which I enjoy finding the answers. Currently I have a B+ and that only motivates me to strive for that A, which I have high hopes of achieving. Oftentimes, as I'm sure anyone reading this can probably tell, I put things that have nothing to do with each other together and make them somehow make sense. It's the way my mind works. During conversations, I tell people that the way I talk and write is due to me having a poetic mind and then I chuckle.

I was thinking about a topic during a Bible study at church recently, where we discussed unity in JESUS, in a world that is divided. We live in a world that clings more and more to immoral ideologies all the time and things only continue to get worse. I could list for days the things that are wrong with the world we live in; some are new, but many are the same things that were going on hundreds of years ago.

The more that time passes, the more people there are living immorally, without love existing as the core value, concept, reason, or whatever you want to call it. With love comes humility, gentleness and patience and this is who we are called to be. The more we strive to be of love, the more we will become who we are meant to be in JESUS.

GOD tells us in His Word that we are all part of the Body leading up to the head, who is JESUS: Unified, working as one for the greatest purpose that exists, which is to love one another. The more we grow in our spiritual maturity, the more we understand and the better we become in everything we do. The more spiritual growth and maturity that is achieved, the more likely one is to be given spiritual gifts, as it is written in the HOLY BIBLE. When GOD sees fit, He grants such gifts and it is by His righteous judgment and through the HOLY SPIRIT that He does so. Seeking the will of God with all your heart and soul greatly benefits your recovery from any form of burden the world puts on your shoulders.

Ephesians 4:11-16
So Christ himself gave the apostles, the prophets, the evangelists, the pastors and teachers, 12 to equip his people for works of service, so that the body of Christ may be built up 13 until we all reach unity in the faith and in the knowledge of the Son of God and become mature, attaining to the whole measure of the fullness of Christ.

Then we will no longer be infants, tossed back and forth by the waves, and blown here and there by every wind of teaching and by the cunning and craftiness of people in their deceitful scheming. 15 Instead, speaking the truth in love, we will grow to become in every respect the mature body of him who is the head, that is, Christ. 16 From him the whole body, joined and held together by every supporting ligament, grows and builds itself up in love, as each part does its work.

For so many years, I was blinded by the world, even after being raised in the church and knowing right from wrong. I was far too immature and too interested in the world's instant gratification, which appeared to help me cope with my pain and burden. The world's influence is a powerful thing, especially when someone is hurting. It always seems so much easier to quench the pain, fear and doubt with the world's "quick fix."

Unfortunately, that "quick fix," or instant gratification, has an expiration date and leaves us feeling more miserable than we did before. This is why so many of us become addicted to various activities or substances. Thank GOD for His patience and the unconditional love He has for us! I'm grateful to the LORD that He granted me the time to seek Him and His will. I want to be better with each passing day and I do actually ask that His will be done in all things, including the writing of this book. My thoughts, speech and actions should be and strive to be what the LORD would have them to be.

I will never claim to be perfect, because I'm not. I am far from it, but what I now have—which I was missing for the majority of my life—is the want, need, desire, passion and longing for GOD's love and a close relationship with Him and to please Him. I know how real a connection with GOD is and what it means to have His favor. It is what I want, both for myself, and for all my brothers and sisters, whom I love. By "brothers and sisters," I mean everyone in this world that makes up the body of CHRIST JESUS with me.

Ephesians 4:1-8
As a prisoner for the Lord, then, I urge you to live a life worthy of the calling you have received. 2 Be completely humble and gentle; be patient, bearing with one another in love. 3 Make every effort to keep the unity of the Spirit through the bond of peace. 4 There is one body and one Spirit, just as you were called to one hope when you were called; 5 one Lord, one faith, one baptism; 6 one God and Father of all, who is over all and through all and in all.

But to each one of us grace has been given as Christ apportioned it.

As seen in the Spirmentical Diagram, a personal relationship with Jesus Christ is the key to life, both here on earth and in Heaven. As scripture states, Jesus is the way, the truth and the life. The Holy Bible states that no one goes to the Father, but through Christ Jesus. Thus, our spiritual well-being is the foundation by which our lives are intended to be built on and Jesus is only one way this can be done. Our physical, mental and emotional states depend on each other, but can be hindered by what we allow ourselves to eat and by a lack of exercise. Eating an unhealthy diet on a regular basis can play a role in developing or be a side-effect of depression and/or anxiety, as well as other negative emotions. Keep in mind that the more we surround ourselves with positive and uplifting people, places and things, the more likely we are to mirror their behaviors. The more we surround ourselves with anything damaging to our relationship with loved ones and, more importantly, with Jesus, via the things we hear, see and consume, the more likely we are to reflect these things in our thoughts, speech and actions, as outlined in the GIGS Diagram. The Lord does not walk away from us, ever. We create separation between ourselves and the Savior when we allow ourselves to fall short of our full potential by living in sin. Jesus is intended to be our rock; our foundation upon which we build our lives.

Lord, thank You for counting me among Your children and writing my name in Your book. Help me, Lord, to be a better servant tomorrow than I was today and let Your light and love be seen in me, Father. I pray this in JESUS' name. Amen

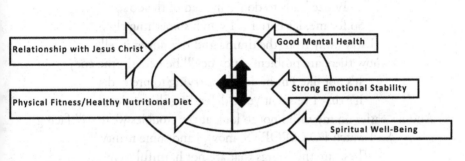

Spirmentical Diagram

The News

If there's one thing I don't watch much of, it's the news.
When I do watch, there's only one network I choose.
They are fair and balanced, so I know I can't lose.
As you've probably guessed, my choice is FOX NEWS.
News leads to stress and stress leads to booze.
Booze leads to don'ts instead of the do's,
So for me, it's better if I watch something else.
I stay away from the drama and the stories it tells.
I know there are problems and they'll be here till the end.
It's not like I'm in denial or trying to pretend;
It's that I've spent years defending this nation,
And it's easier on my mind not to look at the troubles we're still facing.
So I watch FOX SPORTS, movies and some reality TV.
These are the things that are not harmful to me.
Occasionally, though, I like to see some Bill O'Reilly.
From time to time, I like to watch Shawn Hannity.
Other times, I'll turn on a little Glenn Beck,
Or FOX and Friends in the morning once in a while . . . what the heck.
Most of the time, though, I watch shows with my wife.
She doesn't watch the news: only a few times in her life.
So, that is another very good reason.
To watch whichever one of my favorite sports is in season.
When I'm flipping through the channels, it's past all of the liberal
media I cruise.
If and when I watch the news, I choose FOX NEWS.

I t took me years to realize—and actually, my wife noticed it before I did—that by me watching the news on a regular basis, my mood remained in either a down and depressed or short-fused and angry state most of the time, due to the effects of PTSD. Every time my wife warns of things such as this, I go into a phase of denial, because the things she refers to are the things which I enjoy very much.

I used to sit around and watch the news for hours and hours, keeping up with what was going on around the world: in particular, the events that were occurring with the war on both fronts. At the time, I didn't realize what was occurring in my subconscious mind, causing more problems within my physiological self than was necessary. My wife, however, knew that there was a definite change in me every time I watched the news. Most of the time, it was when I would hear anything that involved soldiers getting hurt or killed, while other times my mood was changed by hearing news about our country's economic troubles or various other issues. Basically, if it was bad news, it did not go well for me. My inability to hear bad news and deal with it in a positive manner led me to drinking in excess, as did anything with which I seemed incapable of coping without some kind of chemical assistance. This, of course, was all due to my struggles with PTSD, because prior to deploying the first time to Iraq in 2003, I never seemed to have any problems after watching things on the news.

Over time, my sensitivity to things such as this has become far less, due to my success with recovery, but it has taken some time. These days, it is my preference to not watch the news except for on occasions where I absolutely want to be informed of something I feel is important going on in the world. When I choose to watch the news, I defer from the majority liberal media and watch only FOX News, because they do seem to actually be more fair and balanced than any other network I've viewed. As a whole, I watch far less television than I used to and if it were totally up to me, I would go away from satellite television and only have basic cable in my home, because there are so many negative, worldly views on television and it gets worse all the time. This is my personal opinion and I'm not opposed to going away from television altogether and only watching the occasional family-friendly movie. I'm sure my wife and I will have a few discussions on this matter and one of my arguments will be the importance of spending more time in the Word and putting more and more emphasis on GOD, as we grow as a family in CHRIST.

It's unfortunate that so many people, even Christians, put so much emphasis on the things of this world. We make it seem so hard to break away from our habits, such as our favorite shows. Many of us—and I used to be guilty of this—underestimate the power of GOD and the direct line of communication we have with Him through prayer. I've mentioned some of the experiences I have endured with prayer and the undeniable reality that was clearly shown to me by GOD. My hope for and advice to anyone would be to give it a chance.

You should devote yourself to prayer and communicate with GOD the things you need. Of course, as with all things, common sense applies: Ask that the LORD's will be done and that in all things He be glorified. Most of us have some knowledge of what GOD sees fit and we should pray accordingly. Don't worry so much about the things of this world and try to realize what is truly important in this life. For we who are in recovery, the more we pray and get into the Word, the more we will begin to think clearly and logically in our daily lives. It requires being pro-active and wanting with all one's heart and soul to have a normal life as well an eternal life.

Titus 1:9
He must hold firm to the trustworthy word as taught, so that he may be able to give instruction in sound doctrine and also to rebuke those who contradict it.

Lord, as I grow closer to You, let me be ever mindful of the things of this world which I knowingly can live without and live more freely and purely than I can with them. If I am misguided about anything, Father, may You reveal it and help me cast it away. I pray in JESUS' name. Amen

It Is What It Is

It is what it is, is what I say.
Not living in the past: I'm looking past yesterday.
It's possible that tomorrow will be here in a little while.
I plan to practice what I've mentioned and only wear a smile.
My intention is to create peace in my life for the greater part my days.
Sooner and not later, I still need change in some of my ways.
It is what it is; I cut ties with the so-called friends.
With time, I realize these four are here till the end.
There is so much more for us to look for.
I'm excited about the future and what is in store.
Time to suture the disconnect that exists in my mind.
There is no rewind; my marbles, I will find.
It is what it is: remind me in a week
Not to be weak, but remain focused. A new horizon I seek.
More and more, I'm realizing the potential I always had.
It's much easier to honor them when I'm not feeling sad.
I have a plan and one option to succeed.
We will live without greed and I'll provide for our needs.
With society I will coincide, the process is to heal.
Less often than more, I am emotionless. I want so badly to feel.
Sadly this takes time, but I'm now a patient man.
It is what it is and this is where I stand.
I understand, because of the aid by which I've been assisted.
It is what it is and I'm proud to have enlisted.

t is very interesting to consider what different people consider a personal sense of accomplishment. For some, it is achieving a college degree while for others, it is becoming a professional athlete. Some people are elected to office, while some see their greatest accomplishment as serving their country in the armed forces. For many, it is a combination of things and such is the case with me.

I am proud to have served my country and I will be proud to be a college graduate when the time comes. I have dreams of publishing this book and hopefully someone else is reading this now, which would mean that I accomplished it. I also have hopes of further paying it forward, by speaking to groups of people about the same message I am sharing within the contents of this book.

The possibilities are endless, as far as accomplishments are concerned. Some people want to become doctors, actors, singers, therapists and some even want to perform on Broadway. Then, there are those out there who become inspired to create things that are more or less on the counter-productive spectrum of goals in life. I am not saying anything bad about those out there who create certain products, but what I'm referring to are those who for one reason or the other wish to be remembered when they are gone by the alcoholic beverage they created. I'm not saying that they who create alcoholic beverages are evil people. That is not for me to decide and I'm no longer a judgmental person.

I was at the store not too long ago and I noticed a sign with a man on it who used to be an actor. He was holding a bottle of liquor and the sign stated that this man would be coming to our post, where he would be holding a bottle-signing. The sign clearly stated that he would be signing pre-purchased bottles of the liquor from the company which he owned. This was the first time I had ever heard of something such as a bottle-signing and I thought to myself, "Why would anyone want a bottle signed by another man?" It seemed rather strange to me, but then again I never really quite understood putting others on a pedestal, especially for something as simple as a brand of alcohol.

Once again, I'm not saying anything bad about anyone. I'm simply expressing my personal views on the matter. My thought-process is that when I'm done with a glass or plastic bottle, regardless of the previous contents, I'm usually going to recycle it. I am not going to get it signed by someone.

I try to keep everything in perspective. I guess I could say that when it comes to anything, I now do my best to remain aware of the importance of not idolizing anything. There are various opinions that exist when it comes to idolizing, but the fact of the matter is that anything and anyone can be idolized. When a person puts such importance on something or someone that he or she becomes consumed with it and separation between GOD and the individual is created, that is idolatry.

In a manner of speaking, anyone can worship anything. In a way, the alcoholic idolizes alcohol. There are those who idolize automobiles, jewelry, money and of course false gods and prophets. There are even those out there who idolize men and women. The possibilities are endless. It is written in the New Testament of the HOLY BIBLE:

2 Corinthians 6:14
Do not be yoked together with unbelievers. For what do righteousness and wickedness have in common? Or what fellowship can light have with darkness?

As I mentioned before, if an individual tries to make something in his or her life fill up the emptiness they feel in their lives, they do indeed create separation between themselves and GOD. I have been guilty of living in this form of sin at more than one point in my life, with more than one idol. There's no reason to sugar-coat this: I call it what it is. After all, what is the difference between statues of various sorts mentioned in the BIBLE, or something that holds just as much value in any given person's life? The truth of the matter is that there is no difference, if any given individual is consumed in the same manner to the point that the individual's heart and soul are overcome by whatever it may be.

I can say that, for a large portion of my life, I was overcome by various things at different times. Much of the time, my life has been overtaken by a combination of things, as is the case with so many people. The majority of my life was consumed with drugs, alcohol, and women. For a larger part of my life than that, alcohol and women controlled my life: even after marriage, as I've stated before. If there is one thing that I'm now accustomed to, it is being able to openly confess to anyone the sins that I have committed. What does it matter that another human being knows the wrong I am guilty of? That is the farthest thing from my motives. Rather, I want GOD to know that I freely confess my sins before man so that I will be held accountable by whomever and by whatever means possible. My number one goal in life now and forever is to please my GOD by doing what is right and just in His sight. This means I must possess the ability to cast out evil thoughts immediately upon them entering my mind. By doing this, I drastically lower the possibility of any separation being created between me and my Heavenly Father.

At the same time, because I am not perfect and mistakes will certainly be made, JESUS will always be there to intervene on my behalf, due to the fact that He paid for all of our sins in full when He died on the cross. Of course, as I have mentioned and will continue to mention, this is not a free pass to sin and later ask for pre-planned forgiveness. We will all be held accountable for our wrongs accordingly. It is written in the HOLY BIBLE in the New Testament:

Galatians 5:19-21
The acts of the flesh are obvious: sexual immorality, impurity and debauchery; 20 idolatry and witchcraft; hatred, discord, jealousy, fits of rage, selfish ambition, dissensions, factions 21 and envy; drunkenness, orgies, and the like. I warn you, as I did before, that those who live like this will not inherit the kingdom of God.

Lord, thank You for blessing me with new vision and a clear mind and a heart that now desires Your will beyond all things. In JESUS' name I pray. Amen

One Day Time

Today, I will be better than yesterday. I will start fresh and change my way.
I will listen to the potter, because I am the clay.
I won't worry about tomorrow. I will live in the now.
Self-improvement is my goal, by asking how.
I won't stress about what the future holds. Humbly, I will be shaped
into the mold,
Understanding my purpose, now I have the key.
It is faith, hope and love that are my reality.
I no longer live life as though it's just me.
I go by "one day time," because tomorrow is no guarantee.
I'm grateful for every moment. I miss them when I'm away.
I can't stand being apart even for less than a day.
For as long as time still applies to me
I'll spend as much of it as I can with my wife and our three.
I'm showing my children right and what not to be.
I go by "one day time" and take nothing for granted.
You can't bear fruit if no seeds have been planted.
Labor pains will come and many will groan,
And I for one will bear it until I go home.
I have an ear to hear, so I listened and I heard.
This poetry is for me to share, but seek first the Word.
Don't get me wrong: I'm glad you took the time to read.
Now spend a little "one day time" on your spiritual need.

There are times when I slip and fall flat on my face. There are times when for one reason or another, complacency sets in and I do something I regret. Granted, I don't typically make the mistakes that I used to, but that is not to say that it couldn't happen. I have often used the phrase which I learned in the Army: "complacency kills." The important thing is that I learn from the mistakes I make and I learn how to combat them in this war within myself, this "spiritual warfare." I try to remain aware of the importance of not getting down on myself after slipping, because it only creates more collateral damage. As soon as we realize our folly, it is important that we make the correction necessary. The correction every time is to stop what it is that we are doing, repent and seek the Lord's will in prayer.

Romans 3:23
For all have sinned and fall short of the glory of God

In this life, there is no "too late" in GOD and He knows full well that many of us will fall short and how it is that we will. He also knows that not a single one of us is perfect, which is why Christ, the Perfect God-Man, paid the price for all mankind's sins. As I have clearly stated and will continue to do, being that I am a man of repetition, there is never to be any misconception of pre-plotted prayer. There is no excuse for letting the thought of willfully sinning accompanied by pre-planned repentance enter our minds. That is not to say that if a person does that, this person is damned. After all, there were many times I was guilty of this very thing when I was less mature in my spirituality and I knew that my preempted sin was wrong at the time. The difference now is that I know the consequences of continuously living deceitfully and the foolishness of it.

Romans 7:20
Now if I do what I do not want to do, it is no longer I who do it, but it is sin living in me that does it.

Hebrews 3:12
See to it, brothers and sisters, that none of you has a sinful, unbelieving heart that turns away from the living God.

Cy Mulholland

1 Peter 2:11

Dear friends, I urge you, as foreigners and exiles, to abstain from sinful desires, which wage war against your soul.

I have thought on various occasions, "Why is that in one moment or day I can be doing so well and then the next thing I know, my world seems to have turned upside down?" The thing I have to remind myself of in those times is that, because things are going so well, the evil one does everything in his power to bring us down. During a football game, if an offense is continuously beating a defense with the passing game because of zone-coverage, the defense may then switch to man-coverage so that they can have tighter coverage on the star receiver. It is then that the offense must adapt and overcome. It is in those moments that I need to be strong and go back to the huddle and communicate effectively with my quarterback through prayer.

We are strengthened in the Lord. These are skills that take effort and practice. There is never-ending growth that can be achieved as a Christian. We can and should always strive to be better. Not only that, but there is no reason we shouldn't strive to learn more about who we are and our history theologically.

Now, I know that there are different levels of faith. By that, I mean some people are going to be the Christians who change their lives and go to church and read their Bibles from time to time. Then, there are those Christians who do this, yet still go out to the bars and clubs and get drunk and participate in indecent acts. Lastly, there are those Christians who make the complete change and turn their whole lives over to the will of GOD.

I have been each of those at different times in my life. And I'm not judging anyone. That is not my message here. My message right now is that there is never-ending growth as a Christian. Looking back, I can map out the process of my growth, which continues on today and for the rest of my days. Ladies and gentlemen, it only gets easier in Heaven, when we no longer have to put up with negative influences and temptations from the evil one. Be excited about that Truth, as I am. We should be excited. Knowing this should give us strength and courage to carry on toward our goal.

I will mention that the only reason I am glad that GOD hasn't called me home yet is so that I can teach my children and someday my grandchildren about GOD's love and the Gift of JESUS. Not only that, but I appreciate the opportunity to reach out to as many strangers as possible, so that they may hear the great news of our Lord and Savior JESUS CHRIST.

It's ok to allow oneself to become motivated to do the Lord's will. Be excited. Be dedicated. A person should get situated so that he or she may be vindicated. An individual should not allow anything to deceive him or her as a good time, as fun, as something they are missing out on. Stand firm in the Lord, our GOD: A person should desire with all his or her heart and soul to be where the Savior is and to love.

Psalm 40:2
He lifted me out of the slimy pit,
out of the mud and mire;
he set my feet on a rock
and gave me a firm place to stand.

Colossians 3:17
And whatever you do, whether in word or deed, do it all in the name of the Lord Jesus, giving thanks to God the Father through him.

Lord, let me only speak and write of Your Truths, in hope that anyone who would hear or read would be moved to seek You in Your Word, contained in the HOLY BIBLE. I pray this in JESUS' name. Amen

Spirmentical

What is Spirmentical? What does it mean?
It's about taking care of yourself: it is your well-being.
It is living proper and being in touch with GOD.
It's about morals and values, not being a fraud.
It's about self-improvement and giving your best.
At times, it's about giving to some of the rest.
It's about being healthy and thinking with a clear mind.
It's looking to the future and leaving the past behind.
It is eating right and being physically fit,
And when you've got nothing left, you still don't quit.
It's about body, mind and definitely soul.
For most, it is taking care of you first.
When you fail to do this, you may display your worst.
It's finding something you are passionate about.
It's doing the right thing, without a doubt.
It's honesty and respect and all the gifts from above.
It's about faith and hope, but most of all love.
It's about building you up, not tearing yourself down.
It's about opening your eyes to see what's around.
Indeed, it is your spiritual, mental, and physical well-being.
No longer blinded by the darkness: it's the light that I'm seeing.
A better, safer, sober man is what I'm to be.
It's not only a choice, it is my destiny.

"In recovery place everything in God's hands. Then go to therapy and do your best. My therapy session was only an hour. After I left there I went to the gym for three hours and did more on my own. I spent a lot of time looking in the mirrors learning how to walk again and getting my body in the best shape of my life. Eating healthy, exercise, and prayer have been my emphasis throughout recovery. We have to give God something to work with, I did my part and God blessed me."

—Jerrod Fields, single amputee combat veteran.

Comparing myself now to the way I was before is like comparing night and day. It feels good to feel this. I remember once again, (because I always get a chuckle out of it when I think about it) that when I was younger I used to say that I would never not drink. I truly believed it, too. No doubt I felt that way because I knew no other way to feel. All I knew was that even the hang-over didn't feel as bad as whatever else I felt when I wasn't intoxicated. This was due to the fact that, at the time, I didn't realize where the pain was coming from, but now of course I know it was because I had lost my brother. It had been there for so long that it became the norm.

That is why I feel free now. I finally broke away from the chains of bondage: the chains of hurt, fear, pain, doubt, guilt and sadness. I made a choice: a choice to give it all to GOD. I made a choice to ask JESUS to speak on my behalf and asked Him for His forgiveness. I asked the HOLY SAVIOR to add my name to His HOLY BOOK. I apologized for all of the wrong I had committed. I thanked JESUS for loving me enough to pay my debt in full.

Matthew 11:28
"Come to me, all you who are weary and burdened, and I will give you rest.

Galatians 5:1
It is for freedom that Christ has set us free. Stand firm, then, and do not let yourselves be burdened again by a yoke of slavery.

1 John 5:3
In fact, this is love for God: to keep his commands. And his commands are not burdensome

I have mentioned before that there is nothing wrong for a man or woman to drink and I have referred to those who drink without the purpose of getting drunk. It is when the goal is to get drunk to the point that some negative emotion is masked, or some harm is inflicted that drinking becomes a problem. There really is no purpose whatsoever for getting drunk: however, it is perfectly acceptable if someone has a few drinks for the purposes of relaxing the mood and innocent enjoyment, such as at a banquet or a wedding. Even JESUS turned water into wine at a wedding. His judgment was never clouded and He never fell in the ways we so easily do. He is perfect and all knowing.

The point is that wine is not for getting drunk, which is why there is a penalty that our bodies must pay the following morning for over-doing it. It only makes sense that when one drinks to the point that it causes more sin to enter his life, that he or she must feel the brunt of it. GOD does not bring pain into our lives. We bring our own pain into our lives. Drinking to the point that one is drunk and can no longer control him or herself is indeed sinful. Too often, those of us whose sole mission is to get drunk as a means of blocking memories bring sin into our own lives, and sometimes into the lives of those close to us. We create troubles for others. It is a selfish and careless life-style and I was guilty of this too often, in so many ways. It was the reason for much of my regret. I am so glad that I finally snapped out of that thought-process—with a lot of help and treatment, of course. GOD gives us everything we need for guidance in His HOLY WORD.

Luke 21:34
"Be careful, or your hearts will be weighed down with carousing, drunkenness and the anxieties of life, and that day will close on you suddenly like a trap.

Romans 13:13
Let us behave decently, as in the daytime, not in carousing and drunkenness, not in sexual immorality and debauchery, not in dissension and jealousy.

1 Corinthians 5:11
But now I am writing to you that you must not associate with anyone who claims to be a brother or sister but is sexually immoral or greedy, an idolater or slanderer, a drunkard or swindler. Do not even eat with such people.

1 Corinthians 6:10
nor thieves nor the greedy nor drunkards nor slanderers nor swindlers will inherit the kingdom of God.

Ephesians 5:18
Do not get drunk on wine, which leads to debauchery. Instead, be filled with the Spirit,

1 Thessalonians 5:7
For those who sleep, sleep at night, and those who get drunk, get drunk at night.

Thinking back to the man I used to be, I remember how much a part of my life staying out and getting drunk really was. I remember my sin causing others heartaches and pain. I know now that any man or woman that goes into his friend or family members' homes and causes someone else to sin is even worse off for bringing sin into another life. If one person brings drink to a happy home and leaves that home suffering, than that person is dead wrong. I was guilty of this on more than one occasion. The sad thing is that in situations such as this, the individual who has wronged others doesn't even feel any remorse, most of the time. I didn't until years later.

Luke 17:3
So watch yourselves.
If your brother or sister sins against you, rebuke them; and if they repent, forgive them.

As I've mentioned before, being that I no longer drink, many of the so-called friends that I used to have are long since gone. It's kind of funny, but not really because when I used to drink and get drunk and sin against others, I also drove away many people, because I was also a "so-called friend." It's crazy how we hurt each other when we willfully live in sin, by spreading pain to the ones we are supposed to love. So many don't realize there is a better way to relieve the pain. I know for me, even after coming up in the church, I remained unaware of the possibility of truly letting go of the pain and having peace.

That is a large part of my motivation for writing these things down: to show that it is actually possible to have peace. It takes effort and a person has to actually want something better. A person has to want to be successful and to give, to serve and suffer less. A person has to face reality and realize that he or she is only human and that he or she cannot do it on his or her own. I've been down that road: it doesn't work. It's not even a matter of depending on other humans, though they can be very helpful. There is a spiritual connection that must be established in order for healing to take place. This is the undeniable Truth.

I know there are many who might read this and wonder what in the world I am talking about. Some will read this and think I am absolutely off my rocker, but I am not lying to anyone when I say I have lived it. I'm stating plain and simply that I was a terrible person, who was completely miserable and caused many other people to hurt, on account of my wretched speech and actions. I was a low-down, sorry, selfish, cheating, lying, greedy individual. I was only concerned with the things that were "good" for me. I'm the same person who was guilty of laughing while I killed the enemy, because I was so blinded by the world that it somehow became fun. This only haunted me later on, to the point that I doubted there was a GOD at all. I was a person that let hate fill my heart and become so hard that I actually had thoughts of harming another innocent American, due to the fact that I felt he deserved it for causing discomfort in my life on a far lower level than what I was planning on doing to him. This is who I was.

Then I found peace. I got help. I received help on many levels, but the most important thing and the main reason I was able have sanity back in my life was because of GOD's grace. The Father in Heaven who created us all by His own design made it so crystal clear for me that there was a better life waiting for me. Prior to this, there were so many things I was using to remedy myself that I didn't actually need at all. It became well-known to me that, in a world where we are set up for failure from the beginning if we follow our own instincts, I could be healed by Faith. I am so grateful. I will take peace over chaos any day.

I often say, "I'd rather be bored than have too much fun," and it is completely true. I feel so much better now than I used to when I was so blinded and deceived. I took my future back and we all know what I mean. I was living in sin and I actually was an evil person, to the point that I had an evil glaze over my eyes and was weighted down by burden—both self-inflicted and not—but now I am light and I have the light instead of the darkness. I am free because I have been set free. It's as if someone tossed me a key while I was reaching through the bars of a cell, only to realize that when I picked up the key from the cold concrete floor, there remained on the floor the imprint of the key. It had been there since the concrete had been poured long ago.

It's sad and unfortunate, but some do go too far and do things that land them in jail or worse. My hope and prayer would be that anyone reading this who is struggling with PTSD will stop today whatever it is that is self-destructing. Though you may not know, take it from me: I have been to my rock-bottom and I know how hard it is. I know the feeling of hopelessness. I remember others reaching out to me and for so long, I pushed them away. Some who are reading this might not be as fortunate as I was. Some who are reading this might not have someone who loves him or her, but if someone is reading and someone is or knows someone in need, then love. We are to love ourselves and others. For those who are hurting, reach out for help and later, reach out to help, before it is too late.

Lord, give those reading this the strength and courage to reach out, either for help or to help someone in need. Let us all stop and be conscious of the things in our lives that are causing pain and that are counter-productive. In JESUS' name I pray. Amen

My Vision

Where will I be? What's my vision of me?
I have a good idea of where I want to be
Two, three, four, five years from now.
I know where I want to be and I know how.
I feel better today than I've felt in years.
I have no urge for beers and I have no fears.
So where will I be? What is it that I see? For one, I see me and a
united family.
I see a vision of the man I'm supposed to be.
My kids are a little older and still making the grade;
Maybe some of the bad memories have begun to fade.
My wife, in time, I hope, will smile more often.
I hope her hard outer shell will eventually soften.
I see a long life together, verses me in a coffin.
We'll have a cozy little home out in the Pacific Northwest.
We'll replace the Army with family; it'll be for the best.
My wife and I will provide a good living for Cain, Cenna, and Celeste.
I will be a civilian; hopefully, my mind can rest.
I will continue this journey of going to school:
Military experience plus college can be a valuable tool.
I see myself as one who got his life in check.
No tragedy, but a success story. I'm no longer a wreck.
This is my vision of me and my family. No matter how I picture things,
we are happy.

There once was a man named John, who was an alcoholic. John had attended church very briefly as a child and had a wife who was a Christian, but who had walked away from going to church and carrying herself as a Christian. John drank most days with his neighbor, who lived directly across the street. Together, the two men were sarcastic and arrogant in their drunkenness. Every day, an elderly man who lived a few houses down would walk up and down the street for exercise and whenever he would pass the two men, he always had something kind to say to them. In return, John always had a rude response for the old man. Nonetheless, the old man was always kind.

One day, John came home from the hospital, wearing a cast after breaking his arm. The old man happened to be passing by on his daily walk and called out to John, "Neighbor, what have you done to yourself?" To which John replied, "Mind your own business, old man." Then John walked in his house and after a few minutes, he could hear a noise coming from outside. He looked out the window and saw that the old man was trying to start a lawn mower in his front yard. John walked out to the old man and said, "Old man, I thought I told you to mind your own business." And the old man replied, "Neighbor, I'm going to mow your lawn." For the next few weeks, the old man would come by once a week and mow John's yard. John always thought to himself, "This old man is going to want something in return."

Then, one day, the old man walked up to John's door and told him that he would be going out of town for a few weeks and asked John if he would keep an eye on his house while he was gone and John said, "Sure I will" and did. One day, John heard the mower start up once again in the front yard and when he looked out he saw a teenage boy pushing the mower in John's front yard. John walked out, cast and all, and asked the boy what he was doing. The boy responded with, "My grandpa told me to mow your lawn while he was away." For the next couple weeks the boy came over and mowed John's lawn.

One day, John received a package in the mail which contained a letter and a book from his brother. The letter from John's brother stated that he knew John had a lot of unanswered questions from their childhood because they had only attended church briefly while they were kids and they grew up in a very angry home. John read the book and found many of the answers he had been searching for. After a while, the old man returned home. John walked down the street to where the old man lived and knocked on the door. The old man answered and John said, "Old man, I know why you mowed my lawn." And the old man said, "You do?" John said, "You are a Christian, aren't you?" The old man smiled and began to cry and replied, "Yes I am." Then John began to cry and the two men hugged each other and they became friends and John soon became a Christian.

The previous story is a true one, with the exception of a few changes. The behaviors of the alcoholic man are similar to those of someone suffering with PTSD. The man referred to as "John" did have a very angry and sometimes violent childhood. Many people who have been diagnosed with PTSD are alcoholics or drug-addicts or sex-addicts, while others find even stranger ways to cope then any of these.

As a Christian man, I have come to understand the importance of reaching out to those in need of the good news about the Gospel of JESUS CHRIST. It is one thing to be a Christian standing idly by, only concerned about his or her salvation. It's another thing to fulfill a purpose by getting active, not being hypocritical and reaching out to those in need.

Matthew 9:10-13
While Jesus was having dinner at Matthew's house, many tax collectors and sinners came and ate with him and his disciples. 11 When the Pharisees saw this, they asked his disciples, "Why does your teacher eat with tax collectors and sinners?"

On hearing this, Jesus said, "It is not the healthy who need a doctor, but the sick. 13 But go and learn what this means: 'I desire mercy, not sacrifice.' For I have not come to call the righteous, but sinners."

The better I seem to feel and the closer I get to a normal life by readapting and being able to do the things I used to do prior to Post Traumatic Stress Disorder, the more I realize the importance of not being complacent and selfish by not sharing the good news of CHRIST. I used to think that even though I was beginning to feel better in many ways, I needed more spiritual attention before I could possess the ability to help someone else. I could not have been farther from the truth. I had to realize that it didn't matter how knowledgeable I was about the Word; I could still help someone in need, given the opportunity. As long as I didn't put out false information and lose credibility with those with whom I would potentially be reaching out to, then I could be very helpful.

The important thing for an individual to remember who wants to help someone in need is that before we are able to speak of the good news, we must first listen. We have to be able to listen effectively. For one person to really listen to another person, that person has to actually want to listen. Truly being able to hear someone's story and being able to offer them the reassurance of GOD's love takes love. Once a person has opened him or herself up to GOD's love, then the love of God will radiate from within that individual. I know that by sharing what I know and potentially helping someone in desperate need, I could possibly be saving someone's life.

A large body of research indicates that there is a correlation between PTSD and suicide. There is evidence that traumatic events such as sexual abuse, combat trauma, rape and domestic violence generally increase a person's suicide risk. Considerable debate exists, however, about the reason for this increase. Whereas some studies suggest that suicide risk is higher due to the symptoms of PTSD, others claim that suicide risk is higher in these individuals because of related psychiatric conditions. Some studies that point to PTSD as the cause of suicide suggest that high levels of intrusive memories can predict the relative risk of suicide. High levels of arousal symptoms and low levels of avoidance have also been shown to predict suicide risk.

In contrast, other researchers have found that conditions that co-occur with PTSD, such as depression, may be more predictive of suicide. Furthermore, some cognitive styles of coping, such as using suppression to deal with stress, may be additionally predictive of suicide risk in individuals with PTSD. Given the high rate of PTSD in veterans, considerable research has examined the relation between PTSD and suicide in this population. Multiple factors contribute to suicide risk in veterans. Some of the most common factors are listed below:

- Male gender
- Alcohol abuse
- Family history of suicide
- Older age
- Poor social-environmental support (exemplified by homelessness and unmarried status)

- Possession of firearms
- the presence of medical and psychiatric conditions (including combat-related PTSD) associated with suicide

Currently, there is debate about the exact influence of combat-related trauma on suicide risk. For those veterans who have PTSD as a result of combat trauma, however, it appears that the highest relative suicide risk is in veterans who were wounded multiple times or hospitalized for a wound. This suggests that the intensity of the combat trauma, and the number of times it occurred, may influence suicide risk in veterans with PTSD.

Other research on veterans with combat-related PTSD suggests that the most significant predictor of both suicide attempts and preoccupation with suicide is combat-related guilt. Many veterans experience highly intrusive thoughts and extreme guilt about acts committed during times of war. These thoughts can often overpower the emotional coping capacities of veterans, as reported by the PTSD Support Services.

Though I have never been suicidal, I came to the realization that my life had been saved in the very same manner. My loved ones and I agree that if I had not quit drinking to cope with the painful memories of my past, I surely would have died in sin by drinking myself to death. The power of GOD's Holy Word is not only something that is read and spoken, but it is also felt in the depths of the believer's heart and soul. It is when the Word is believed and spread to others that the HOLY SPIRIT descends upon the believers and they are changed forever. For some reading this that have never heard anything like this before, this could be a lot to take in and could be overwhelming. I can assure you that this good news is Truth. As one who has been to combat and proceeded on to hell on earth and traveled the long journey back to peace, hope, faith and love, I can tell you that there is new life in JESUS.

Acts 1:8
But you will receive power when the Holy Spirit comes on you; and you will be my witnesses in Jerusalem, and in all Judea and Samaria, and to the ends of the earth."

There are those in the world who are crying out for help and many who read this are among those. No matter where you are in life, there is action to be taken and it would be my hope and prayer that hesitation will be avoided. Reach out. Reach out for help or to help. Let the tool that you are reading right now be of help, but more than that, seek the Word of GOD and pray for the Lord to move in your life. Believe in JESUS' name and I promise you it will be done. GOD calls us all for a purpose. Pray for your purpose to be revealed and it will be done.

One of my purposes was to write this book and I said when I started that if even one person is saved, it will be worth it. I am not finished here. I will continue to reach out, as others reached out to me when I was broken and hopeless. I am grateful to GOD for answering my loved ones' prayers and for showing me who I really am and what my purpose is. We must not be complacent. No one is unworthy of the Grace of GOD. Exchange meanness for kindness. Allow yourself to be loved and to love.

Lord, show me someone I can help who is hurting. I pray in JESUS' name. Amen

CHAPTER EIGHT

FAMILY FRAME OF MIND

The war is in the mind. The home is in the heart.
Love is the only thing that can set the two apart.

Through the Trees

—Carleeh Mulholland

tossed and turned all night. The excitement is just too much for me to bear. Soon, I will be able to touch his face and kiss the lips I have been dreaming of for fifteen long months. The clock slowly ticks from one hour to the next, like the swing of a pendulum. It is finally morning and I have five hours 'till I will be seeing my love, in the flesh. I stay lying in bed for just a few more minutes and roll onto my left side; I look at his side of the bed and smile. Soon, he will fill the spot that has been waiting for only him. As I rise, I catch a glimpse of my perm-a-grin in the mirror across the room and bust out into a happy dance; I jump up and down, clap my hands and giggle profusely. "YESSS, he he, uh-huh" is all I can say.

I feel like I am levitating off the ground: quickly, I am back on the floor and the multitude of all the things I still have to do is heavy on my mind. Shower, shave my legs, paint my nails, wake the kids up, get them dressed . . . but my dress and make-up have to be last, so I look fresh. I feel the nerves all over, but especially in my stomach . . . like I have one of those plasma balls inside me.

I have everything prepared. I have banners hung on the front door and at the field, and one to hold up and wave. The house is spic-n-span: all of his belongings are washed and ready to be worn, and his freshly-waxed car is waiting to hug the corners of his favorite roads, while a little scented tree hangs from the mirror, hiding the staleness of the unused air. I have spent the whole year prepping for this day. I have money set aside for our anniversary trip to Jamaica, and I spent five days a week at the gym toning every inch, and had a ritual of SPF-coated tanning poolside since spring.

I make sure to take a peek out the front door to check the weather. Perfect! It is sunny and warm, just like the forecaster promised. Even Georgia has a freakish rain storm in June. The sweltering heat is in hibernation for this special occasion; I think Mother Nature owes me from the last redeployment, since I had to sit in a stuffy, foul-smelling gymnasium with 300 other eager families.

As I close the door, I hear my alarm ring-a-dinging in my room. It's time to wake up the kids. Cain and Cennady practically jump out of bed and run into the hall to meet me. It is funny to me how their reactions are so close to my own, upon waking. I guess they are ready for Daddy to finally take his role back. I send them off to take showers. While I wait for them to finish, I assemble their clothing and shoes. I notice the time and head off to get myself showered.

After I am finished, I get my robe on, apply my makeup and blow-dry my hair into his favorite style. I have bright blonde highlights and smooth bronzed legs to spark his desire. I walk to the closet and pull out my "BAM! Dress." It has a plunging neckline and is thigh-length black with a silver-spotted design, and it fits like it was made for my body. I throw my three-inch black stilettos on to complete the look. They make me almost five-foot eleven-inches tall, which is his height. At this moment, I know my vigorous gym routine was well worth the pain. I have never felt more stunning.

I decided to go the patriotic route with the kids: White dress on my daughter, with red, white, and blue ribbon dangling from her blonde pig-tails. My son is wearing his favorite Red Sox hat, a blue-and-white collared shirt and a pair of khaki shorts.

Once again, my alarm sounds. I have it set it to notify me fifteen minutes before I need to leave. I start to scramble, throwing together the last minute details. I dust shimmer powder from head to toe. Check. Grab my purse and cell phone. Check. Get kids into the car. Check. Make final inspection around the house and in the mirror. Check. Check. We are off!

As I head to post, I swing into the local coffee shop (my home away from home) to order a huge decaf mocha and to snap some "before" pictures. My friend meets me there, so she can follow me. It is better to have a team of friends who are welcoming their soldier home to sit with, for support.

Back on the road, we pull up to the main gate and head towards the parade field, which is set up for the welcome home ceremony. There are families everywhere, and the stands are filled with smiling faces and energetic children. As we park, I realize my whole body is shaking like I am freezing, but since it is 98 degrees out, it must be all the excitement that is buzzing through me. I feel like a giddy child on Christmas morning. I hear the Army band playing "Proud to be an American" and the realness sets in. I am really going to see him. I am really going to be able to hold him and I am really going to have my husband back safely. For a moment, every emotion is running through me and tears are welling up. I have to remind myself "Don't ruin your make-up, Carleeh".

The field is large and the green grass is perfectly mowed. The big stands are adorned with flags. Across from them on the other side of the field is a 3rd Infantry Division patch sign and behind it is a line of large, groomed trees. Around the entire field is the Warriors Walk (rows of trees planted in memory of Fort Stewart's fallen soldiers.) We make our way over to take a seat. I chose the bottom bleacher to the right of the stage, perfect for running onto the field and getting back to the parking lot quickly.

As I chat with a couple friends, including my best friend (who came to support me, even though her husband is still in Iraq,) my cell phone rings. It is my husband calling from the bus to tell me they are down the street! I start jumping up and down, screaming. The announcement "five minutes out!" reaches the crowd. A surge of joy fills the stands. It seems like only seconds go by and I hear a woman yelling "BUSES, I SEE BUSES!" and all of a sudden screams break out all over the field.

I grab my children onto my hips and frantically search. Just then, I catch a glimpse of a white bus. There is nothing more breathtaking at that moment than the line of white buses passing in front of our eyes. They round the corner and stop behind the line of trees. I look down at my daughter, as tears run down her face. She doesn't understand the emotions, but she does know her Daddy is so near. Everyone is holding up their handmade signs and waving their flags. Boisterous shouts and hollers dance in the air.

At this second, I cannot tell if I can feel anything but a single drop of sweat rolling down my back, and I have no idea if it is from the humidity or the extreme situation. Other than that, I am numb. I stare at the tall, slender, and pointed barriers. I cannot take my eyes off them, for I know any second he will come marching through the trees. Seconds feel like hours and out from behind the greenery step the colors, being held so high. The red, white and blue in all its majesty waves, as if every twist is wrapped around my heart.

Next come at least two hundred of America's finest in digital print, camouflaged into each other to look like one tactical team. They march proudly in the distance and stop in front of the speaker's podium. A man comes over and hands my son a microphone and tells him to shout to his Daddy to hurry up. The presenter starts his speech and rambles on. I don't hear a word he says because I am scanning the masses for the one familiar face, the one I could trace in my sleep. I cannot find him. Where is he? Which one is he? It has been so long. What if he doesn't recognize me? The speaking stops, and resumes with simple words "Fall out".

The crowd takes off. I stand in shock, then begin sprinting toward the dispersing formation. A swift and speedy movement catches the corner of my left eye. The most beautiful smile I have ever seen rounds a group of lingering people. I let go of little hands and run into the arms of my hero. I am lifted and spun, a dance I never want to end. As I am lightly set down, I am reaching for more. I have to touch him again to make sure he is real. I smell his scent and feel his skin. I savor every second and make as many memories as I can. I am reminded I have to share him when small arms wrap around his waist and tiny lips shower him with kisses.

Finally, it is my turn. I look up to him and see those piercing eyes and run my hand over the curve of his face, and with everything I have in me, I kiss his lips. No one else is there. It is just my love and I. His life was spared and he will fight no more. This is the day that we get to start forever, again.

The BIG If

If I don't come and she hears the news, will she stand there crying or
will she fall to her knees and stare at nothing?

If I don't come home, will she look at the sky and remember me or will
she hate the world for delivering me?

If I don't come home, will she lie down at night and dream of me, or
will she wake up screaming, wondering what really happened to me?

If I don't come home, will she hold our kids and tell them stories about
their Dad, or will tears roll down her face daily while they ask her,
"Mommy, why are you so sad?"

If I don't come home she could be bitter, but I know she never would.
My wife is the kind of woman that would stand up proud: More so than
I ever could.

If I don't come home, my wife will go on, just like I'd want her to. She'd
keep me in her heart and she and our children would find something
worthwhile to do.

If I don't come, some day she may find love after me, but that's ok
because we are true love and in her heart she'll never replace me.

Our kids will grow up and my wife will grow old and I'd hope they'd
have a wonderful life.

No matter what happens, always remember, you are my happiness, my
love, my wife.

One of the hardest things for a soldier who is a father and/or a husband to think about before he leaves his loved ones to go off to combat is whether or not he will make it back home. I couldn't stand the thought of not watching my children grow up and not getting to experience the joy of being a grandfather someday. It scared me to think of the possibility of my wife hurting because I would no longer be in her life and the possibility of her finding love with another man.

I can't help but think now that those were foolish thoughts. It's hard not to, but I don't think that is the way a Christian man should think. If I had been as strong in the Word then as I am now, I would realize that with GOD on my side I could never go wrong. As I've written before, I kept a laminated copy of Psalm 91 in my left breast pocket over my heart. It made me feel at ease. I know GOD was watching over me and know that it was part of His plan to bring me home. I also know that now that I have a better grip on my PTSD, I will not take the time I've been blessed with for granted.

So many of my friends and battle-buddies did not make it home and I can't imagine the pain their families had to go through. I know it hurt badly enough for me just to know that they were gone. I will never forget a single one of them. It seems as if the price of freedom will never be paid in full.

Each time I came home from the war, I was that much harder. I seldom smiled and I didn't realize how fortunate I was to have made it home to see my wife and my kids. My thoughts were clouded by the memories of the ones I had killed and the brothers in arms that I had lost. Instead of honoring them by making good memories with my family and having good times, I created a continuous drunken sadness with my anger that seemed to have no end.

That was the madness of my PTSD and I could not see past it. I didn't even know that I needed to reach out for help or that I had a problem, but my family, feeling the brunt of my issues on a daily basis, did. It wasn't until 2009 that I really began to get help and head down this path of recovery. I can proudly say that I am honoring my fallen brothers and sisters the way I should be today.

2 Timothy 2:1
You then, my child, be strengthened by the grace that is in Christ Jesus

Cy Mulholland

Lord, please bless and comfort all those families and friends that have lost and will lose a loved one in the name of freedom. Let us not forget, Father, that the cost of sustained freedom is high and let us always honor those that have given the ultimate sacrifice. I pray in JESUS' name. Amen

I Don't Want to Miss a Thing

I don't want to miss a thing.
I don't want to die here and waste my life for nothing.
I don't want to miss my wife's smiling face when I come home.
I don't want to miss leaving the house for a moment and feeling alone.
I don't want to miss their yell for me, when they greet me with a hug.
I don't want to miss holding our daughter, 'cause she's our little love-bug.
I don't want to miss all the nights when my wife makes me melt.
Those are the nights when comfort, peace and happiness is all I felt.
I want to coach my son's baseball teams and cheer with my daughter.
When my wife gets thirsty, I want to fetch her some water.
But if I never get to see them again, then I am eternally grateful for the
time I had with them.
I'm not a hero, but at times I've been a zero. I'm just a man who is in
love with his family and if our time together is over, then I guess it was
destiny . . .
Though it wouldn't seem fair and what purpose could it bring?
Just remember, I love you all so much and I don't wanna miss a thing.

wrote the previous poem "I Don't Want to Miss a Thing" while on my second tour in Iraq in 2005. My unit, B Co 1-64 Armor, was based out of what was called Camp Cuervo. It was formally known by another name, but for the life me I can't remember how to spell it. Anyhow, I wrote the poem because I was very lonely and I thought about my wife and kids back home all the time. I called home as often as I could and I even wrote letters from time to time to my wife and kids. My wife still has those letters today. There are some things that can be written that just wouldn't be the same in an email. And what woman doesn't love to receive a real love letter anyway, right?

I was thinking of all the memories that would be missed if I didn't come home. I thought about it every day and I remained in prayer daily because of it. Not that it was the only reason I prayed, but it helped when I was in combat and I wanted nothing more than to be back in my cozy, warm, loving, dust-free, sand-free, smell-of-death-free home. I wasn't so much worried about the fact that something could happen to me, but more so worried about my family's well-being.

I wanted to have an influence in my kids' lives. I wanted to watch them grow up and participate in all of their functions. I wanted to be there for my wife. I wanted to be the only love of her life. I wanted to grow old with her and spoil our grandchildren together. Those were the dreams that I wanted to see come true. I didn't want to miss a single thing. I guess I could say I was kind of greedy, but at the same time I kept everything in perspective. I knew at all times that life happens and we never know what that's going to be from one moment to the next, so I have to cherish each one as if it's my last.

Though I know I'm going to a better place when I leave this world, that doesn't mean I shouldn't make the best of this life while I'm here. On another note, I always keep in mind the fact that not everyone made it home to carry out the dreams and goals that I have the opportunity to carry out. I will never forget.

2 Thessalonians 2:15-17
So then, brothers, stand firm and hold to the traditions that you were taught by us, either by our spoken word or by our letter.

Now may our Lord Jesus Christ himself, and God our Father, who loved us and gave us eternal comfort and good hope through grace, 17comfort your hearts and establish them in every good work and word.

Lord, help me always be mindful of everything You have blessed me and my family with. Let me always remember the children who have lost their mothers and fathers in defense and security of our nation. I pray in JESUS' name. Amen

Never the Same

It will never be the same and I'm the one to blame.
I didn't focus on her needs; it was my wants I could not tame.
I remember the days she used to greet me with a kiss.
I remember a time when it never felt like this.
She used to bat her eyes and bite her lip.
She used to come up and nudge me with her hip.
Everything changed when the truth came out.
I lost her respect: she will always doubt.
It'll never be the same and that's a shame.
I am the only one that I can blame.
I no longer know what this marriage is about.
Often, it feels we are traveling down two separate routes.
There were days, a long time ago, when she would run outside as soon as
I got home—
The look of sincere happiness all across her face because I was home.
Now, she only wonders where I am when I'm gone.
It's entirely my fault; it's because of what I've done.
I took advantage of who should have been my only one.
It's almost as if someone died—
Not someone, but part of something has died.
She's always been everything that I need.
I wish I had turned away from my greed.
I chose to live the high life at a real fast speed.
In a home full of beautiful plants, I'm the only weed.
I missed out on so much; I'm always out of touch.
She doesn't owe me a thing.
I'm surprised she still wears her ring,
She doesn't look at me with a smile. It's been a while.
I constantly feel guilty in this never-ending trial.
She is no longer playful; she's always busy with something.
The fault is my own, I did the wrong thing.
I can't say that I'd blame her if she found another someone.
We used to call each other soul-mates, but maybe I'm not the one.

Right here and now, I'm feeling so down.
At this very moment, she's nowhere around.
It will never be the same and I'm the one to blame.
I messed everything up, because I'm so lame.
I have no doubt she loves me, but she no longer likes me.
If I tickle her, she says stop: I don't think she wants to be close to me.
It's easier said than mended, you see.
I ruined everything; I did these things behind her back.
I was never the husband I should have been before and after Iraq.
Damn it! I wish I could take it all back.
It will never be the same, it's not a game.
She feels hurt and doubt and I feel guilt and shame.
I was taught better than this, but I let her down.
I'm supposed to be the head of the family. I'm no king, I have no crown.
Do you know what I mean? There's no twinkle in her eye.
I ripped her heart out, but she didn't die.
I created a river of tears when I made her cry.
I have always loved her, but always lived in lust.
It's amazing she's still here; she could have left me in her dust.
Part of me feels she stays to take care of me.
She likes me a lot, so she won't leave me.
What a damn shame, I am not a good man.
There are far better out there, more deserving of her hand.
When I kiss her, she stops me; when I hold her, I'm too close. She
probably regrets that I'm the one she chose.
She tells me what is best for me, like a life-coach.
I'm the obligation that leads to her frustration.
No one has ever made me feel better than she has,
And I've brought her the most pain.
She's stronger than I am. If she'd done what I did, I'd go insane.
Is it love or the kids that keep us together? LORD knows, she deserves
so much better.
It will never be the same: this is not a game.
There's no one for her lack of forgiveness that I can blame.
Only me, so go ahead and boo.
I thought I could have my cake and eat it too.
Does she still love me and if she does, why so?
These are the things I'll probably never know.

Cy Mulholland

When she speaks, I feel her anger and hate.
It's because of me she never sleeps well or feels great.
I don't know how to face her family in her home state.
I do love her so much, but for her I've never been there.
For me to make her smile is extremely rare.
I took advantage of her, why would she think I care?
She calls herself a touch-me-not.
She's not at all proud of me, but I'm proud of what I got.
She and our children are the good part of who I am.
The other part is a combination of things that make me an ungrateful man.
We have an all-American family and these days that's sad.
Things could have been great, but I made them all bad.
It will never be the same and I'm the one to blame.
We should have been on the same team, but I played the wrong game.
I deserve to drive myself insane.

One day, but not only one day, my family and I took too much time getting ready and were late to church. But "better late than never" is what some say and I agree. I was so glad that we made it, because like the Sunday before and all of the Sundays I attended previous to that, I heard exactly what I needed to hear. Our regular pastor was out of town visiting family, so that day we had a guest speaker from Fort Knox. He is a chaplain there and he spoke to us about family and how GOD intended our family to be. He was so correct with everything he said, because it was as the Bible says. He was a good speaker and I could tell that the Lord worked strongly through Him. It seems to me that I can always tell when GOD has truly anointed someone to share his message. Both our regular Pastor, Pastor Curtis and this gentleman have such an anointing. He made several valid points.

The main point that he made was that we have wealth in our children. We have far more wealth in our children than any riches this world has to offer. Our children will be a direct reflection of who we are. I know that today I am a far better parent than I used to be, but there is still much room for improvement. I want to do daily devotionals with my family and pray with my children before they go to bed at night, among many other things that I'm going to implement. I want my children to be good, strong, Christian people, because that's what they saw in me; this motivates me to do more and be better with each passing day.

Another valid point he made was that adultery is a major offense. He noted that back in the old days, people were actually sentenced to death for such an offense. That's how serious it is. I am guilty of wronging my wife this way and she did leave me and she did forgive me, but like the pastor said, "There is nothing worse one can do in a marriage to harden one's heart." That is so true. I am guilty as charged for that crime and a crime is exactly what it was. Thank GOD we are capable of forgiveness.

To this day, I am tempted by the evil one as we all are, but I am overcoming temptation. I will never be perfect, but knowing this does not give me or anyone a free pass to sin. What does this have to do with my recovery? Everything. Not only does my PTSD affect me, but it hurts the people I love. Stress, depression, anxiety, anger and all other symptoms of PTSD or any other disorder or disease that causes negativity and leads to sin is from the evil one, Satan.

The world is dying because of the sin he influenced into it and he wants all of its inhabitants to die as well. The sooner we realize that, the better off we will be at combating it. We can break free from these various different chains that the world tries to bind us with, by developing a personal relationship with Jesus. We find peace in Him and Him alone and we find hope in His Word and comfort through His Holy Spirit. One should not go on carrying burdens for another day. He has taken it already and forgiven us and if one lifts it up to Him through prayer, He will give them peace. My brothers and sisters, JESUS is the living Word promised by GOD Himself. He is the way, the truth and the life, as it says in the Holy Bible. The previous poem was written when I was feeling down in the dumps and thought that things would never be the same after my mistakes, but today my wife and I and our children are happy and have peace, because we have the love of Jesus Christ. Amen

1 Thessalonians 3:13
So that he may establish your hearts blameless in holiness before our God and Father, at the coming of our Lord Jesus with all his saints.

1 Thessalonians 3:8
For now we live, if you are standing fast in the Lord.

Lord, give me the wisdom to share Your message in the manner that You would have me to. Let me only speak Your truths, Father and always Lord, Your will be done. I pray in JESUS' name. Amen

The Grass

I called to talk about things other than the grass.
Regardless of that fact, I really showed my a**.
She has other things on her mind, like me not being home.
She wants me to get help, even if it means being alone.
Why is it that I'm wired so much different than her?
Sometimes, it's like she likes the idea of me or as if she's not sure.
As far back as I can remember, she has wanted me to change.
Why would you devote yourself to someone you felt was so strange?
Regardless, I know you want what is best. There was no reason for me to
get so upset.
I just wish we could stay on the same page.
We miss each other when I'm gone and together, we rage.
Are we both actors? Do we belong on a stage?
With a fuse as short as mine, maybe I belong in a cage.
Just like most times, before I called I was excited to talk to you.
A few wrong words and the conversation was through.
Still, I don't know what I'd do if I didn't have you.
Best friends do fight; we're the pain in each other's a**.
Even over stuff like mowing the grass.
I shouldn't have got upset; I should have given you a pass.
We made up and everything is well.
One thing is for sure and it's not hard to tell:
There will be more phone calls and we will put each other through more hell.

t used to be that I took everything I have in life for granted. It used to be that I took my life, my wife, my kids, my health, my job, my faith and so many other things for granted. So often, I lived under the assumption that those things would always be there, no matter what I did. The truth is that if I'd done too much of some things, I would have lost many things.

If I had refused to make changes for the better, than my life definitely would have progressively became worse. It is the domino effect. For example, if I had not quit drinking and had continued to get in trouble, it is pretty safe to say that I would have continued to cheat and my wife would have left me permanently. If my wife were to leave, then she most definitely would have taken our children with her. If she were to take herself and our children away from me, then I most definitely would have drank heavily. If I were to go on a drinking binge, then it is certain that I would be arrested, then jailed or hospitalized. And if I would have put myself in too many situations like this, then I would have definitely damaged my health, my career and my faith, among other things. It would be a vicious cycle multiplying negativity until a tragic ending . . . most likely in death.

Thankfully, I have more sense than that and I finally got my act together. I no longer take so many things for granted. I'd be lying if I said I didn't take anything for granted. We all do and I'm certainly not perfect by any means. I still make mistakes. I still fall short. I still sin, but I do make a constant effort to do the right thing. I no longer intentionally plan to sin. Today, I choose a better quality of life for my family and I. Today, I choose the easy right over the hard wrong. After all, I'd rather be bored than have too much fun.

Colossians 2:6-7
6So then, just as you received Christ Jesus as Lord, continue to live your lives in him, 7rooted and built up in him, strengthened in the faith as you were taught, and overflowing with thankfulness.

Lord, thank You for Your spiritual guidance. I truly feel Your presence every day and for this I am grateful. I pray in JESUS' name. Amen

My Definition

What is it that defines me?
It's definitely not the Army.
So what is it? What could it be?
Is it good, bad, or ugly?
The truth is I know it: I'm a hard worker and a poet.
Most of the time, I'm a good man: sometimes, I even show it.
Oftentimes I worry, though I could possibly outgrow it.
I thank GOD for my dad. He took great care of me.
When I look at him, the best man I know is all that I see.
For everything he has done, I will be grateful eternally.
Without him, I haven't the slightest clue exactly where I'd be.
He showed me values like honor, loyalty, and respect.
To say that I first received any of these from the Army would not be correct.
He gave me courage. He gave me strength and that I will never forget.
So as you can tell, it's easy to see, I'm a man after my dad's own heart.
Someday when he leaves this world, we will still never be apart.
He knows how much I love my old man and he will always be in my heart.
My definition was written by my Dad: a great man wrote his too.
I love you, Dad and I know for certain that I'll always be a part of you.

Cy Mulholland

My dad and I have always been very close. He's the hardest working man I have ever met. He made sure that my little brother and sister and I had a good life. He made sure that we had a better childhood than he had. I won't get into details about his childhood, but he too had great parents. The difference is they were poor and their quality of living was far less than ours. My dad made sure of that.

Today, he is sixty-five-years-old and he's still the hardest working man I know. He showed me the importance of working hard and taking care of what's mine. He played the biggest role in shaping me into the man I am today. He taught me morals and values such as honor and respect and he taught me manners. He taught me the importance of having a personal relationship with our Lord and Savior Jesus Christ.

He showed me how important it is to have a home filled with love and a family that sits at the table together for every meal. The holidays were always a special time in our home. He taught me that family comes first. He and my mother have been married for more than thirty-five years now and they have always been a good example of facing adversity together and keeping the marriage strong. He's told me many times that the most fun times he ever had have been with his children. Indeed, we did have so many good times and I hope to have many more. My dad gave me my definition and I love you so much, Dad.

Philippians 3:16
Only let us hold true to what we have attained.

Lord, thank You for bringing me into this world under the direction of the honorable and wise and loving man that my dad is. I pray in JESUS' name. Amen

My Love

What is my love? I'll tell you who it is.
It's the one who loves me, not only what I give.
She's the first thought in the morning that enters my mind.
Compared to all the treasure in the world, she is the greatest find.
It used to be when guys would look at her, my teeth would start to grind.
For someone not to do a double-take on her, they'd have to be blind.
Unconditional love is all I feel, every time I hold her close.
My love has a beautiful face and beautiful eyes; she has the cutest
Italian nose.
I love my girl and she loves me. We've had rough times, but we are happy.
It's been eleven years now, I want eleven times eleven more.
I love my baby so much, she's my bestest friend for sure.
My love brings me up when I'm feeling down.
She's there for me when there's no one else around.
She's the first and loveliest thing I see when I wake up in the morning.
She doesn't mind if I steal a kiss from her without warning.
I'm so blessed to have her in my life.
I'd be a lesser man if she were not my wife.
She gave me my pride and joy. She's the mother of my children.
It's been so much fun; I'd definitely do it all over again.
I'm so lucky to spend the rest of my life with you.
I know how much you love me; you feel the same way, too.
My love, Carleeh, I miss you. I can't stand being apart.
You are the only one in the world that holds the key to my heart.

Cy Mulholland

My wife and kids were once in Georgia visiting her parents and some of her friends for a week. It was a short Monday through Friday visit and then they planned to be back here in Kentucky, but I missed them so much the moment they drove away. Every time I have to be apart from them, there is a huge void in my life that can only be filled by mine or their return, depending on the situation.

My wife, Carleeh, is the best wife I could ever ask for. I know a lot of people probably say that, but I mean that one hundred percent. She has been through so much in the last eleven years and she always has remained right here by my side. In some ways, the war has been harder on her than it has on me. For one thing, she has had to put up with me and my PTSD. So many marriages don't make it in the military. I'm not about to go quoting statistics right now, but I for one know that the percentage of marriages ending in divorce in the Army is very high. I know people that have been married for more than twenty years in the Army and get divorced. That could leave me with a feeling like no marriage is safe, but it doesn't.

My wife and I know we will always be together. We married young and we married for life. We have been through some very tough times and we've made it through them all. We know that there are tough times ahead and that we are going to face them together. Marriage is something I have to work at every single day. Like most things, I can't get complacent. I can't lose focus, because if I do, I am going to lose so much more. I speak from experience as one who has lost focus and nearly lost everything, but by the grace of GOD and my wife's love and forgiveness, we are still parenting our children together. I truly am blessed.

I make it a point to remain aware of everything I'm blessed with every day now, after taking things for granted for so long. These days, it's all about my family and GOD. That is my focus. They are my life. Sin is going to happen, but I'm going to put a stop to as much of it as I can. These aren't just words. It is the way I'm living. Today, I know that to get well and be the man I'm supposed to be, I have to want it. I do want it, so I am pro-active in my recovery. I make sacrifices and because of that, I have a more fulfilled and rewarding life. I no longer concern myself with the supposed friends, the party, and being cool. I choose my family.

John 20:29
Then Jesus told him, "Because you have seen me, you have believed; blessed are those who have not seen and yet have believed."

Lord, thank You for today and my family, because even though they are away I still have a family to miss. I pray in JESUS' name. Amen

No Need to Wonder

Everyone has certain things that they ponder.
There are certain things about which I don't have to wonder.
Like whose bed have her heels been under?
I'm a lucky man and I am so grateful.
I know I'm the only man with whom you are playful.
Those heels have remained right where they belong:
In our closet or matching whatever dress you have on
You were always waiting for me, every time I came home.
It feels good to have someone, as opposed to being alone.
Countless days spent apart with hours spent on the phone,
I always knew you were here, taking care of our kids.
I never had to wonder about what you did.
It feels so good to be loved by you.
I'm so glad you know how much I love you, too.
Never have I had to wonder in more than eleven years.
At times, I feel overjoyed; my eyes fill with tears.
I don't have to wonder where you've been or where you're going.
I don't have to wonder who you're with or try to be all knowing.
We have the same goals in mind and we're constantly growing.
I'm proud to call you my wife and I'm grateful for all you did.
You are so precious to me. Without you, we wouldn't have our kids.
That is the greatest gift that only you can give.
I'm so happy you're with me in this life that we live.
We have a bright future, because you were able to forgive.

've written several times about my five deployments overseas, but I haven't written much about everything that took place in between those deployments. There are certain measures that have to be taken prior to deploying overseas: certain training that has to be fulfilled in order to properly prepare for any given mission.

As previously stated, I was in the 3rd Infantry Division for ten years straight. During my time there, I went to many gunneries and field training exercises. Most of the time when my unit and I went to the field for training, we did things such as force-on-force, where we would match one platoon up against another, using everything we had been trained on to defeat each other. We were highly-trained with our equipment: we learned the abilities to shoot with precision fires and call in indirect fires and to move tactically, utilizing terrain to our advantage. We communicated within the platoon, higher echelon leadership and parallel units in order to accomplish mission success. We spent weeks and sometimes months at a time in the field, with few breaks, to ensure that we were fully prepared for whatever mission we could possibly be called upon to execute while deployed.

Another and easily the most fun type of training one could possibly do as a Tanker or, as it's more formally known, as an Armored Crewman, is Tank Gunnery. Tank Gunnery is more than just training. It's a competition. It is the Super Bowl of the tanker world. If you shot high tank within your company, you were "the man" or actually "the crew." If you shot high tank in the battalion, then you were considered the best of the best, the elite and you had bragging rights over all others in the battalion.

There are a total of a thousand points possible. Any given crew had to score a minimum of at least 700 points out of a thousand to qualify, but that's not all: Every crew had to also score seventy points out of one hundred on at least seven engagements out of ten. It is very competitive, like a sporting event and a lot of fun. It is one of the things I will miss most about the Army.

There were various other training exercises I took part in, depending on what overseas mission was ahead of me. On five separate occasions, I deployed within the continental U.S. to Fort Irwin, California, known as the National Training Center (NTC). This was a month-long training mission and was usually the final training we would receive, prior to leaving the country for a longer period of time. I also went to Fort Polk, Louisiana two times for month-long training exercises known as the Joint

Readiness Training Center (JRTC). Both times, I went in the summer and both times, it was hot and muggy and miserable, but I survived.

Somehow, I've survived every place I've ever gone during my time in the Army and every time, I returned and my wife, my best friend was right there waiting for me with open arms. She is a truly wonderful woman, with morals and values. She's a Christian woman and loves GOD with all her heart and soul. I have never had to wonder about a thing she was doing, because I know she has always had our family's best interest in mind.

Galatians 5:10
I have confidence in the Lord that you will take no other view than mine, and the one who is troubling you will bear the penalty, whoever he is.

Lord, thank You for blessing me with my soul-mate. I know whole-heartedly that we were meant to be together because You intended it that way. I pray in JESUS' name. Amen

I was just talking to my wife the other day about where I would be without her. When it comes down to it, I don't know quite where I'd be, but none of the scenarios I went over in my mind had positive results. We were married at a very young age and oftentimes that creates a lot of trouble for couples. Indeed, it caused some very tough times for us, but I wouldn't change a thing. For some, I believe there has to be trying times like those in order for the relationship to grow and be tested, to see if it is strong enough to survive. There is so much divorce in the world today and it's getting worse all the time. It seems as though no marriage is safe these days. I know people that have divorced after twenty and thirty years. Getting married and later divorced these days is like breaking up used to be. For some, that could be discouraging.

For my wife and me, it is motivating. We don't have a crystal ball and we can't tell the future. However, we do work very hard at our marriage and we believe that our toughest obstacles are behind us. At the same time, we don't let ourselves get complacent. So it is what it is. I wanted and needed her at a young age and forever and she feels the same way.

Then there's the fact that we have three of the most amazing kids in the world. I know a lot of parents say that. That's how we feel. My wife got pregnant with our son before we got married and I wouldn't trade him for anything. Then, after only dating for four and a half months, we got married in Wyoming. My son is my best buddy. Then of course, we have two beautiful daughters. I'm sure they are going to give me some grey hair when they get older, but we are bringing them up right.

It is so important that love be our foundation for healing. The ability to love and be loved is the most valuable tool we can ever have.

1 Corinthians 16:13
Be watchful, stand firm in the faith, act like men, be strong.

Lord, I am so grateful for my wife. She grounds me, she takes care of me and she loves me. I care for her the same. I am eternally grateful to You, my Father in Heaven, who has blessed me with such an amazing family. I pray in JESUS' name. Amen

She Said

She said I'm more than the choices that I've made.
She said I'm more than the price that I paid.
The things she said helped me realize who I am.
I beat myself up, but she said I'm a good man.
She made me feel better about the sacrifice.
She helped me realize the importance of thinking twice.
She said "Look at everything you have to live for."
She asked me to open up, and not close the door.
Thanks to her staying by my side, I am not alone.
Through the good and the hard times, our relationship has grown.
Often I stare off into nothing, because my thoughts tend to roam.
She says "Come back to me baby, come back home."
She said she sees the man I can and used to be.
I remember that man, but I can't yet see me.
My lack of vision makes it hard to agree.
Hopefully, I didn't spend too much time on the other side of the sea.
She said she loves me beyond my mistakes.
I nearly brought this marriage down with several of my quakes;
Before it was too late, she said it was time to hit the brakes.
She held us together with the remedy that she makes:
Bless her heart and its many little breaks.
She said we have to live for GOD, it's the only way,
And so that is where we find ourselves today.
She said "I love you Cy, a little more each day."

The biggest toll my mistakes have taken throughout the years has been on my wife and kids. They've had to witness my unruly behavior in the past. I've come a long way since then and today I can say that my life is manageable and that everything gets a little closer to normal each day. Despite my actions and everything I've put my family through, my wife has always been there for me. Every time I deployed, she was right there waiting for me to get back and I never had to worry about her being unfaithful while I was away. When I went outside of our marriage, she was able to forgive me. She and the kids left at one point to go stay with her parents after she found out about my wrong doings, but we were able to work things out. We are together today and for the rest of our days and we are happier than ever, because we live our life through JESUS CHRIST our Lord and Savior. It is so very important for us all to forgive and seek forgiveness.

Romans 15:13
May the God of hope fill you with all joy and peace in believing, so that by the power of the Holy Spirit you may abound in hope.

Lord, thank You for my wife and our children and for forgiveness. I am so blessed. I pray in JESUS' Name. Amen

Eleven in Eleven

One thing is for sure, I am so blessed. I have great kids: Cainen, Cennady, and Celeste;
And of course, my wife of eleven years since our "I do's."
It's kind of crazy, but it didn't take her long to choose.
I was never going to marry, but she came after me.
It didn't take me long to realize it was meant to be.
We got married on June 21st two triple zero. She was my lady and I was her hero.
We were so young, but we wasted little time.
Soon, a baby boy joined me and my partner in crime.
Most of the time, things are great. Other times are hard.
When we are dealt a bad hand, we choose to discard.
I'm the first to admit that she is the family's rock.
She's this family's foundation, the price of our stock.
She gave me two lovely girls who we love so much.
When I messed up, she forgave me and helped me throw out my crutch.
It's 2011 and we've been married for eleven years.
And throughout, there's been a pretty even mix of smiles and tears.
Between deployments and my mistakes, I'm lucky to have her by my side.
Because of this Army life, many marriages don't survive.
So here we are, happy and recovering together.
We are focusing on us and our kids forever.
Together till the end; this marriage is tougher than leather.
What we have is true love; it's so much more than fair weather.

I am so blessed and it so obvious to me that GOD brought me and my lovely wife together. He made sure that he paired me with a strong-willed and strong-hearted woman who could put up with me and love me throughout my struggle with PTSD. I believe that just before the point that she would not be able to tolerate any more of my foolishness, I finally came around. Carleeh always had faith, as she told me that the man she married was still inside my hardened outer shell. She was right. It's often easy to be right, when one's faith is in JESUS. She prayed a great number of hours throughout the years in hope that I would one day come around and as always, GOD answers prayers. Thank you JESUS, for finding humanity worthy of sacrifice.

I was having a conversation with a gentleman who I used to work with at a soccer game. His son and our son play on the same team. We were talking and in a way comparing the differences that were taking place in our lives recently. He had a lot to say about how things were not going the way he'd expected them too and I was sharing with him how things are going so well for my wife and I, but I explained to him that this wasn't always the case.

He made it evident that he didn't have an active relationship with GOD. Finally, I told him, because I didn't want it to appear as if I was boasting about my own doing, that the defining moment when everything turned around for my family was when I whole-heartedly turned my life over to JESUS and the will of GOD. He looked at me and said, "I might have to look into it." I agreed that he should and explained how GOD blesses those who follow him.

If we pay attention, we can all clearly see that when we live for the world out of greed or whatever the case may be, things never go according to plan. If an individual or group live a life of riches and fame, but never have GOD, they do not inherit the kingdom of Heaven when they die. The alternative is far less enjoyable and enticing. My point—and I cannot express this enough—is that with our free will, we have a choice and if we choose darkness over light, then we choose our own fate.

A person might say, "Having money, fame, women and alcohol among other pleasures of this life is not evil" to which I would tell that person that if we allow anything in this world to consume us, then we are acting out of evil: Not righteousness. The world has everything and anything to offer those who are in need or of greed, but with these worldly pleasures comes an expiration date which only GOD the Father knows. It is then that we all shall reap what we have sown. Some pleasures are not bad in themselves: it is when they are sought in an idolizing or evil way that sin is committed.

People fail to realize that they can have blessings abundantly from the Lord by living according to His will, but too often they choose to sell themselves short and accept the easy handout from the deceiver, who doesn't require anything except sin. He too has an expiration date and even though he doesn't want to be alone in the end, he will be unable to see anyone in the darkest pits of hell. I refuse to sugar-coat it. It is what it is and it is my hope and prayer that anyone reading this will seek first the will of GOD through His Word, found in the Holy Bible.

Amos 5:14
Seek good, not evil,
that you may live.
Then the LORD God Almighty will be with you,
just as you say he is.

Mark 9:47
And if your eye causes you to stumble, pluck it out. It is better
for you to enter the kingdom of God with one eye than to have
two eyes and be thrown into hell

Lord, thank You for my family and all other blessings. I pray in JESUS' name. Amen

CHAPTER NINE

RECOVERY AND ROUTINE

——•——

To lack knowledge is a weakness. Strength is found in healing.

Rock-Bottom

Where is rock-bottom? I thought I was there.
I thought I hit the bottom and I thought I didn't care;
Then I climbed back up with time to spare.
I believe rock-bottom is death, or life in jail with no parole and dying in hell.
Dying without forgiveness is the final nail.
Rock-bottom is a place of extreme sadness.
Rock-bottom is a place of bitter loneliness.
Rock-bottom has to be a place of misery that seems endless.
I know it is a place that I refuse to go.
I increased my chances by breaking contact with the foe.
Life is dangerous when it's fast; I prefer it to be slow.
Rock-bottom can be a man on the street with no home.
It can be a hitcher on the highway, able only to roam.
Possibly a drug-deal gone badly, with hot lead in your dome.
To some, rock-bottom could be a way of life.
I thought rock-bottom was cheating on my wife.
Reality cut through that like butter after a hot knife.
The bottom of a rock is a dark and dreary place.
It's cramped and uncomfortable; there is a lack of space.
No one likes to be stuck between a rock and a hard place.
Are you getting anything out of this? There's a point . . . can you see?
I'm not trying to waste paper or be rock-bottom for a tree.
This may not help you, but it's sure helping me.

don't know how to truly define rock-bottom, but I know I've been in some very tough situations. I suppose rock-bottom could be different for everyone. In a manner of speaking, we choose our own rock-bottom. Either that, or we compromise with our descent and choose to climb back up. Or, we choose death, or to spend the rest of our days in jail. For those who don't know, an individual can be jailed both behind prison bars and in his or her own mind. This is how it was for me. I was trapped in my own head. My struggle with PTSD was taking me farther and farther down all the time and much of this was due to the fact that I didn't understand fully what was going on with me. It wasn't until I received the treatment I needed and was educated by experts that I was able to climb out of my personal rock-bottom.

This week in my public speaking class, I gave a speech about coping and survival skills in order to recover from PTSD. For coping skills, I spoke about the things that, over time, I have learned are useful tools for those suffering with PTSD: tools to be utilized in recovery, instead of drinking, drugging, gambling and acting out, among the many other destructive ways to cope with PTSD. I expressed the importance of finding coping mechanisms that are productive in recovery, as opposed to the various forms of masks we use to hide our problems. I explained that my coping skills consist of writing poetry, furthering my education and physical fitness.

For survival skills, I outlined the skills identified by Charles W. Hoge, MD, Colonel, U.S. Army (Ret.) in his book, Once A Warrior, Always A Warrior. This book has been one of the most valuable learning tools I have come across and I have learned more about recovery from Colonel Hoge than from any other doctor or therapist I have been treated by in person. The reaction I received from the class was amazing. My classroom audience was very tuned in to what I was saying and I realized all the more how much people really do want to be educated about this disorder, whether they have it or not. In his book, Colonel Hoge also gives valuable information about mild Traumatic Brain Injury (mTBI) and its effects on the human body. Recently, I had to take another bite of humble pie. I was once again faced with adversity in the form of another individual projecting anger toward me. I realized later that, though I initially thought I was being wronged, I could have prevented the entire situation if I had relied on my fundamental beliefs and values. The important thing is not what happened, but acknowledging that I was wrong in the way that I reacted to negativity. I was reminded of how human I am and how on guard I must remain in my daily life.

I learn something every day about myself. Sometimes it's good and sometimes it's bad. This week, I learned that when I intentionally do not put on my scripture dog tags and my cross dog tag, I am not in the right frame of mind. For me, it means that something is eating away at me or I am feeling guilty about something. Oftentimes in the past when I stopped reading my Bible and praying, it happened because I was letting myself be involved in things that I shouldn't be, such as trying to meet random women on dating websites. These were dark times when I allowed myself to be deceived by the evil one. It is in these times that I need to go directly to GOD with whatever the issue is. It means I'm desperately in need of reading my Bible and getting down on my knees and praying for guidance and healing. I believe it is important for everyone to be able to recognize when they are falling short and intervening not only with self-help, but also praying for spiritual assistance.

Today and for the rest of my daily interaction with everyone and everything, I will emphasize within myself the importance of remaining humble when faced with adversity. I will make it a point to not create adversity for myself or others.

Romans 8:37-39
No, in all these things we are more than conquerors through him who loved us. 38For I am sure that neither death nor life, nor angels nor rulers, nor things present nor things to come, nor powers, 39nor height nor depth, nor anything else in all creation, will be able to separate us from the love of God in Christ Jesus our Lord.

Lord, give me the courage to follow my faith, beliefs, values and moral standing with actions. I pray in JESUS' name. Amen

A Smile

Like so many things, Satan is a smile.
I have only been aware of this for a little while.
The more I pay attention, the more I see. Everywhere I go, Satan smiles at me.
He finds our weaknesses and then he issues temptation.
This is the cause of my frustration.
I can't go to the store; I can't go get a coffee.
Everywhere I look, she's looking right at me.
He gives me her number and makes me want to call.
I know that if I do, I'm going to hit the wall.
This entire process will only lead to guilt and shame.
This vicious cycle is the evil one's game.
I hate him: he's tricky. He plays with my mind.
He tempts me to explore. I feel the urge to find:
To find something I feel I'm missing out on.
I seek it until it's conquered and then it is gone.
Satan finds me in many ways—sometimes it's a song.
He can be a wink, tight clothing, or even a thong.
If I remain aware of this perspective, I won't go wrong.
He wants to see me fail, so that I join him in hell.
He knows I won't drink so I won't go to jail.
He'd like to end my marriage and send my kids down this path.
I'm fully aware of his plots; I've already done the math.
I'm ahead of the game: I've arrived at last.

Cy Mulholland

2 Corinthians 5:17
Therefore, if anyone is in Christ, the new creation has come:
The old has gone, the new is here!

I am the new and the old has gone and I am strong. I will state again that in order to be whole, we must be spiritually-sound. This is where all our strength comes from and we must be able to love: Not just our blood-relatives and close friends, but everyone. The Bible mentions that with faith the size of a mustard seed, we can move mountains. The Bible also states:

1 Corinthians 13:2
If I have the gift of prophecy and can fathom all mysteries and all knowledge, and if I have a faith that can move mountains, but do not have love, I am nothing.

We, as those who have suffered from PTSD, are not always aware of what we have lost because of this disorder. A few of us become aware when we actually open up to treatment and love. Too often, we do not open up to treatment and because of our actions, we do not receive love either. It's not the fault of those close to us; yet the fault is not solely ours either. We are only human and have experienced inhumane situations. So where does this leave us?

Well, it's easier said than done, but we have to find some level of self-control before we go too far and someone gets hurt. Those of us with PTSD become angry and violent and explosive and we snap within a matter of seconds. The individual suffering from this disorder has to, at some point, open the door just enough to let someone or something—such as a program, or even a book—act as a guide to initially head down the path to recovery. Even better, try to actually see a pastor or a therapist in combination with some kind of program or book. As long as we become open enough to the idea of getting help before it is too late, then lives can literally be saved.

If I had given in to temptation and taken the easy way, my rehab would only have taken longer and I would have gotten less out of it.
—Bryan Anderson, No Turning Back

So whether you are the one causing pain or the one who is being hurt, if you truly love someone, you won't give up on him or her and you will keep showing love to that person: and sometimes, love is tough. Of course, this is easier said than done, and it is understandable to leave if the safety of anyone is being threatened, or if children are being exposed to too much aggression. Separation doesn't have to mean divorce. All too often, especially in the military, spouses give up on each other too quickly. They look for a permanent solution to what could be a temporary problem and while PTSD requires a life-long commitment, so does a marriage. Most couples do vow to stay together through the good times as well as the bad.

It is a well-known fact that many soldiers are too proud to accept help, because they are afraid of looking weak. That outlook is not easy for any spouse to break through, but it is worth the effort. For years, I was one of those soldiers and a Non Commissioned Officer who was too "hard-core" to accept help, until it became essential. My advice to any soldier—and for that matter, to any person who has experienced a traumatic event—would be to humble yourself and talk to someone.

To the family members: don't give up hope and pray for your loved one. Somehow, someway, get reconnected if the relationship is struggling, whether it is a marriage or some other relationship. If your mother or father, grandmother or grandfather, aunt or uncle, cousin or friend is hurting, then reach out to that person and show that person love.

Lord, let me love and be loved and most of all, thank You for Your love. I pray in JESUS' name. Amen

Cy Mulholland

The Do Not Conform Diagram is a basic breakdown of our decision-making process and the benefits of properly utilizing our free will, versus allowing complacency and deceit to detour us. This diagram expresses this without taking into consideration technical brain chemistry that occurs within our physiological beings. Indeed, God did make us very complicated and adaptive: however, this process is too often made more complicated than it has to be. It comes down to seeking our Lord and Savior Jesus Christ, as opposed to worldly pleasures for instant gratification.

Through His Word, the Lord tells us that He will never give us more than we can handle and He is always with us. We make the mistake of taking difficult situations of various types into our own hands and forming our own solutions. Often, we self-medicate, which can be done by much more than just substance alone. Self-medication can be done through any of the senses and through the blood stream: all of these can be equally destructive. We are not intended to let the pressures of the world over-power us. Rather, we are to put our hope and faith in God, who loves us and to seek His reassurance in His Holy Word. We are to reach out and cry out to Him in prayer. Only we create separation between ourselves and Jesus by taking matters into our own hands. Only we allow the pressures of this dying world to overwhelm us and drive us to willfully turn away from God's saving grace.

Don't get me wrong: the good Lord does not nickel and dime us and tally every mistake we make, as if there is some kind of checklist that we must uphold. Worrying whether or not we have sinned so much that there is no more grace left for us is a waste of time and energy and there is no fear or doubt in Jesus. There is a difference between giving up and falling short. There is a difference between messing up, catching ourselves and repenting, versus willfully planning to sin and preplanned repentance. It is very important to put our trust in the healing power of Jesus and to not allow ourselves to conform to the negativity of this world.

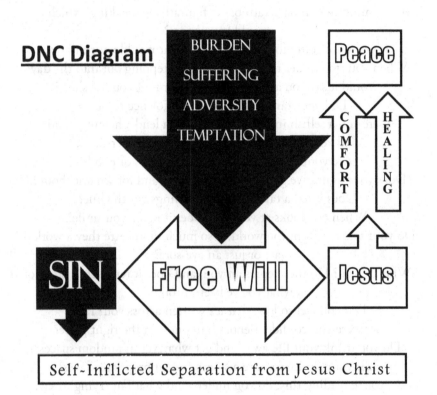

DNC Diagram

BURDEN
SUFFERING
ADVERSITY
TEMPTATION

Peace

COMFORT
HEALING

SIN

Free Will

Jesus

Self-Inflicted Separation from Jesus Christ

Glow-in-the-Dark Ink

In my mind, we all have tattoos, so figuratively speaking, which one
would you choose?
If you were going to tell your story, what would your ink say,
When you step under the black light like stepping out into the day?
Would it say you are a good person, or that you fell short?
Did you stand for peace, or to violence resort?
Were you a selfish individual, or did you lend a helping hand?
Did you shun those in need, or try to understand?
Are your tats of angels or demons, evil or good?
Does your figurative glow in the dark ink stand for what it should?
Does it tell a tale of regret, or things worthwhile?
When one looks at your ink, does it make you smile?
Do your tats represent the world or so much more? Are they a work of
art or just an eye-sore?
Who are you? Do they represent you, and does it represent a story of
what you've been through?
Did you feel so low, that it's written across your face,
Or were you confident enough to put it in the right place?
Do you drink your life away and get whatever in random spaces?
Is it your choice to have a stamp in inappropriate places?
As you're reading this, do you understand what I'm trying to say?
Are you able to sift through the words I wrote today?
What does your glow-in-the-dark ink imply, whether it's there or not?
Do you tell a story of life, or will you eternally rot?
Will you hate and be hated: will you judge people on the spot?
Or will you love and be loved? What was it you were taught?

There are many out there who can see no other way for existence than evolution and that somehow, this entire universe appeared on its own. They believe that our occurrence is by chance, or by some kind of accident. For many scientists and archeologists, this is the case. They believe in their interpretation of their research and studies so much, that they can see no other way for existence. Creation makes no sense to these unfortunates.

There are, however, those who believe in evolution and creation. Then there are those that would tell you that the Bible is nothing more than a metaphor. I'm here to tell you that while the Bible does contain metaphors, such as Jesus being the Lamb of GOD, it is so much more than a metaphor. JESUS is indeed the Lamb of GOD. He is the Son of GOD, who was sent by GOD to be sacrificed for the sins of all mankind. In order for us all to be saved, righteous blood had to be spilled, because the price of sin was that high. It was not only for those that lived in JESUS' day, but He paid for the sin of all man that had lived, were living and were yet to come. That's a lot of sin. There was no other offering capable of paying such a high price that had to be paid in order for us to share in JESUS' kingdom. GOD, because He loved us so much, came to walk on the earth in human form and to die a mortal death.

That brings me to my point. The nonbelievers and those confused by religion are those that, for the most part, do not want to be held accountable for their actions. If there is no GOD and everything goes black and blank when our lights go out, then one can be a drunk every day if one so chooses. One can do drugs and have multiple relationships with many women: steal, cheat, lie and do everything else that is morally wrong.

The fact of the matter is that we all know the difference between right and wrong. And where did we get this notion of the two? Why is it that wrong isn't right? Why is it that good conquers evil? It is because everything good comes from GOD. This is an important lesson that I had to be re-taught.

As I've written before, trauma can cause PTSD in individuals who have had to remain in a fight-or-flight frame of mind for lengthy periods of time. This can develop a disconnect in their brain, separating the communication between the upper and lower brain. For many, this causes sensations of being untouchable and bullet-proof, which leads to wrong-doing. A person suffering from PTSD may become rebellious to all authorities. These individuals may regularly have episodes of rage and be quick to argue with family members, friends, coworkers, and bosses and many times, they possess the potential to be violent. The morals and values for life that a person may have once had have to be relearned or remembered: Preferably before the individual gets themselves into situations that they may regret. It is vitally important for anyone suffering from PTSD to get help. Many people don't realize they have PTSD, so it is important for loved ones of trauma victims to watch for signs and symptoms of PTSD.

1 Thessalonians 1:3
We remember before our God and Father your work produced by faith, your labor prompted by love, and your endurance inspired by hope in our Lord Jesus Christ.

Lord, thank You for putting helpful people and resources in my path so I could receive the help I needed before it was too late. I pray in JESUS' name. Amen

The Cloud

The place where expectations are too high, the place some go to over-try.
Most clouds are white, but others are pink.
These are those that dissipate in a blink.
The inhabitants of these often do not think.
They, for some reason, feel their trash doesn't stink.
The pink cloud, as it's called, is no place to go.
A misconception of "I've Figured It Out" is nothing to show.
Staying sober is no easy line to tow. "I'm no longer addicted" will help
the beer flow.
Relapse is not normal, but it may happen.
I'm telling you the truth, I ain't rappin cappin.
If you're on that cloud, come back down to earth.
Experience a new life through a new birth.
Value your life and explore your self-worth.
It may seem selfish, but it's important to put yourself first.
You've made bad decisions, but you've not made the worst.
Despite what you've heard, there's only one higher power.
There's only one GOD: He is the high tower.
My recommendation is to make Him your foundation.
To Him, devote your focus and concentration.
This is what I'm doing and it's working for me.
It's been a long time since I've been this happy.
By putting sobriety first, things are better for my family; my future is
brighter as far as I can see.

I remember having a false sense of certainty. I remember sitting in groups and having conversations, stating variations of having it all figured out. I was sober and I was there to stay: yeah, right. I spoke confidently with a smile on my face and to others in early recovery, I probably appeared well put together, but my false motivation offered little deception to any old-timer who was no stranger to real sobriety. I was white-knuckling my half-hearted attempt at staying sober, but it was a lesson that had to be learned: A lesson that if a person truly wants a new way of life, then that person has to genuinely change those old thoughts, behaviors, people, places and things that act as enablers for alcohol, or drugs, or sex, or anything else a person may be addicted to. This is a point that I make time and time again, but it is a valid point that needs to be driven into the mind of an addict.

It's not going to be easy, but it does get easier with time and effort. For those that become motivated and dedicated to their purpose, they will begin to realize how much better they feel and how much more productive they can become. It's hard to say goodbye to the people we drank with for so long and we feel that we are going to be missing out on so much. When I stopped deceiving myself and arrived at my true sobriety, I began to pick up new hobbies and behaviors that were positive and productive. These new activities became coping skills and are far more enjoyable than drinking and being miserably hung over.

Aside from writing, I put a lot of emphasis on my physical well-being. I began working out on a daily basis and paying more attention to what I ate. I bought a bicycle and started riding and soon took an interest in mountain-biking, which has become one of my favorite hobbies. I now appreciate the outdoors more than I ever imagined I would. My wife, our kids and I go hiking and on family walks around the neighborhood on a regular basis. Most mornings, my wife and I go to a local track to run and walk together after the kids go to school. I'm in college now and I love it. For me, college would have been a waste of time and money when I was drinking, because as an alcoholic I would have been more focused on getting drunk than I would have been on doing my homework.

So here I am: A better, happier, easier to get along with, more fun to be around version of me and any alcoholic can have what I have if they truly want it. We have to be true to ourselves. We have to live in truth. It will not work if we deceive ourselves. We have to want to change and be better. We, as alcoholics, all have potential to live positive, productive, fulfilled

Cy Mulholland

lives. Today, I am a better man for me and my family. I know that there will be hard times. I know that adversity is coming, because the evil one is always working, but GOD is bigger and He is working in me.

Matthew 6:24
24 "No one can serve two masters, for either he will hate the one and love the other, or he will be devoted to the one and despise the other. You cannot serve God and money.

Lord, be with the addict reading this book and give him or her strength to change his or her life. I pray, Father, that they will find their strength in You and serve only You. I pray in JESUS' name. Amen

Patience

Patience is a virtue, but it's something I don't always do.
It's good for me; it's good for you.
If it weren't for patience, I don't know what I'd do.
When I practice patience, it's better for you, too.
A patient without patience is a bad combination.
It leads to irrational behavior when you need focus and concentration.
If someone wears on my patience, it's time to change locations.
One man speaks when he's supposed to listen.
Another man listens, but never speaks up.
He remains patient, when he wants everyone to shut the bleep up.
Which one is more likely to fill his cup?
If you have an ear, than let yourself hear.
When you come across a patient without patience, you best stay clear . . .
And that's very common in places like here.
Inpatient or outpatient are both good places to be.
Give it some time and you will see
That learning to be patient is a valuable key:
A key, as in a tool to put in your bag.
I don't mean to boast, I don't mean to brag,
But I'm soaking up patience as if I were a rag.

There was a time when I never would have thought that I would learn patience. There was a time when I never would have thought that I would not have a short fuse and meet adversity head-on with a fight, rather than a solution. I had a chip on my shoulder: an attitude problem. I would rather fight than work something out peacefully, even if it meant getting beat up. My thought-process was completely irresponsible.

I always took care of business in other aspects of my life. I paid my bills on time. I showed up to work and worked just as hard as anyone else. I just didn't deal well with adversity and I didn't respect authority. I carried myself as if I had it all figured out and I actually thought that I was untouchable for many years.

For a long time, I had this idea in my head that someone or something was looking out for me and that it was a good thing. To better explain this, let me rephrase this. For the majority of my life, I did not live the way I should be living and I thought it was a good thing that someone or something was looking out for me while I got away with it. Is it possible that Satan can have influence over people, places, and things that should not influence your life? It is certainly true. There are two sides to everything. Day is to night. Life is to death as good is too bad. Big is too small as white is to black. There is no grey area when it comes to good and evil.

On one side, there is Jesus, who will have great influence over your life if you just ask and live as He would have you to live. To live for Jesus is to do right and live a life of love. On the other hand, there is Satan, who is more than willing to have negative influence over a person's life if given the chance. I see it all the time. As for myself, I lived in sin for the majority of my life and I only truly gave my life over to the will of GOD this past year.

Throughout this entire book, I talk about Satan and his influence in my life and how I am able to overcome him and his evil ways through God's grace, but as I mentioned, I still make mistakes. Sin is inevitable, but it's the constant will to overcome that we must strive for. Greed is one of the biggest problems there is in this world and it has been that way since the beginning of time. People want money, riches, fame, land, women, power . . . and did I mention money? Our Father in Heaven tells us through His Word time and time again that we will reap what we sow, both here and in the life hereafter. That is not what many people want to hear: Many want to believe that we are here by chance, because it makes it easier for them to live however they want to live. Indeed, each and every single one of us who has ever walked the face of this earth will be held accountable. We will reap what we have sown, regardless of what our belief systems are. I wrote the previous poem while I was inpatient at a behavioral health hospital. I was struggling with patience, but getting better at it at the same time.

Psalm 73:24
You guide me with your counsel,
and afterward you will receive me to glory.

Lord, thank You for blessing me with patience. Please help me to continually grow in the ways explained by Your Word. I pray in JESUS' name. Amen

My Coping Skills

My coping skills have been replaced. So often, I've been a waste with bad taste.
For the majority of my childhood, I depended on drugs.
My loved ones, I shrugged: I missed out on many hugs.
We all know I drank beers for so many years.
I drank whiskey and bourbon the entire time I was serving:
Drinking on the job and living like a slob.
Still taking care of business, but it's my family I robbed.
No need to be selfish; a problem creates problems.
They multiply and bounce around in my mind like a hundred tiny goblins.
With time and inpatient, I've come to realize
You can't live a lifetime with glossed-over eyes.
Your liver and then your life eventually die.
Then everyone you loved will cry, but they will go on and so you died for nothing.
Or I will die for nothing; now isn't that something?
We make everyone's life harder, because we did the wrong thing.
No way, it doesn't have to be this way.
We can stand up and make a change today:
Take care of mind, body and spirit and really mean it.
For me, it's easy. I'm going to be who I want to be, a fitness enthusiast and a poet.
And for you, I will show it: I do have some talents, but I didn't even know it.
We make it hard, but it's easy, you see.
Take the time to search and find out who you want to be.
Find purpose, set some goals, love and be free.

In a world that at times, seems upside down and without rhyme or reason, writing to release tension, emotions and expression is brought about by tragedy and conflict. That conflict is of the mind, and unlike a physical injury that can heal and be seen, the pain and sorrow of the mind takes a different and at times a dark path. To find the strength to write about conflict, sorrow, healing and emotional or inspirational topics comes from places that many people don't know they have inside of them. That release can flow at different rates and at the most unusual times of day or night. The spirit that leads you to express many different feelings has no rules or regulations, makes no sense or perfect sense, and most importantly comes from the heart and soul. Writing novels, short stories, poems, biographies, plays or fantasy epics takes the mind to uncharted territories and places where dreams and nightmares live. Pictures may say a 1000 words, but words form a picture.

—*William Koch Jr., Author of* Casualties of War

Segment of the poem "Bleeding of Ink"
Have they this night saved this soul to march on too
A versifier with blue collar roots that no one knew
An old man now of pain and emotional distress
Takes to the language of rhythmic for his address

Passing on tributes to heroes that protect this nation
Teaching at the same time young minds for salvation
Life and death using words and letters as their link
Feelings and emotions from a heart bleeding of ink
by William Koch Jr., Hollow Sorrow 5-30-2011

One of the most important things I ever did was discover the things that trigger me. I had to find out what exactly made me want to drink. It turned out there were many things, simple and complex, that make me want to drink. No matter how simple or complex my triggers are, they all stem from one thing: PTSD. And they all lead to my desire to drink. As I've written before, I began drinking at the age of twelve, shortly after my brother took his own life. It was from that point on that I chose drinking as a coping skill. Drinking alcohol was always my first choice to supposedly help guide me through adversity. Later, after going through three deployments in Iraq, my symptoms were amplified by traumatic events and combat stress. Let me take a step back and explain some of what I call my "simple triggers."

My simple triggers can be anything I perceive as negativity in my life. That is the excuse I make for myself, anyway. It could be anything from an argument with my wife or having words with some random stranger. It could also come from something as simple as getting cut off in traffic, or noticing someone cutting in line. Many times, I would make something that was none of my business, my business, knowing full well that there would be a confrontation, instead of doing the right thing and minding my own business. It's one thing to help someone in need or duress; it's an entirely different thing to let something simple bother me to the point where I think I need to get involved when I don't. More times than not, poking my nose in others' business only makes things worse.

Most of the time, simple triggers are a result from trauma-related stress. Trauma-related stress causes what I call "complex triggers." Complex triggers for me are just that: complex. They come from some form of trauma-related stress and take some form of treatment for recovery. For me it was the stress of losing my big brother at an early age: then, when I was still recovering from that loss, I experienced more Post Traumatic Stress by enduring more than three years of combat stress.

The first time I deployed to Iraq was in 2003 for the invasion, for a total of fourteen months. I deployed to Iraq the second time in 2005 for twelve months, and the third deployment to Iraq was for fifteen months. I won't go into the details of everything I experienced in the war at this time, but it was very intense and chaotic. I've seen a lot of carnage on both enemy and friendly sides. The memories that remain with me on a daily basis: the flashbacks; the zoning out and being in another place in my mind; the mistaking of things on the side of the road or elsewhere while driving, being put back in a dark place in my mind by any of these events, are all examples of what I call complex triggers. As stated, they can lead to various forms of other triggers, due to stress. One of the most important decisions I ever made was to get help.

There was a point in time where I realized I had to get treatment. Treatment for me came in many forms. I began seeing a therapist, a psychiatrist, a substance abuse counselor and most importantly, I went back to church and got back into the Word. It was still a very rocky road for a long time and life will always throw challenges my way, but today I have positive coping skills to counteract my triggers: my two favorites, of course, being writing poetry and physical fitness.

Revelation 22:11
Let the evildoer still do evil, and the filthy still be filthy, and the righteous still do right, and the holy still be holy."

Lord, thank You for guiding me and giving me a purpose in life. I pray in JESUS' name. Amen

The Trigger Path Diagram is completely interactive and explains the pattern of the multiple possibilites of trigger paths. These triggers, whether simple or complex, all share the same origin, Post Traumatic Stress resulting from a traumatic event. For the struggling individual, triggers are various forms of adversity.

What we consider adversity can be different for everyone and the more we become aware of what our triggers are, the better we can combat them. Much of the time, our extreme behaviors cause our own grief and guilt, as well as the grief of those around us. An example of a trigger path could be troublesome information received, such as the loss of a loved one. This could lead to a drinking and/or a drugging binge and/or acting out by other various means of instant gratification and/or confrontation. This in turn, more times than not, will lead to more adversity, consequence, and sometimes voluntary or involuntary treatment.

There was a situation previously described in this book when news of soldiers deploying drove me to drink—which led to my arrest—which led to my hospitalization. One's trigger path may be longer or shorter depending on the situation, but if you are aware of your triggers and have faced simialar situations, take a few moments to map out your own trigger origins and trigger paths on the diagram and decide what can be done in order to avoid going down the same path in the future.

Learning from our mistakes is one of the most valuable tools we can place in our bag, as opposed to carrying out the same counter productive behaviors over and over again and expecting different results.

Trigger Path Diagram

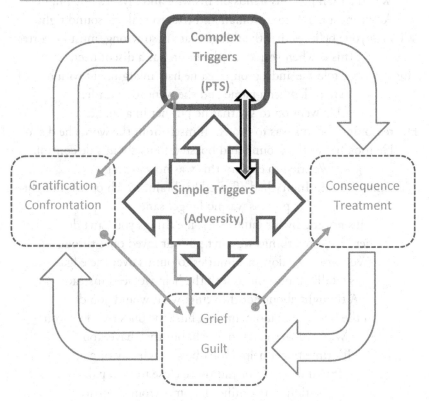

Cognitively Distorted

When a man puts his hands on his wife and says it's not a fight;
Any time a man hits a woman and tries to make is sound right;
When anyone believes that the things that are so wrong, must be correct;
This is when you know the brain has a disconnect.
This guy once told me and a group that he had an argument with his wife.
He called her a name and she went for a knife.
He went on to say that he put her in a choke.
His reasoning for this was to protect himself from the words he'd spoke.
He took her to the ground and boasted to us about side control.
We tried to explain this was no way to go.
Traumatic Brain Injury had affected his brain. Much of his thought-process was no longer sane.
It's not totally his fault, but some things you can't do.
There are some things we can't put our loved ones through.
We must not allow our injuries to put us over the edge.
It's vitally important to seek the help we need instead.
A thought about not thinking: what would you do,
If in the heat of the moment, you hurt the ones that love you?
We have sacrificed so much, but they have, too.
It's time to get help. Don't be a tough guy or gal.
It will benefit you and those close to you, pal.
Distortion of the mind: it comes from combat.
If your brain is injured, it's time to get help for that.

Cy Mulholland

One night, I was sitting at home watching television and drinking while my kids were playing and my wife was sitting on the front porch with our friend Jill. It was a typical evening back then, until I walked outside to see what my wife and Jill were doing. As soon as I stepped out of the front door, my wife asked me if I had heard the loud noise. She said it sounded like a car accident and couldn't be any further than just right up the road. I told them I would go and check it out, so I got in my car and drove about a block and a half up the road to see what the matter was. Right away, I could see a car wrapped around a telephone pole and skid marks leading from the street off of the road to the pole. I walked up to the car, where I could see two other bystanders trying to wake the driver of the car, whose head was now leaning on the passenger side door. I walked up to the vehicle, took one look at the fellow inside and told the two standing there, "No use trying to wake him: he's dead."

They looked at me as if they'd never seen a dead body before and replied, "Oh, no. He is." They went on to tell me that they had already called 911 and that an ambulance was on the way. I thought to myself, "This guy never had a chance for an ambulance, going as fast as he was . . . and to be able to wrap a car around a telephone pole the way he did." Fortunately, there was no one walking the neighborhood street where he was driving at the time, or there very well may have been more casualties. I later learned the individual driving the car had been very heavily intoxicated.

Looking back, I think about how that alone could have been a wake-up call for me, but it wasn't. I mean, really? I was drunk and I jumped in my car to go check on another unfortunate individual who just died because he was driving drunk. Back then, I didn't even give it a second thought. Back then, I probably thought to myself that I would just be sure to not drive fast and reckless when I'm drinking and driving. As if drinking and driving wasn't reckless to begin with. That was the insane way I viewed things back then; not only could I have ended up like that guy, but I didn't even take into consideration that I could possibly kill someone else or someone else's child. I couldn't imagine life after losing my child at all, let alone to something like that.

Now, with a clear mind, I would never want to put anyone through that much pain. It's a proven fact that mind-altering chemicals, such as alcohol, slow down reaction time, but for some reason thousands of people every day make the decision to drive while impaired, because they think that it won't happen to them. I know, because I used to be one of them. To this day, I don't know how I never got a DUI, but I sure deserved to have. With the insane way of thinking I used to possess, I actually considered it fun to drink and drive. The alcoholic mind believes completely that nothing will go wrong for him or her; the alcoholic soldier, after surviving combat often, believes he or she is super-human and above the law. That is, until the Police Officer who is still on his mission to Protect and Serve enforces the law and puts the drunk in the back of his car and hauls his or her butt off to jail, before that individual can cause any more harm during at least that drunken escapade. I've been arrested plenty of times for offenses while intoxicated and now that I no longer drink, I often mention to others that I am allergic to alcohol because when I drink I break out in handcuffs.

So much time is wasted under the illusion that alcohol and drugs are the best way to cope with painful memories and trauma. So much time is wasted by living by the cop-out of "you don't understand" and "if you'd seen and done the things I have, then you would drink too." So much time is wasted that could have been spent with family, friends and children. So much time is wasted to black-outs and pass-outs that could have been memories worth remembering. To anyone reading this: it's not too late to change. I did.

Revelation 21:8
But as for the cowardly, the faithless, the detestable, as for murderers, the sexually immoral, sorcerers, idolaters, and all liars, their portion will be in the lake that burns with fire and sulfur, which is the second death."

Lord, may You bless anyone reading this, who is having a second thought to take it seriously. In JESUS' name I pray. Amen

Passing Time

I call it passing time, but the day is passing me.
I'm lying on my bed, staring out the window at a tree,
Meaning that the only part of me moving is my hand.
I'll write a few more lines and maybe you'll understand
That whether we are still or in motion, time passes on.
We do not pass the time. It's here, then it's gone.
Where does it go? Time, we cannot see;
That is, unless you close your eyes. Time is a memory.
Time is mortal life. It is not eternally.
You could say it is a test you must pass in order to be free.
Nonetheless, it passes on, though at times we wish for pause.
Some wish to rewind and blame it, as if it were the cause.
They say don't waste it, but who are they?
I am entitled to how I spend each day.
It's my time. Not a waste. I happen to enjoy this place.
What one calls boredom, I call peace. My family still fills my space.
Day leads to night and night to an alarm: or the crow of a rooster, if you
live on a farm.
Time is always moving; it will constantly roam,
But the clock is still on the wall of my home.
Like me, it's passing time while I write this poem.
I meant time is passing it and my thoughts are beginning to roam.
So, for now I'll be done. I'll let time pass me another way.
Perhaps I'll let time pass me while I write later on today.

We are all accountable for how it is we spend our time. It took me what will probably end up being more than half of my life to realize that we receive the result of how we carry on. While we are not the sum of our past mistakes, we do indeed reap what we sow in the present. Knowing this, I have still fallen short and I know I will fall short again and every time I do, I am quickly reminded that I have messed up. But every time, I come right back to the Lord and repent. This is the process of growth, because I am constantly getting better.

Many of my mistakes from the past are not repeated and the ones that are, are not to the same extent. We will not be without sin, ever in this life: If this were the case, then there would be no reason for a Savior. As it is, in a sinful world, accompanied by a sinful nature with a weak free will, we do fall short of the glory of GOD and give in to temptation. This is why JESUS came to intercede on our behalf. He loves us so much that He took on human form and died the worst human death, in order to save us from our own sin. He paid the price we would have paid. That doesn't mean that we are not disciplined in much the same manner that we discipline our own children. While the Lord does not inflict all pain directly onto our lives, nothing touches us which doesn't pass through His hands first, as is clearly stated in His Holy Word.

Proverbs 3:11
My son, do not despise the LORD's discipline,
and do not resent his rebuke

Consider this: do the hardest, most difficult times in anyone's lifetime come while we are living righteously, or when we are living in a worldly way? This is a question of personal experiences, not outside influences, such as a loved one dying or things which are obviously out of our control. I'm referring to the things that make one ask, "Why is this happening?" Depending on the situation, we are impacted by various different disciplines and such will be the pattern until repentance and change are implemented.

I know first-hand and as an example, I will refer to the times when I was being unfaithful in my marriage. Now, for some who may be reading, this may sound a little far-fetched, but it is the truth. For me, during my times of unfaithfulness, I was constantly experiencing troublesome situations, or "disciplines." GOD would at times reveal things to my wife, as a means for her to investigate and at other times, He would impact me directly.

For example, if I was using a certain vehicle to meet other women in, I would have vehicle troubles and then, when I would repent and cease my misbehaviors, somehow the vehicle issues would disappear. Another example: I wear a wedding band and under my wedding band, I also have a tattoo of a wedding band around my finger. When I would leave the house to meet up with these other women, I would remove my wedding band and put band-aides around the tattoo, so that it was no longer visible. On one occasion, while shutting the door of the vehicle in the same manner which I had hundreds of times before, somehow my finger got caught in the door and crushed my finger to the point that the meat from inside my finger burst out the tip of my finger and my finger nail came off. After cleaning the finger and taking some aspirin for the immense pain I was in, I then dressed the wound with the same band-aides which I had bought to cover my wedding band tattoo. As I placed the box back in the cabinet, I stared at it for a moment and it was then that I realized what had happened. I immediately repented of my sins and the burden was lifted. Just as in society, the Lord has different disciplines to which He sees fit for the sins which we commit. We not only commit these sins against each other, but more than that, we commit them against our Father in Heaven.

The other side of this is that while we are disciplined, we are also rewarded and blessed by our Father in Heaven. The more we live pleasingly unto the Lord, the more bountiful our blessings will be. If we commit our lives to Him and live in obedience in the same manner which we would have our children to live, then our Father will most definitely look after us, His children. If we love one another, give to those in need, give offering, share the Lord's message, have faith, and let our light shine, then the Lord our GOD will shower us with a multitude of blessings. By allowing the Lord's light to shine in us, we cast away all fear, doubt, anger and temptation. The road map to life eternal is in GOD's Holy Word and is my recommendation for anyone reading, if you haven't already, to make your foundation on the Rock who is JESUS CHRIST. Amen

Hosea 10:12
Sow righteousness for yourselves,
reap the fruit of unfailing love,
and break up your unplowed ground;

for it is time to seek the LORD,
until he comes
and showers his righteousness on you.

Revelation 14:12
Here is a call for the endurance of the saints, those who keep
the commandments of God and their faith in Jesus.

Lord, let me be ever mindful of who I am and who I am to be. I pray
in JESUS' name. Amen

PTSD General Stats
70 % of adults in the U.S have experienced some type of traumatic event, at
least once in their lifetimes. That's 223.4 million people.

Up to 20% of these people go on to develop PTSD. As of today, that's 31.3
million people who have had or are struggling with PTSD.
- ➢ An estimated 1 out of 10 women develops PTSD; women are
  about twice as likely as men.
- ➢ Among people who are victims of a severe traumatic experience
  60-80% will develop PTSD.
- ➢ 50% of all outpatient mental health patients have PTSD!

Somewhat higher rates of this disorder have been found to occur in African
Americans, Hispanics, and Native Americans, as compared to Caucasians in
the United States.

Combat PTSD Stats
- ➢ Lifetime occurrence (prevalence) in combat veterans 10-30%.

In the past year alone the number of diagnosed cases in the military jumped
50% and that's just diagnosed cases.

Studies estimate that 1 in every 5 military personnel returning from Iraq and
Afghanistan has PTSD.

20 % of the soldiers who have been deployed in the past 6 years have PTSD.
That's over 300,000.

17% of combat troops are women; 71% of female military personnel develop PTSD due to sexual assault within the ranks.

Source (www.winoverptsd.com)

Lord, let me no longer waste time and reach out to as many as I can with helping hands and I pray Your will be done in my life and in all things. I pray in JESUS' name. Amen

Don't Take It from Me

Hold back what needs to be held back. Don't let judgments
continually stack.
Let out what needs to be let out.
Don't waste time with the scream or the shout.
Find positive ways to cope with the fear and the doubt.
Don't let your low self-esteem take away from others.
Remember, we are all sisters and brothers.
Don't forget to be understanding and listen.
When we talk too much, there's a lot we are missing.
Don't look at others' faults when you can't see your own.
At times, we need only use the speaker part of the phone.
Don't forget to love and lend a hand.
I've learned that helping others helps me understand.
Don't forget to reflect on what you value in life.
For me, it's my faith, my kids, and my wife.
Don't rely on isolation or chemicals to cope.
There are so many other better ways to find hope:
Hope, not despair, but you have to care.
Put recovery first, or nothing else will be there.
Don't just listen to me—after all, I'm talking to myself.
By putting my thoughts down on paper, I improve my mental health.
I now have an abundance of spiritual wealth.
Thank you, Lord. I listened and I heard.
Thank You so much for giving us Your Word.

Cy Mulholland

One time, but not only one time, I was reminded that there is an entity in the world who wishes for me to fail. This is how it is for all of us. So often, when things are going so well, I get blind-sided by adversity. Because of this, I try to remain aware that, regardless of how good things seem to be going, adversity is coming.

For example, I woke up one morning to a call by which I received some very good news. I won't go into details about the news: the point is, the news caught me by surprise and the day was off to a good start. The day proceeded on and more good news followed and I was becoming very motivated. Going on into the afternoon, my wife went with me to an appointment, where I was to see a social worker with a doctorate in therapy. This is where things began to get a little strange.

Throughout the course of my appointment, where the focus was supposed to be on me, somehow the focus was put on my wife in a manner in which she was being blamed for some of the minor issues that existed in our marriage. The fellow who was politely grilling my wife and digging into her past had previously not even known that she was coming to my appointment with me. He questioned her to the point that she was very uncomfortable and crying.

My wife and I walked out of the man's office at the end of the appointment confused and upset. We went home and the cheerful mood we had both began the day with had been dashed away by the incident and we could make no sense of what had just taken place. Time passed and our kids came home from school, did their homework and went outside to play.

It wasn't long before we heard something going on outside and went to see what the matter was. It turned out that our children were having a dispute with another neighborhood child and the other child's dad took it upon himself to yell at my kids. Then my wife and I proceeded to have an argument with the neighbor. It just so happened that this happened just prior to us leaving to go to our Wednesday night Bible study. While driving to church, Carleeh and I came to the realization of what exactly had taken place: the evil one, Satan, had gotten to us in areas where he knew we were vulnerable that day.

We went on to have a great Bible study and prayed about the events which had taken place and the day was salvaged. Once again, this is a prime example of spiritual warfare. Just because we grow as Christians doesn't mean that Satan is going to stop manipulating us for his purposes. It is when things are going well that Satan becomes the most enraged and ready to attack the faithful followers of Christ. Satan will try to influence us, no matter how devoted we are to God. We must try to avoid becoming weak or complacent, because he will use that moment to try to keep us away from the grace of GOD.

I can only imagine how many times would-be Christians have been turned away, because we give into temptations and appear as hypocrites to the potential believer. This can be said for the Christian who is hung over from getting drunk late Saturday night, sitting in the pew, struggling to stay awake and hear the message, all the while wishing he or she was still home in bed. This also goes for the Christian who is having an affair and is sitting in the pew as well for Sunday morning worship. The same can be said for the Christian sitting in the pew not singing, while the rest of the congregation is praising—or while another Christian, who gambled his or her money away the previous night, turns away when the offering plate is passed. I must confess, I have been the Christian guilty of all the above at one time or another and so it is utterly important that I remain on guard in all situations, regardless of how good or bad things seem to be going.

When we are down, we have to find the strength and courage to pull ourselves out of it. It is during those times that we must lean on Christ and wash away the funk with His Cleansing Blood. The enemy works in deceitful ways. He lurks and he uses guerilla warfare tactics. He ambushes us when we least expect it, but we have access to armor. We are to wear our armor all of the time: A soldier without armor is a soldier whose heart is pierced easily. So put on the whole armor of GOD. Walk in it, eat in it, sleep in it and speak in it. Let everything you do be while you are wearing the armor that GOD Himself has given to us. Then we will indeed win the battles of the war which has already been won. Amen.

GOD has set us up for success and we owe it to ourselves and to Him to take full advantage of it. We stand in His ranks because He loves us and has hand-picked us because we are the finest soldiers. Let us love Him back and follow our King into battle. Let us stand on the frontlines and strike down the enemy as Psalm 91 proclaims we shall and not a single one of us will fall. Amen.

Ephesians 6:10-17
Finally, be strong in the Lord and in his mighty power. 11
Put on the full armor of God, so that you can take your stand
against the devil's schemes. 12 For our struggle is not against

flesh and blood, but against the rulers, against the authorities, against the powers of this dark world and against the spiritual forces of evil in the heavenly realms. 13 Therefore put on the full armor of God, so that when the day of evil comes, you may be able to stand your ground, and after you have done everything, to stand. 14 Stand firm then, with the belt of truth buckled around your waist, with the breastplate of righteousness in place, 15 and with your feet fitted with the readiness that comes from the gospel of peace. 16 In addition to all this, take up the shield of faith, with which you can extinguish all the flaming arrows of the evil one. 17 Take the helmet of salvation and the sword of the Spirit, which is the word of God.

Lord, may we stand firm among Your ranks and be seen as the disciplined soldiers we are to be in Your army. I pray in JESUS' name. Amen

Good Times

I have so many reasons to be happy, so much meaning in my life.
There are times when I feel so much joy:
No pain or doubt or fear.
These are the times when I live for the moment; when I don't linger in
my own head.
I look at my children and I feel peace.
So much love . . . they are my reason.
There are times when I'm so happy, the madness fades away;
No loneliness is near.
These are the times when good memories are made, when I see my wife
smile.
I look at her beautiful face and realize how good I have it; so much
patience and forgiveness.
There are times when I forget about all that is bad.
No anger, no tears.
These are the times I wish had no end, when time seems to stand still.
I look at pictures of our life and see only good times: so many fond
memories.
There are times when nothing else matters: when love is the only
emotion present.
I remember the good times and they outweigh the bad.
These are the times in the front of my mind
When there are only good times.

Cy Mulholland

The Lord has blessed me with so many things and I am not ashamed to say out loud or to write down that I am overjoyed to be a Christian. Jesus loves me, this I know, for the Bible tells me so.

Amazing grace, how sweet the sound that saved an alcoholic, traumatized individual, such as me. Thank GOD that today I am coping with PTSD in a positive manner, that I still have my family and that I am clean and sober for another day.

Thinking back, my wife and I have, of course, enjoyed having our kids so much. As a parent, I know I need them every bit as much as they need me. We have had so much fun throughout the years. The good times definitely outweigh the bad times, both in my marriage and in the family as a whole. More than any amounts of money or possessions that I could ever have, my children are my wealth. This is as the Lord intended. I have come to realize that the home IS where the heart is and what that really means.

For so many years, I put my family second to so many things. For years, alcohol and even drugs were more important than my family. I remember drinking with my friends and occasionally partaking in some other recreational chemicals without telling my wife, so that I didn't get chewed out. Many times, she found out anyway and I deservingly felt the brunt of it. I am so fortunate to have such a loving and forgiving wife. Carleeh is the nails that hold our house together. She is the glue that has held us all together through our toughest times: most of which were primarily my fault. I am so very blessed. I have my wife, our two girls and our son and our best days are yet to come. We just keep getting better, thanks to a loving and forgiving Father in Heaven. We are blessed to live in the United States of America, where we are free. It is my belief that as long as this country remains one nation under GOD, we will continue to be a blessed nation. I am grateful to the Lord that I am so blessed. And as for me and my home, we serve the Lord.

Revelation 3:5
The one who conquers will be clothed thus in white garments, and I will never blot his name out of the book of life. I will confess his name before my Father and before his angels.

Lord, thank You for all of the many blessings You have bestowed on my family and I. May I be ever reminded of the importance of giving, but not being given to. I pray in JESUS' name. Amen

I'd Rather Be Bored
than Have Too Much Fun

I'd rather be bored than have too much fun.
I'd rather not lose, but it doesn't matter if I've won.
You may think that I'm boring, but I'm number one to my son.
I'm a simple man that's living a simple life.
I have everything I need; my boy, my daughters and my wife.
We're an all-American family with a cat and a dog.
Too much fun can create a fog.
That will only make it hard to see things clearly.
Currently, I'm working on that; baby, I miss you dearly.
Good thing for me I didn't wind up in jail.
LORD knows, I put my wife through hell.
I'd rather be bored and take care of business.
Too much fun can make misery limitless.
Too much fun has been the majority of my life.
For years, I didn't stop having too much fun, even after I met my wife.
And you know what: I've never had more fun with anyone else in my life.
I'd rather be bored; too much fun leads to no fun at all.
Drinkin' and drugging and havin' a ball leads to my downfall.
Once I start, I'm bound to crawl.
Time after time, I've done the dinosaur call.
I've had big and tall expectations of all sorts,
And every time I did, I always fell short
Like an important mission that I had to abort.
In the end, facing the music, to inpatient I report.

Cy Mulholland

I used to the think that the party never ended, until the day I died. There was once a time when I never had any plans for my life. Even after I joined the Army, I guess you could say that my plan was to work hard and play harder. I never wanted to get married and I definitely could not see myself having kids. Then I met my wife. It's kind of crazy, but she came after me. I met her cousin first and then her cousin introduced me to her.

One day, I got off of work after working in the motor pool all day doing tank maintenance and went to my barracks room to get cleaned up. I believe I was a Private First Class at the time. I was a tank driver in B CO 1/64 Armor. Anyhow, after I was freshened up I went over to Carleeh's cousin's house. I was going to her house, because at the time I was trying to date her. What I didn't know was that once I got to her house, she called Carleeh, who lived across the street with her parents and told her she had the perfect guy for her and that she was going to bring me over and introduce me to her. Carleeh hadn't been feeling well for several days and tried to convince her cousin not to bring me over, but her cousin told her to hurry up and get ready and hung up the phone.

After a few brief moments, we strolled across the street and walked into Carleeh's parents' house. I walked through the living and on through the kitchen as if I owned the place, but not in a rude way. Then I noticed an open door, so I poked my head in and there I saw Carleeh sitting up on her bed with the covers over her legs, looking beautiful as ever. We shared a smile and we both said hi and then her cousin formally introduced us to each other.

The rest is history and we have been married for more than eleven years and have three beautiful children together. No one could have ever told us that the first ten years of our marriage would prove to be some of the most trying years of our lives. No one could have ever told her that being married to me would be the most difficult challenge she had ever faced. I've described many things I have put her through throughout the course of this book and one thing is for sure, for the first ten years of our marriage, I was never bored and I had entirely too much fun.

My personal opinion is that I have much more fun when I am spending time with my beautiful wife and our three amazing kids, as opposed to wasting my life away to the party or to the poorest and most ineffective coping skill: alcohol.

Revelation 2:17
He who has an ear, let him hear what the Spirit says to the churches. To the one who conquers I will give some of the hidden manna, and I will give him a white stone, with a new name written on the stone that no one knows except the one who receives it.

Lord, thank You for another day clean and sober, where I have the ability to think with a clear mind and acknowledge the many blessings— such as my loving family—that You have bestowed on me. I pray in JESUS' name. Amen

I Want More Of It

I like it, I love it and I want to be heard.
I'm going to apply this to many things, because I'm a nerd.
I'm going to write down the things I want more of.
I want things like peace, happiness and love.
I want to be successful and to have a happy family.
I want to be the husband and the father I'm supposed to be.
I want to live right, do right and be free.
I want to be the Christian I am called to be.
I want more happiness by casting aside the guilt and the pain.
I want to realize it doesn't matter who is to blame.
I want to be a part of what's real and stop playing games.
I want to keep things simple and stay away from complicated.
I want to stay away from stress and everything related.
I want more of my kids and more of my wife.
I want more of everything that gives me purpose in life.
I want to be more giving and more forgiving.
I want to want no longer, 'cause I'm spiritually strong.
I want to love and be honest and do right over wrong.
I want to hang on to what I have today because it's better than yesterday.
I want peace and wisdom and to learn more along the way.
I want to remain sober and be the best I can be, day after day.
I want this feeling to last forever. I need to be more than ok.
I need to realize it's about more than what I want; it's about the truth,
the life and the way.

I am only human, but it's not an excuse for me. It's not an excuse for anyone. It's a copout. At the same time, I know just how easily distracted I truly am and it's with that knowledge that I now put emphasis on staying on the beaten path. We all have a path or a road that we are constantly traveling. Occasionally, we come to a fork in the road and have to make a decision about which way to go. Sometimes, we choose the wrong path because the map is complicated and other times, we choose the wrong path because it looks more adventurous.

We look down both paths in the fork in the road and we see that one path looks very clear with an occasional bump in the road, but free of any obstacles that would prevent safe passage. Mountains may pop up on this path from time to time, but the descent on the other side always seems to be very gratifying. Down the other path, we see tall mountains that are difficult to climb, with overgrown thorn bushes cluttering the path. This path is dark and dreary. The road has pitfalls and wild beast, hungry and waiting for someone, anyone, to pass by. We look back at the smoother path. It is much more pleasant and still has its challenges, but because there is a bright light shining at the end of the road, the entire path is illuminated, ensuring safe passage. Why do we so often choose the dark path?

This path allows us, the sinner, to do as we please, though we make things harder on ourselves. Much of the time, people don't even realize that by living in darkness, we put so much more pressure on ourselves, because we attempt to negotiate the hardships we inflict upon ourselves all by ourselves. By choosing not to believe that there is a GOD and only one true GOD, many people think they are making it easy, because they are "unaccountable" for their actions. But really, living in sin has consequences not only in the next life, but here in this life as well. It is then that people wonder why they have so many problems. Most nonbelievers will spend the majority of their time blinded by the world, investing all of their time into trying to find a worldly solution: As if we, as humans, have control over our lives. The actual solution to all of our problems is not complicated, but not necessarily easy at first, either. However, it takes putting faith in Someone much greater than oneself.

The answer to any problem anyone could ever imagine is faith and a new life in JESUS CHRIST. Yes, it is the same answer I give time and time again throughout the contents of this book, but He is indeed the only answer to every question of doubt, fear, loneliness, anger and regret. I will mention that, (though I'd like to think this book I've put together may help at least one person suffering with PTSD get pointed in the right direction toward successful recovery,) the real answers to any problem, disorder, or troubles of any kind are found in the Holy Bible. The New Testament is where JESUS the Savior has outlined the way we are supposed to live our lives. It is the map that clearly shows us all how to navigate our paths properly and successfully.

Revelation 2:11
He who has an ear, let him hear what the Spirit says to the churches. The one who conquers will not be hurt by the second death.

Lord, thank You for the knowledge and insight to utilize the practice of asking for abilities through prayer and being able to effectively use these gifts in my daily life. I pray in JESUS' name. Amen

Forgive Honestly

When it's time and you are ready.
Don't rush forgiveness. Take it slow and steady.
To those out there who would say "I forgive you"
Only to turn around and not let it be true:
Shame on you. Only say it if it is so. Take it from me; this is one
thing I know.
I've felt the pain of being forgiven over and over again.
Not for multiple offenses, but the very same sin.
Because one has hurt is no reason to hurt back.
Vengeance is worse. There's no need for attack.
Forgiveness is essential in order to be forgiven.
I know this to be true. It's by the Word I am driven.
It is so valuable. It has so much worth,
Though it's getting harder to do all over the earth.
Now, it may take a while and shouldn't be rushed.
You'll know when it's right and if not, then be self-hushed.
I forgive easily. I hold a grudge never.
I accept all for who they are and some, I keep out forever.
Just because you don't allow someone into your life doesn't mean
failure to forgive.
It simply means that by sustaining separation, it makes it safer to live.
Does that make sense? Is it as clear as dirt? I've been through it before. I
even have the t-shirt.
It's simple, you see. There's a peaceful way to live.
One thing we must do is honestly forgive.

Revelation 2:7
**He who has an ear, let him hear what the Spirit says to the
churches. To the one who conquers I will grant to eat of the
tree of life, which is in the paradise of God.'**

Lord, let me forgive as I have been forgiven. I pray in JESUS' name.
Amen

As I mention elsewhere in this book, my anger grew to an uncontrollable state while serving my third tour in Iraq, after some of my closest friends had been killed by a suicide bomber. My frustrations and inability to cope with the loss ruined relationships with my soldiers and fellow Non-Commissioned Officers. Years later, as I advanced in my recovery, I often wondered how some of those guys were doing and eagerly wanted to make amends. At a minimum, I wanted to reach out to them and apologize, whether they would be able to forgive me or not. Much to my surprise, not a single one of them refused to forgive me and for that I am grateful.

It just goes to show the character of men I already knew them to be. Not many men and women who put on the uniform lack strong and admirable character. I was able to reach most of these guys I served with during Operation Iraqi Freedom V on Facebook. It seems that just about everyone has a Facebook and some of these guys who served with me on my crew and in my platoon even accepted me on their friends list. If any of you guys are reading this, thank you and GOD Bless you. I hope you all are doing well. Many of the men I served with have since left the Army and moved on to jobs or college. It won't be long until I rejoin society as a civilian and I am very excited for that.

During the worst times in the struggle with PTSD, it is hard to see past ourselves to care about anything other than ourselves. It becomes second nature to lash out at close friends and family. The insane thing is that much of the time we place blame on those around us, who oftentimes never had anything to do with the situation at hand. We allow our frustration and anger to spill out onto others and usually do not take the time to go back and apologize. In our minds, we tell ourselves that the fault is not our own, when indeed it is. I put so many people I care about through a lot of anguish and left them wondering "what just happened?" So many times when I was to blame, I ruined birthday parties, get-togethers, family dinners and so on. And I always blamed the situations on someone else. Most of the time, I was highly intoxicated and I was always completely irrational. The only way to get past the regret and the guilt we feel for putting those we love and care about through so much misery is to:

1. Repent, ask GOD for forgiveness
2. Forgive yourself
3. Seek forgiveness from others

Asking for forgiveness requires humility and GOD calls us to be humble. Seeking forgiveness doesn't only have to be from a family member or friend, or even anyone we know very well at all. The only requirement for the need of apology is to have done someone any form of injustice. Any thoughts, speech, or actions that are not done out of love or in a loving manner could justify an apology. However, it is impossible to make amends to everyone everywhere that we have done wrong by. Therefore, it is essential that we repent and seek forgiveness from GOD, who loves us so much that He sent His only son, His righteous right hand to save us from our own sins. Lastly, it is important to forgive with all one's heart when forgiveness is asked of us. Thank you, JESUS! Amen.

Matthew 15:11
What goes into someone's mouth does not defile them, but what comes out of their mouth, that is what defiles them.

Matthew 15:17-19
"Don't you see that whatever enters the mouth goes into the stomach and then out of the body? 18 But the things that come out of a person's mouth come from the heart, and these defile them. 19 For out of the heart come evil thoughts—murder, adultery, sexual immorality, theft, false testimony, slander.

Philippians 2:14-15
Do everything without grumbling or arguing, 15 so that you may become blameless and pure, "children of God without fault in a warped and crooked generation." Then you will shine among them like stars in the sky

Colossians 3:13
Bear with each other and forgive one another if any of you has a grievance against someone. Forgive as the Lord forgave you.

Lord, I praise You and thank You for Your guidance and forgiveness. I pray in JESUS' name. Amen.

PTSD AWARENESS

CAUSES, INCIDENCE, AND RISK FACTORS

PTSD can occur at any age. It can follow a natural disaster such as a flood or fire, or events such as:

- Assault
- Domestic abuse
- Prison stay
- Rape
- Terrorism
- War

For example, the terrorist attacks of September 11, 2001 may have caused PTSD in some people who were involved, in people who saw the disaster, and in people who lost relatives and friends.

Veterans returning home from a war often have PTSD.

The cause of PTSD is unknown. Psychological, genetic, physical, and social factors are involved. PTSD changes the body's response to stress. It affects the stress hormones and chemicals that carry information between the nerves (neurotransmitters).

It is not known why traumatic events cause PTSD in some people but not others. Having a history of trauma may increase your risk for getting PTSD after a recent traumatic event.

SYMPTOMS

Symptoms of PTSD fall into three main categories:
1. "Reliving" the event, which disturbs day-to-day activity
   - Flashback episodes, where the event seems to be happening again and again
   - Repeated upsetting memories of the event
   - Repeated nightmares of the event
   - Strong, uncomfortable reactions to situations that remind you of the event

2. Avoidance
   - Emotional "numbing," or feeling as though you don't care about anything
   - Feeling detached
   - Being unable to remember important aspects of the trauma
   - Having a lack of interest in normal activities
   - Showing less of your moods
   - Avoiding places, people, or thoughts that remind you of the event
   - Feeling like you have no future

3. Arousal
   - Difficulty concentrating
   - Startling easily
   - Having an exaggerated response to things that startle you
   - Feeling more aware (hypervigilance)
   - Feeling irritable or having outbursts of anger
   - Having trouble falling or staying asleep

You might feel guilt about the event (including "survivor guilt"). You might also have some of the following symptoms, which are typical of anxiety, stress, and tension:

   - Agitation or excitability
   - Dizziness
   - Fainting
   - Feeling your heart beat in your chest
   - Headache

SIGNS AND TESTS
There are no tests that can be done to diagnose PTSD. The diagnosis is made based on certain symptoms.

Your doctor may ask for how long you have had symptoms. This will help your doctor know if you have PTSD or a similar condition called Acute Stress Disorder (ASD).

   - In PTSD, symptoms are present for at least 30 days.
   - In ASD, symptoms will be present for a shorter period of time.

Your doctor may also do mental health exams, physical exams, and blood tests to rule out other illnesses that are similar to PTSD.

TREATMENT

Treatment can help prevent PTSD from developing after a trauma. A good social support system may also help protect against PTSD.

If PTSD does occur, a form of treatment called "desensitization" may be used.

- This treatment helps reduce symptoms by encouraging you to remember the traumatic event and express your feelings about it.
- Over time, memories of the event should become less frightening.

Support groups, where people who have had similar experiences share their feelings, may also be helpful.

People with PTSD may also have problems with:

- Alcohol or other substance abuse
- Depression
- Related medical conditions

In most cases, these problems should be treated before trying desensitization therapy.

Medicines that act on the nervous system can help reduce anxiety and other symptoms of PTSD. Antidepressants, including selective serotonin reuptake inhibitors (SSRIs), can be effective in treating PTSD. Other anti-anxiety and sleep medicines may also be helpful.

SUPPORT GROUPS

You can get more information about post-traumatic stress disorder from the American Psychiatric Association—www.psych.org.

EXPECTATIONS (PROGNOSIS)

You can increase the chance of a good outcome with:

- Early diagnosis

- Prompt treatment
- Strong social support

COMPLICATIONS
- Alcohol abuse or other drug abuse
- Depression
- Panic attacks

CALLING YOUR HEALTH CARE PROVIDER
Although traumatic events can cause distress, not all feelings of distress are symptoms of PTSD. Talk about your feelings with friends and relatives. If your symptoms do not improve soon or are making you very upset, contact your doctor.

Seek help right away if:

- You feel overwhelmed
- You are thinking of hurting yourself or anybody else
- You are unable to control your behavior
- You have other very upsetting symptoms of PTSD

You can also contact your doctor for help with problems such as repeated upsetting thoughts, irritability, and problems with sleep.

PREVENTION
Research into ways to prevent PTSD is ongoing.

REFERENCES
1. Bisson J, Andrew M. Psychological treatment of post-traumatic stress disorder (PTSD). *Cochrane Database Syst Rev.* 2007;3:CD003388. [PubMed]
2. Stein DJ, Ipser JC, Seedat S. Pharmacotherapy for post-traumatic stress disorder (PTSD). *Cochrane Database Syst Rev.* 2006, Issue 1. DOI: 10.1002/14651858.CD002795.pub2. [PubMed] Review Date: 3/5/2011.

Reviewed by: Linda J. Vorvick, MD, Medical Director, MEDEX Northwest Division of Physician Assistant Studies, University of Washington, School of Medicine; and David B. Merrill, MD, Assistant

Clinical Professor of Psychiatry, Department of Psychiatry, Columbia University Medical Center, New York, NY. Also reviewed by David Zieve, MD, MHA, Medical Director, A.D.A.M., Inc.

Words To Live By

Smile and don't live in denial.
Recovery must be pro-active, not reactive.
God is love, so do your best to mirror the One above.
Don't live a life of greed. It's not about wants, but needs.
As far as those lost, properly grieve them. Set goals and achieve them.
Get your life in order. Don't be controlled by Post Traumatic Stress Disorder.
Cling to your family and keep the home happy.
To be addicted is to be self-restricted.
Don't be a tool bag, but utilize the tools in your bag.
Let your personality be one of speaking, acting and thinking rationality.
Let the moral of your story be to value your morals.
It is important to be motivated, dedicated and communicated.
GOD gives faith, hope and love. The most important of these is love.
On yourself, never quit. Remain Physically, Mentally and Spiritually fit.
You must be forgiving if you want to be forgiven.
To learn resilience is to achieve brilliance. The more you listen, the less
you'll be missing.
Don't be he or she who over-contemplates when the evil one temptates.
Even though I am not worthy, GOD is trust-worthy.
There's a lot of wealth in controlling oneself.
Empty your bin of sin and be forgiven.
Pray and meditate and you will feel great.
It is fundamental not to be judgmental.
It's ok to be a nerd. Educate yourself in the Word.
Replacing wild with mild, seek the heart of a child.

One thing I definitely have learned over the course of the last couple years is that the truest, most real friendships are the ones made in Christ's church. I have never felt more loved in a congregation than I do at Stithton Baptist Church in Radcliff, Kentucky just outside of Fort Knox, Kentucky. As I have mentioned before, my near and dear friend Pastor Curtis, an instrument of the Lord, has helped me a great deal in my recovery with PTSD. He once spoke of interruptions: the interruptions by which the world disturbs us with on a regular basis. He presented the question, "When we are interrupted, will we trust the Lord and follow him?" This got me to thinking about "interruptions" and what exactly was the cause of my interruptions and why do I allow them to distract me from following the Lord, when those are the times I need to dig in and focus on what is right and good? Many fail to realize that, whatever their downfalls are, these mistakes or discouragements or sins are the reaction to deception, accompanied by a lack of faith. These negative situations come into existence because we replace faith with fear and doubt, which leads to depression, anxiety and anger. This makes complete sense in the cases of we who suffer from PTSD, because these are a large part of the symptoms involved with PTSD.

Case in point, my brother took his own life when I was a child and I became traumatized. The problem in that situation was that there was no one around to properly point me in the right direction and help me to focus on what the Lord had to offer. Being that I was just a child without the direction I required at the time, it became simple for the evil one and his deception to fill the void.

Another example is serving in combat. The difference is, in this case, I was an adult and instead of not having proper direction, it was a matter of losing faith that had previously been established. In this situation, where one becomes "lost," it becomes essential for loved ones to reach out and help by whatever means possible. This requires prayer as a part of reaching out, because GOD truly does answer prayers. When we pray, GOD listens and answers if it be His will and inserts people, places and things into the life of the one prayed for, where He sees necessary.

When we encounter interruptions in life, it is so important to have faith and to keep walking and following JESUS. I am forever grateful to the Lord for putting the many resources in my life that He has to assist me in successful recovery and for allowing me to share with others what truly works for recovery of any kind: namely, healing through the power of JESUS, who said, "Follow Me." Amen

Mark 5:35-36
While Jesus was still speaking, some people came from the house of Jairus, the synagogue leader. "Your daughter is dead," they said. "Why bother the teacher anymore?"

Overhearing what they said, Jesus told him, "Don't be afraid; just believe."

Joshua 1:9
Have I not commanded you? Be strong and courageous. Do not be afraid; do not be discouraged, for the LORD your God will be with you wherever you go."

Lord, I pray that those reading will understand the importance of not being complacent in recovery and vulnerable to deception. I pray in JESUS' name. Amen

10 WAYS TO RECOGNIZE POST-TRAUMATIC STRESS DISORDER

After a loss, it is normal to go through a natural grieving process. Sometimes, however, after a tragedy, such as a sudden traumatic event, feelings of loss surface several weeks or months after the tragedy occurred. This is called post-traumatic stress disorder (PTSD). Recognizing these symptoms in yourself or others is the first step toward recovery and finding appropriate treatment.

1) *Re-experiencing the event through vivid memories or flash backs*
2) *Feeling "emotionally numb"*
3) *Feeling overwhelmed by what would normally be considered everyday situations and diminished interest in performing normal tasks or pursuing usual interests*
4 *Crying uncontrollably*
5) *Isolating oneself from family and friends and avoiding social situations*
6) *Relying increasingly on alcohol or drugs to get through the day*
7) *Feeling extremely moody, irritable, angry, suspicious or frightened*

8) *Having difficulty falling or staying asleep, sleeping too much and experiencing nightmares*
9) *Feeling guilty about surviving the event or being unable to solve the problem, change the event or prevent the disaster*
10) *Feeling fears and sense of doom about the future Source-(www. mental-health-today.com)*

1 John 2:27
But the anointing that you received from him abides in you, and you have no need that anyone should teach you. But as his anointing teaches you about everything, and is true, and is no lie—just as it has taught you, abide in him.

1 John 1:9
If we confess our sins, he is faithful and just to forgive us our sins and to cleanse us from all unrighteousness.

Lord, keep me mindful that others are suffering as I have suffered and let me always reach out and help them. I pray in JESUS' name. Amen

CHAPTER TEN

THE GUARDIAN

Healer, Redeemer, Savior

Open Door

The door is open. The light clearly shows it.
Will I walk through it or will I close it?
There is a room on each side of the door.
The light shines from one room to the others' floor.
Standing in the shadows, there's a choice to make.
For some it's very hard, but it's one I can't fake.
The dark room has no light to turn on.
To get to the light, I must step into the dawn.
Where there is light, there is life that is new.
I wouldn't have written this if it weren't true.
I know what's there, but I feel so heavy.
Something's holding me back, but I want to be ready.
Standing outside, there are no rooms: just a door.
I can feel the light in the depths of my core.
There's still no going around it. I must walk through.
My family is there: I want to be there, too.
At night, I close my eyes and the door is open.
Someone is telling me what to put my hope in.
I feel a sense of joy and then I'm pulled back.
My peace is gone and the nightmares attack.
In the morning, I wake in this shadowed room of mine.
The light shines through the window and allows me to unwind.
Peace has come over me with the new day.
For strength and courage to walk through the door, I will pray.

After I lost my older brother to suicide when I was a child, the first year or so was filled with mostly depression. After that, I can remember how certain things were different about me. It was then that I began to do things I would never have done before. In some ways, my sense of humor changed and not for the better. I developed a darker and trickier side to my humor and it was often not appreciated. There was one time that I gathered up some string and a thumbtack and went to my room. Then, I made something that resembled a noose and stuck it to the ceiling. I stood on the end of my bed and waited for my little brother to come downstairs, because we shared a room in the basement of our house. After a while, I could hear him walking down the stairs, so I got ready by slightly bending my knees and putting the string around my neck to create the appearance that I had hung myself.

My brother came walking in the room and saw the illusion which I had created. He called my name and tried to shake me, but I didn't budge. I could hear the fear in his voice as he began to cry. He turned and ran out of the room to go and get help, so I jumped down off the bed and went have after him to tell him it was only a joke before he could tell my mom. He was very upset, but he didn't tell on me. He stayed mad at me for a while after that. I felt bad for what I had done and realized that it was a terrible prank. However, that didn't keep me from pulling similar pranks in the future.

There was another time, when my younger brother and I were arguing and it turned into a fist-fight, as it often did. Fist-fights between siblings are not uncommon, but I possessed the ability to turn a fist-fight into a scare-tactic. So there we were, punching each other and at one point, my brother hit me in the side of my head with his fist. Thinking quickly, I immediately put my hand over my eye and began crying out that my eye had popped out and that I was holding it in my hand. I threw myself on the ground in our room and cried out for help and made the whole thing very believable. My brother panicked and tried to see if I was ok. I could hear the fear in his voice and I knew that he believed I was hurt. I screamed and carried on, and he turned to run for help. As he made it to the stairs and was about to run up to get our mom, I stopped him and told him that I was only kidding. Once again, he was very angry with me for quite some time.

Even as an adult, after being married for several years, I made attempts to prank my wife. Thinking back now, I realize that it wasn't until after I came back from the war that I began these prank attempts on my wife. I say "attempts" because she would often call me out on them and tell me how funny they were not. At one point, she made it very clear that she did not want me to trick her any more. I never played another joke on my wife.

She explained to me just how demented joking with people in that manner is. Clearly, I was not in the right state of mind when I pulled these ridiculous pranks on the people I loved, but the question, once I had a clear mind, became: what was my reason for pranking in such a dark and evil manner? I came to realize that I was projecting the pain I was feeling—initially from the loss of my brother and later from the war—outwardly onto others. I wanted them to hurt as bad as I did, so that I wouldn't be the only one feeling so much pain.

I didn't take into consideration that my brother, as well as the rest of my family, was hurting in the same manner I was. I didn't take into consideration that my wife didn't deserve what I was doing to her. The fact of the matter is that when I was doing these acts, I wasn't aware of why I was doing them. As a child, it simply became another way for me to cope with the pain. This is the very same reason that many others who suffer hurt as children go on to live a life of various crimes.

Anyone suffering from PTSD must get the proper treatment in order to recover from a traumatic experience—or experiences, as in my case. Self-medication does not work and oftentimes leads to death: Not only death for the one suffering, but possibly even death for innocent bystanders. Many times, PTSD becomes a chain reaction of terrible situations that could have been avoided. It becomes laughter for the evil one, because of his success at our expense.

An individual experiences a traumatic event and tries to self-medicate. Then that individual becomes an alcoholic and drinks whenever and wherever he or she can. Then the individual requires more alcohol to achieve the desired effect. The individual gets into his or her vehicle and drives to the liquor store to get more liquor or beer to drink. After the individual leaves the liquor store, he or she gets into a head-on collision with an unsuspecting family of three, leaving two parents dead and a child alone who will never be the same and will struggle with PTSD for the rest of his or her life. That child grows up to be a criminal or a drug addict, and either dead or in jail, after affecting several other families in a negative manner. This is just an example, but a very realistic one of how the evil one achieves victory over us if we don't get the help we need when struggling with Post-Traumatic Stress Disorder.

2 Peter 1:11
For in this way there will be richly provided for you an entrance into the eternal kingdom of our Lord and Savior Jesus Christ.

Lord, I thank You and praise Your HOLY name for not allowing me to be lost to the deceptions of the evil one. I pray in JESUS' name. Amen

Only One Knows

There's a lot you don't know about me.
Don't matter who you are.
There's a lot you don't want to know.
No matter who you are.
There's a lot I don't understand about me.
There's so much I need to find.
I need to find myself.
I don't want to be left behind.
Wait, Someone knows all about me.
He knows who I am.
He knows me better than I know myself,
Though I do not understand.
You do not want to know.
You would not understand.
My dreams would give you nightmares.
He's willing to take my hand.
You don't want to know what I know.
You'll be happier if you don't.
I will not show, I will not tell.
I will only learn to cope.
He's the One who's always been there.
Without Him, He knows I won't
Won't cope, won't care and won't even be here.
He's my life-line, He's my hope. Amen

I am able to do things now that I was unable to do a short time ago, but there are things I still cannot do. Allow me to explain. Recently, I was able to participate in the Run for the Fallen at Fort Knox. There was a time that I wouldn't have been able to do that, because there were too many painful memories connected with the loss of some very close friends of mine in combat. My wife asked me if I would like to participate with her and to her surprise, I quickly agreed. She even bought shirts for us and decorated them herself, so we could properly represent the fallen soldiers we knew. She spent several hours on them, carefully printing out the designs she wanted and then ironing them onto the shirts. They turned out to be very nice.

When the day came and it was time to get up and ready to leave for the event, I began having some reservations about my decision to go. For a short time, I got irritable with my family, which was typical in a situation like this. It had always been a mechanism of mine to spark an argument and then use it as an excuse not to go along with the previous plans made with my family.

My wife quickly called me out on what I was doing, because she is so familiar with my PTSD symptoms. She pleaded with me to get control of myself and to preserve the eventful family time we were all to participate in. She recommended that I pray and I did and I told the evil one to get behind me and soon after, a burden was lifted. We loaded up in the car and headed out.

We had a good time and there was a good turnout. I ran up ahead of my wife and our kids. She pushed our youngest in the jogging stroller and ran along-side one of her friends, who was also pushing a stroller. Once I finished, I waited for them all at the finish line. There was lots of cheering and clapping and everyone got the opportunity to remember specific memories of their fallen soldiers and to stand up for their families—many of whom were in attendance. We all had the opportunity to support our soldiers who have fallen. It was another step in the right direction for me. Now that I proved myself able to participate in an event that focuses on my fallen brothers, I will be a regular participant. There are still things I struggle with, but this never-ending journey in recovery requires constant maintenance and growth.

We can't always control what happens to us. The only thing we can control is how we react to it. Life is meant to be lived forward, and you can't do that if you spend all your time looking backward.
—Bryan Anderson, *No Turning Back*

I still can only be in a store or restaurant for about a half hour, maximum. I still can't be in crowds that are hard to see through, let alone walk through. I still have a hard time driving down cluttered or flooded roads. I still feel anxious in all these situations, as well as when I see factory smoke stacks of any kind. I still scan every room I ever walk into and I know where every available exit is. I still get edgy and anxious when I hear of a service member getting killed in combat. Despite all of this, however, I am like night and day when it comes to who I was even six months ago and who I am now. I am so much better off than who I was a year ago; everyone that I maintain close contact with has noticed a positive change in me.

That doesn't mean it is time to stop going to therapy. It doesn't mean it is time to stop taking my medication. It doesn't mean that all of a sudden, I possess the ability to drink responsibly. It doesn't mean it's time to walk away from the coping skills and survival skills that helped me get to the point I'm at today. It definitely does not mean that I should stop going to church and should turn away from GOD. Actually, it is quite the opposite.

It means it is time, more than ever, to maintain my progress and continue to get better. I know full well that if I walk away from even one of these essential recovery tools, stress will take its place and the domino effect of self-destruction will be initiated. The most important factor to this entire equation is to not allow myself to be so deceived that I turn away from GOD. That would be the simplest way for the remaining pieces in my recovery to fall apart.

With GOD, all good things are possible; without Him, all things are perishable. Therefore I will remain pro-active for the sake of my salvation, my overall health and the welfare of my family. I will shield us all from complacency. I will properly maintain and sustain my growth in recovery. I will be a better man tomorrow by remembering yesterday. I will think about more than myself today. I will love and be loved. I will give and not worry about being given to. I will pray and I will receive the Lord's will. I will use sound judgment and remain morally sound and spiritually fit and I will never quit. I will hope and I will have faith. I will love.

John 3:17
For God did not send his Son into the world to condemn the world, but to save the world through him.

Romans 5:10
For if, while we were God's enemies, we were reconciled to him through the death of his Son, how much more, having been reconciled, shall we be saved through his life!

Colossians 3:16
Let the message of Christ dwell among you richly as you teach and admonish one another with all wisdom through psalms, hymns, and songs from the Spirit, singing to God with gratitude in your hearts.

John 14:6
Jesus answered, "I am the way and the truth and the life. No one comes to the Father except through me.

Lord, You alone are my source of healing. It is through Your will that anything good has come to me. For this, I thank You and praise You. I pray this in JESUS' name. Amen

I Am Forgiven

I've always wondered if I could be forgiven for the things I've done.
Could I be alone? Could I be the only one?
I know better than that, but the guilt eats away at me.
I also know there's a disconnect in my mind from PTSD.
I've talked to more therapists than I know what to do with.
They all mean well and they all share their coping myth.
Only once was I fortunate enough to speak to one who was a veteran.
He had gone somewhere that was much like where I'd been.
That's where I learned that writing was my best coping skill.
I feel the more I do it, the less I feel ill.
The question is still there: am I forgiven or not?
I feel I did so much wrong, even after I was taught.
I know the blood of JESUS is how my salvation was bought.
Regret and the guilt in my mind continue to rot.
I know good and well that a just war is allowed.
Were my actions justified when I engaged that crowd?
That's what I've been told, but I was there.
There may have been lives I could have spared.
I'm trying to live right and with my whole heart repent.
I want to do nothing other than honor the One GOD sent.
I am so blessed to have returned from the places I went.
At the same time, there are still so many things I resent.
GOD'S forgiveness, though, is how I am driven.
When it comes down to it, in my heart, I know I am forgiven.

This morning, my family and I went to church, as we do every Sunday morning, to hear Pastor Curtis preach more about GOD and His will for our lives. The Pastor has a way of capturing his audience's attention and holding on to it. He is able to do this, because He has been anointed by GOD to spread the word of GOD. The Pastor often tells stories with a powerful message as a part of his sermon and today he told one of a man in the desert.

The man had been in the desert for quite some time: long enough that he was completely dehydrated and nearing death if he did not drink water soon. He was at the point when he knew he could envision mirages and so he thought that he had when he crested the top of a very large sand dune. As he looked to the base of the hill, he could see a man standing there with neckties draped over his arms, shouting, "Neckties, free neckties. Get your free neckties."

When the parched man reached the bottom of the hill, he couldn't believe his eyes and ears when he discovered the man giving away free neckties was real. "I don't need a necktie. I need water," he said in an aggravated tone to the man and he continued on in his search for water. The man walked and walked and after a while he noticed something in the distance. As he got closer, he realized there was a restaurant right there in the middle of the desert. The man staggered up to the door where the greeter stood and said, "I have to go inside. I need water. I must have water." The greeter replied, "There is a dress code here, sir. You must wear a tie to enter."

God gives us the opportunity to reach Him and to reach happiness, and a lot of the time we're too blind to take it. We don't realize what He's doing, and assume we can do it better. Silly us.

Pastor Curtis went on to explain—and how true it is—that GOD loves us so much that He sent Heaven's Crowned Jewel to bear the sin of the world, though He was perfect, so that we would not receive the punishment that we so deserve. We will never fully understand the price that was paid, but I am grateful. JESUS offers life to all that will accept it. He paid the price for our sins. There is nothing left to pay. The sin of the world from every generation since time began has been wiped clean, because He loves us more than we can fully comprehend. We are forgiven when we confess our sins and ask for forgiveness in JESUS' name. I myself have lied and cheated in life, and killed in combat. Many of the things I've done were in large part due to the negativity introduced to me by traumas throughout my life and I have been forgiven. I am human and I am not perfect, but that is not an excuse for me. I strive to be better every single day.

1 Peter 1:4-7
to an inheritance that is imperishable, undefiled, and unfading, kept in heaven for you, who by God's power are being guarded through faith for a salvation ready to be revealed in the last time. 6In this you rejoice, though now for a little while, if necessary, you have been grieved by various trials, 7so that the tested genuineness of your faith—more precious than gold that perishes though it is tested by fire—may be found to result in praise and glory and honor at the revelation of Jesus Christ.

Lord, thank You for leading me to those You have chosen to share Your word with me. Be with me as I share Your message with others, Lord. I pray in JESUS' name. Amen

Lay It Down

Freeze, don't make a sound.
Put the burden down and get on the ground.
I wish it were that easy: arrest me please.
Take this burden away; I'm down on my knees.
I never thought I would ever be so weak.
Help me please—a normal life I seek.
This life of mine is one long losing streak.
Thank GOD for the blessings He's bestowed on me.
If it were not for my LORD, I don't know where'd I'd be.
He brought me my wife and our one, two, and three.
My Savior gave me a reason to live.
He saved me from my sins with the gift that He gives.
I have to admit, I really must confess:
Though I think I'm hot, I'm merely a mess.
I tend to put forth my worst, when I should be giving my best:
My best for my wife and our children too—
Most of all LORD, my best for You.
I'm going to lay my burden down, because You tell me to.
So here I go, I'm on my way.
I'm going to lay it down. Tomorrow leads to new days.
No "one day at a time"—I must live it always.
Thank you, LORD, for taking the pain I would have had.
I have no right to hold this burden and that's my bad.
When I remain conscious of You, I no longer feel sad. AMEN

Cy Mulholland

So many times, I have forgotten to love the Lord first. So many times, I've forgotten that if I love my Lord first and remain conscious of Him, everything else will fall into place. So long as I seek Him and allow Him to be the influence over all my decisions, I can't go wrong. So many of us go to church on Sunday and worship and fellowship and feel great and do as we should while at church, but as soon as we walk out of the doors, something changes. It's as if we put on a cloak as soon as we walked in those doors to the church that morning and just before we stepped out into the world, we took it off.

I had to make a decision, a life change, to leave my figurative cloak on at all times, throughout every day. I decided to let my speech and actions be more like what they should be. I also made changes for me and my family, such as not listening to secular music. Thankfully, we all agreed on the change. Another change I made for me personally was to stop wearing clothes that displayed whatever message any given company wanted to display. I stopped wearing clothes with company logos on them as well. After all, none of those companies were paying me for advertising. So, being that I still needed shirts to wear, but didn't necessarily want to wear plain white t-shirts, I did an online search for Christian clothing and apparel. I discovered that there are very cool Christian shirts out there for everyone. My favorite websites are c28.com, sanctifyclothing.com and gratefulapparel.com. And to keep things in perspective, we are all being paid to advertise the Lord's message, with eternal life.

Don't get me wrong, now: not every day is easy. There are still challenges and obstacles thrown at me on a daily basis. The important thing for me is to not get complacent and I do feel peace every day: A peace that I didn't use to have, a peace that comes from knowing that GOD is in control and that as long as I seek Him first in my daily life and with all of my decisions, I can't go wrong.

James 5:11
Behold, we consider those blessed who remained steadfast. You have heard of the steadfastness of Job, and you have seen the purpose of the Lord, how the Lord is compassionate and merciful.

James 5:10
As an example of suffering and patience, brothers, take the prophets who spoke in the name of the Lord.

James 1:25
But the one who looks into the perfect law, the law of liberty, and perseveres, being no hearer who forgets but a doer who acts, he will be blessed in his doing.

Lord, please bless my wife, son and daughters and keep them safe from all harm. Let us all be mindful of You throughout every day and live as You have called us to live. I pray in JESUS' name. Amen

Who Am I?

Who am I? I'm figuring it out.
I'm a healthy person, without a doubt.
The best thing going for me is definitely my GOD.
He loves me when I do wrong; He loves me when I'm odd.
My family is here for me. I have their support.
Their love is unconditional: a love I can't distort.
I'm loving, giving and selfish too. I live in black and white.
I'm usually hard, but sometimes soft. I strive to do what's right.
Most times I do wrong, but it's certainly not out of spite.
If there is one thing I know, it's that I am loved.
My family is still around and I've done things you'd never dream of.
I'm somewhat successful. I have wonderful kids.
My mission is to show them not to do the things I did.
I pay my bills and I provide. When that's complete, I isolate and hide.
I prioritize outward, but not on the inside.
In GOD I'm rich, because I believe.
I must stop living the way I do before it's time to leave.
I'm intimate with Him and my wife is my best friend.
I need to adhere to the advice they lend.
I do more than break the rules: I continually bend.
With a husband like me, how can I be her best friend?
I could talk about a lack of good behavior 'till I'm blue in the face.
I never stay on the right path. It's quite a waste.
I do love those who are close to me.
Can I love them more? I guess we will see.
I value what's good and I value life.
The more I think about this, the more I value my wife.
Everything evil in this world points to death.
If I live the way I have been, I will have nothing left.
I demand that I provide, that I give and that I live.
I demand that I strive for GOD'S will and lose the guilt I live with.
I demand I do the right things to feel good, because I've felt bad for so long.

If you think I'm feeling sorry for myself, then you are dead wrong.
I am one who clings to my LORD, gives to those in need and takes care of my family too.
I know that is who I am. Now tell me, who are you?

My life has been a strange one. On the one hand, I have been up to no good since I was a preteen, often drinking and doing drugs. On the other hand, I was always an athlete and going to church with my mom, my brother and my sister. I never got strung out on any chemical so much that I couldn't somewhat function at school. I guess you could say that I did just enough to cope. I did just enough sex, drugs and alcohol to "help" get me through the day on the worst days and I did just enough school to keep me enrolled.

School was the least of my worries, but being as crafty as I was in my sinful nature, I found every way that I could to manipulate the system. I knew just how many days I could skip school without them kicking me out and when I did go to school, I did everything but the school work. I knew what the minimum for grades was to stay in school and many times, I went to my girlfriend's classes instead of my own. This thought process hurt me several times though, because I was an athlete and much of the time I was not eligible to play.

It ended up that I barely graduated on time and so I had to take one college course on the side at the last minute and con two of my teachers to pass me with a D-. I graduated high school with a 1.8 grade point average. The only thing I cared about was that I graduated. I had no real plans of furthering my education or joining the military. I really only had plans of working whatever job I could and partying in my off-time and that's exactly what I did.

Now, aside from all those troublesome behaviors that began as a child and continued on into my adulthood, I was always a caring individual. I would give anyone the shirt off of my back. My parents did bring me up right. As I have mentioned before, they taught me morals and values and respect. They taught me to make the Word my foundation, though for the majority of my life I did not. I never in my life hurt anyone intentionally. That was never my goal. I just didn't know how, or have the strength, to say no to the things that made me feel better, because I always felt so bad. It took me a long time to admit this, but I had low self-esteem, so I acted out to get attention. Really, I was lost for the majority of my life. I had no true sense of who I was: Until this last year, when I discovered that my purpose in life is to be a Christian man and lead my family in the ways explained in the Holy Bible.

I realized that I cannot let this PTSD that became my life when I was child be my undoing. I realized that just because my brother took his own life didn't mean that he took mine. Today, I am sober and just tonight my wife and I and our three children grilled out in the back yard and then made 'smores. It was a lot of fun, and it was something that would not have taken place last year around this time, because I was too busy drinking. Tomorrow morning when I wake, I will state that I am a nondrinker and begin my day with prayer.

Hebrews 6:11
And we desire each one of you to show the same earnestness to have the full assurance of hope until the end,

Hebrews 3:6
but Christ is faithful over God's house as a son. And we are his house if indeed we hold fast our confidence and our boasting in our hope.

Lord, thank You for another day, clean and sober. Be with me tomorrow, Lord, as I face another day and its challenges. I pray in JESUS' name. Amen

Meant To Be

I wondered, though I'd killed, if I'd be forgiven.
It was not by evil ways that I was driven.
Today, I stand firm and I know in my heart
That I'm no longer in the fight: I set that apart.
There were those few of the many that died by my hand.
A few engagements that were hard to understand.
I saw a weapon, a man in a crowd.
Now, they all knew this wasn't allowed.
He did not face me; maybe he didn't know I was there.
I pulled back on the trigger without a care.
Or did he know, but he was not a threat?
Decisions like these are ones I used to regret.
It took a long time, but today I know I was justified.
The fault was theirs and that's why they died.
I used to have doubts about my war-time frame of mind.
It's taken so much time and I still have much to find.
The war cost so much. Some things I wish I could rewind.
It cost my family; they felt they'd lost the old me.
Now I'm coming back stronger than I ever used to be.
When I took life, I knew not what I was getting into.
I didn't have a choice. At the time, it's what I had to do.
I've lost so many friends at the hands of the enemy.
I believe GOD has a plan, so this is how it has to be.
I've written before and this is what I see.
I'd kill again in defense of the free.

Forgiveness is so very important throughout this entire process of recovery with PTSD, which as we know gets easier with time and effort, though it lasts a lifetime. I find it is essential and beneficial to reflect on where it is we have come from, so as not to forget why it is we are where we are now. By remembering the bad times, we enable ourselves to preserve the good times. A past that is not forgotten is much more likely to not be repeated. During my MEB (medical evaluation board), which was the process I went through to separate from the Army,—I was no longer retainable due to my PTSD—my wife was asked by Doctor Andrews to write a narrative of what our family has had to endure as a result of living with my PTSD. The following was written by my wife Carleeh and is a reflection of some of the behaviors and events that my family had to witness throughout some of my struggles.

"Prior to the numerous deployments my husband has completed while in the Army, he was a much different man. He was vibrant, fun-loving and known for his infectious smile. He was a man who loved his career and was active in his family/social life. He was compassionate and optimistic. Ever since his combat tour to OIF I for the invasion into Iraq, he has greatly changed. He no longer saw himself as innocent and there was a hardening that he didn't let people past. He became standoffish, and alienated his loved ones. He views everything in black and white: what little sense of purity he had in the world before was gone after Iraq. His focus was no longer on enjoying his life, but on how to erase bad memories and drown painful experiences. He had a hard time being around the loudness of a family home that included young children. He would often take off for hours at a time to escape from us, usually to be with people who understood what he was going through and would accept and welcome his heavy drinking.

On many occasions, he woke up thrashing/deep sweats from nightmares and sometimes I would find him sitting on the couch in silence, staring at nothing. If I spoke to him, I was shushed and told to go back to bed. There were even times when he heard or saw things that made him uptight or anxious during the night. Unexpected noises, loud children, and the television (news) would cause him to become overwhelmed. Over time and with additional deployments (OIF III, OIF V) the violent behavior, aggressive actions and seclusion increased. You could see the thoughts of war in his face, or sometimes all you could see was a vacant stare. His drinking became more than a brief break from reality: it became a way of life. There were days when the children and I were scared to be in the same house with him while he was intoxicated: the fear came from him yelling and breaking our belongings.

I guess somewhere deep inside, I was scared that he wouldn't be able to control himself and would accidentally hurt one of us. There were times when he was drunk that I would grab the kids and run to the car when he wasn't paying attention and leave. One time, he found me pulling out of the driveway and chased the car: he jumped on the car and climbed the hood, screaming and threatening. We were so scared he had snapped. When he finally got off the car, he went inside and passed out. After I dropped the kids off with my parents, I returned to check on him. I found our front door wide open and he was sprawled on the floor with our living room and kitchen torn apart (he was looking for his car keys). Glass was shattered everywhere, décor had been ripped off the walls, and our entertainment center and TV were destroyed. I have never been able to leave him alone when he is drunk; I always feel that he needs me to keep him safe. I feel like it is my job. There were many situations like the one I described, though this was by far the worst.

I have had to call ambulances two times for excessive drinking and three times for anxiety attacks. He has been arrested a few times, been in some fights and has been in trouble in his company/squadron a couple times due to his "attempt to forget" drinking: None of which were followed by any optional or mandatory medical/ personal help from his chain of command. Over the years, I have watched my husband struggle with untreated PTSD and lose interest in holidays, family functions and his job. He doesn't ever want to go and do things with us or get festive for the kids anymore. He just wants to sleep or zone out. He talks about how he can't stand his superiors and how they ride him constantly. Sometimes, he even makes up stuff to get out of working. There are numerous times when he comes home angry or with alcohol from work. He is unable to detach his work stresses from the house. I have witnessed a secure man struggle with insecurities over looks, worth, job, finances and marital-related problems. I watch a man who was once so sure of his future, stress over what he wants out of life and what he will do to provide for his family.

There isn't a day that goes by without the weight of Iraq on his shoulders or the talk of how much he can't wait to be done with this Army way of life and forget it all. I used to know my husband; we used to be happy and full of hopes and dreams for our family's future. Now, I feel like I live with a stranger. He pushes me and our three kids away to keep from letting us in or hurting us. But he isn't a lost cause: I do see hope in him. He wants to change and bring back pieces of the old him—he is trying to stop drinking, and he seeks help. Even though our past has been rocky, encouragement can also create change. I love this man and even though he is so different, I/we stand behind him. I just wish he could see himself with the prideful eyes I/we see him with. His sacrifice, strength and courage are not over-looked. He truly is our hero."—**Carleeh Mulholland**

It is important for those of us struggling with PTSD, military or civilian, to face the reality that substance use and acting-out do not mix with our troubled minds. It's not a matter of how severely the trauma has affected one individual from the other; it's a matter of the traumatized mind not being able to function properly, once it has been further altered. Also, substance use is not something "we" can learn to control again with time. It doesn't matter how much time passes and/or how well we have progressed in our recovery: once we pick up using again, we start up right where we left off. Only next time, because of the amount of time which has passed and the progression of our alcoholism, we react to the overwhelming loss of motor skills and thought-process much more poorly and are likely to meet very negative consequences.

Isaiah 64:5
You come to the help of those who gladly do right,
who remember your ways.
But when we continued to sin against them,
you were angry.
How then can we be saved?

Ezekiel 36:31
Then you will remember your evil ways and wicked deeds,
and you will loathe yourselves for your sins and detestable
practices.

Lord, let me not forget that, though I repent and ask Your forgiveness, I do not have the right to continue on neglectfully in that very sin; nor shall I undermine Your all-knowing, all-powerful knowledge and wisdom and what You state in Your Holy Word:

Galatians 6:7
Do not be deceived: God cannot be mocked. A man reaps what he sows.

Lord, let me be ever mindful and ever grateful for what You have done for me. I pray in JESUS' name. Amen

Faith Keeps Me Here

Faith keeps me here. This is definitely true.
The struggles of this world make it hard to do.
Some people experience more pain than others.
Cancer kills mothers and guns kill brothers.
Various other traumas affect the others.
There have been times when I considered checking out.
It can be overwhelming, living in misery and doubt.
It's hard to steer yourself down the other route.
My brother took his own life, he chose his own fate.
He changed my life forever; it put me in a bad state.
I considered following his lead, but instead I rebelled.
As a child I drank, did drugs and slept around. My morals, I withheld.
I went to war and nearly shut the door, but I realized I have so much
to live for.
First of all, my Savior died for me.
He sacrificed everything so that I could be free.
To dishonor my LORD would not be right.
When times get tough, I must reunite.
I've been so blessed with a beautiful wife and great kids.
I could never leave them; I'd be wrong if I did.
Love is the reason I stay; I have so much invested.
I will press on, no matter how much I'm tested.
This world is a cruel place, but I am willing to hear.
The Son of Man died for us all, and it's by that faith I am still here.

Cy Mulholland

A feeling is the general state of consciousness considered independently of particular sensations. An emotion is an affective state of consciousness in which joy, sorrow, hate, or the like is experienced. With that being stated, hopelessness is a powerful feeling. Sadness is a powerful emotion. For the majority of my life, I had this intense inner sadness and at times I did feel hopeless. Even when I wasn't focused on a past trauma, it was always there in the depths of my subconscious. The subconscious mind is a powerful thing that I for one do not fully understand; however, I do know now that there is a lot that goes on there chemically and spiritually, both when we are awake and when we are asleep. Our senses act as gateways to our mind, body and soul. Through sight, touch, hearing, smell and taste, we learn so many things.

I know that sounds like common sense, but what is not common knowledge is the way these things affect us. We were created with feelings and emotions, but at the same time we were created with no intention of being negative beings. What I mean is that we were created after GOD's own image and, though He knew we would be weaker than sinful influence, He installed free will within us. We are so complicated, but our understanding is simple. Because of our simplicity, we don't understand our own thought-process.

For example anger, greed, and jealousy: They are all different, yet much of the time they go hand in hand. Stay with me here. Something may happen in the morning of any given day, such as a rude email or text we may receive at home that angers us and, because we are multitasking sinners, we move on with our business to something else, such as work or exercise. We may do many other things throughout that day and night and the entire time, there may have been something eating away at us: Something that was just burning up inside us, making us angry. All the while, we may not be able to figure out what it is that is making us miserable, until the end of the day when it comes back to hit us in the face and then we dwell on it all over again. This might not be so bad, but it's not only us that we affect. Negative feelings and emotions within an individual become like a domino effect.

For example, one person wakes up on the wrong side of the bed and is unable to get past the negativity he or she is feeling. That same person walks down the street and bumps into a stranger and rudely tells the stranger what he or she thinks of that person. Now that stranger goes into the office where he or she works and is greeted with a request from a coworker and answers the coworker with an abrasive, disrespectful response. This type of behavior is much more common than kindness and that is sad.

The world would be a better place if there were more acts of kindness. A friend of mine conducted an experiment once. She smiled at a stranger she was passing, then turned around. They were walking on a busy street, and that stranger didn't have time to get rid of the smile before another stranger caught his eye, and it made that person smile, too . . . it went on and on. Smiles are contagious.

However, anger is more and more common with every single passing day. Learning this and realizing it for what it is has helped me in dealing with my PTSD. One of the keys to my happiness in daily life has been the realization that my purpose on this earth is to love. What a far better place this could be, if we would all just stop only looking out for ourselves! We would live in a much safer and happier world if we did a little more giving and stopped worrying about taking and being given to.

"And so, my fellow Americans, ask not what your country can do for you; ask what you can do for your country."

—*John F. Kennedy*

2 Timothy 2:3
Share in suffering as a good soldier of Christ Jesus.

2 Timothy 1:13
Follow the pattern of the sound words that you have heard from me, in the faith and love that are in Christ Jesus.

2 Timothy 1:12
Which is why I suffer as I do. But I am not ashamed, for I know whom I have believed, and I am convinced that he is able to guard until that Day what has been entrusted to me.

Lord, thank You for this sense of wisdom that allows me to share Your message with others, while I maintain in my heart that if even one more person will be counted among Your children on account of this, then You are glorified that much more. I pray in JESUS' name. Amen

Have Faith

I said, "Have faith," when you looked at me with that face.
That look in your eye told me you feared you might die.
The doubt drew you near. It was as if I could hear your fear.
Steel rain fell all around us and you froze in place.
"Driver, move out, there's no time to waste."
You shook the fear and that's what got you home.
I told you, brother, you were not alone.
An emotional soldier is a dead soldier.
If you lose your head, then it's all over.
What you feel inside is something serious.
Share your experience with me, because I am curious.
Don't try to minimize, but normalize.
The things you tell me will come as no surprise.
Have faith, you are among brothers.
You can depend on us, but don't tell the others.
Anger and fear will drive you; faith will take you farther.
Allow yourself to get help; try not to make your life harder.
I mean this for myself too. That's why I am here.
I need to separate being down range from being in the rear.
So often, our minds operate in fight-or-flight.
The truth is we need to take flight from the fight.
We need to get ourselves right for the LORD'S sight.
I mean, don't run from your problems: make them run from you.
This is exactly what I'm trying to do.
Have faith, man. I know you can.
We need to adhere to someone else's plan.
I know fear gives you an edge and anger helps you control it.
When we are home is not the place to show it.
Adrenaline will rush you, faith can slow you down.
I'm trying to be grateful when I take a look around.
Most of the time, I feel detached and numb.
I no longer feel comfortable: I only feel numb.
Being on edge sometimes drives me to the edge.

At times, I feel like I'm hanging from a ledge.
Have faith: a lack thereof can be your killer.
It may tighten your rope or pull your trigger.
Stay alert and you may stay alive, whether you're here or on the other side.
Maintain your faith and you will live forever.
Put your trust in your faith and you will perish never.
Think of yourself like a real fast car.
Stay on that red line and you won't go far.
Maintain situational awareness and have faith when times are hard.
You never know when the LORD above will pull your card.
There are few good neighbors and State Farm won't be there.
Just shine some light on any situation and remain aware.
I'm going to be a good neighbor and for my brothers, I'll be here.
I will sustain my faith, because I know He cares.

We had just walked out of a four-story building that was our combat outpost into the motor pool. Of course, we had walls all around our COP, but there were neighboring buildings that stood higher than our walls. They were high enough for a spotter to observe everything he needed to, in order for him to call in indirect fires on us when we were outside the safety of the building. It was almost a daily occurrence for us to receive mortar attacks from the enemy. We kept the trucks ready so that it took minimal effort to prep them for any given mission, because if we stayed out in the open for long periods of time, we ran a high risk for a mortar attack or even a sniper attack.

So as I was stating, we had just walked out and I had just stepped into my gun truck and closed my door when a mortar impacted just outside my door and they began dropping all around us. It was obvious that someone had been watching us from a nearby building. Thankfully, the mortars were a tad bit late. Several trucks were damaged, including mine, but not a single soldier in my unit lost his life that day. My truck sustained four flat tires, extensive body damage and an extremely cracked windshield. I was sure glad that glass was bullet-proof and apparently mortar-proof, to an extent. I thanked GOD.

In the midst of the attack, I looked at my driver and looked back at the rest of my crew, who looked worse than if they'd seen a ghost. I could see the fear in their faces. I looked at them all and I said, "Have Faith." Then instantly, they seemed to be comforted, as if they knew they were going to be alright. I then told the driver to move out and take us to the other side of the building, where we would most likely be safe, because there was a vehicle entry where we could drive inside the building and begin maintenance. That was the first of six times that my crew and I would be hit throughout my third tour in Iraq, but fortunately for me, every single one of my soldiers made it home.

Psalm 91:5
You will not fear the terror of night,
nor the arrow that flies by day,

Lord, thank You for the truths written in Psalm 91. Please bless the men and women defending the free world today and beyond. I pray in JESUS' name. Amen

Colossians 1:21-23
21 Once you were alienated from God and were enemies in your minds because of your evil behavior. 22 But now he has reconciled you by Christ's physical body through death to present you holy in his sight, without blemish and free from accusation—23 if you continue in your faith, established and firm, and do not move from the hope held out in the gospel. This is the gospel that you heard and that has been proclaimed to every creature under heaven, and of which I, Paul, have become a servant.

Lord, let those who hear Your message receive it and not be deceived. I pray in JESUS name. Amen

Like a Window

Have you ever looked through a window you couldn't see through?
Not knowing what's on the other side, but knowing someone is
watching you.
What if this was something close to the realm of heaven?
Some things aren't for us to understand, such as the number seven.
It is fun and exciting to dream, try and imagine.
Someday we'll go away and leave behind the sin.
How do we explain the mystery of space?
We can't, but I'm going to share a thought for you to chase.
We know there are first, second and third.
I assume the atmosphere and the universe from the Word.
I'm not sure, so I'm going to guess.
The universe, they say, is vast and endless.
It probably is, so where is our God?
It's all hard to fathom; it seems rather odd.
Could it be it's like that mirror we've seen?
We can't see through, but we are viewed, if you know what I mean.
Perhaps our side is seen as a work of art.
Put in its proper place, it all does its part.
Have you ever wondered why there are so many things in the sky?
And how most of them are perfect circles that fly?
How is it possible that so much can orbit just right?
Why do so many things project so much light?
Could it be that this is all some kind of accident?
Do we know where we came from and where our loved ones all went?
Or do we know who we are and where we want to go?
And is it possible that GOD is watching us through His window?

Philippians 1:27
Only let your manner of life be worthy of the gospel of Christ, so that whether I come and see you or am absent, I may hear of you that you are standing firm in one spirit, with one mind striving side by side for the faith of the gospel,

Lord, thank You for the many people You utilize in powerful ways to encourage others such as me about Your truths. More than any human, Lord, thank You for Your Holy Spirit. I pray in JESUS' name. Amen

Live, Love, Laugh

Life is charitable, but it is perishable.
Life is a gift from the One above.
We are given this gift through unconditional love.
Love is not controlling, so we are given free will.
Will your cup overflow or will it spill?
We have the choice to turn away from the lie, the cheat and the kill.
Life comes from One and One only.
If you live a life of love, you will never be lonely.
He who loves you is the light everlasting.
He is the way, the truth, the life and the light shining through the
darkness evil is casting.
Life doesn't end here, if you choose to die never.
He loves us so much, He will let us live forever.
Eternity you will see, if you live not in the dark.
Our Creator calls us to live our life like a spark.
Let your light shine throughout the entire journey on which you embark.
Do so and you will experience greater things than Louis or Clark.
Life is much more than a box of chocolates, though you never know
what you're going to get.
We know the One who gives life. Don't worry that He hasn't come
back yet.
Live a life of love and you will live worry-free.
Be the one He calls you to be. Live and love and you will be happy.
Don't worry about who you can and can't see.
Someday, we'll leave this place and there will be life after.
So while you're still here, live a life filled with laughter.

There are so many scriptures that help me get through each day. I reflect on various scriptures to help me get through certain difficult situations. It is good to spend time reading the Word in the Holy Bible a portion of every day. Reading the Bible along with prayer are the healthiest things a person can do for his or her spiritual well-being. Meditation and fellowship with other Christians are also great daily practices, but reading the Word accompanied by prayer is how we keep our personal relationship with GOD the Father strong, asking that His will be done in the name of JESUS CHRIST, His Son, our Lord and Savior. The following scriptures from the Holy Bible help me know that no temptation will be placed in front of me that the Lord will not allow me a way out of and for that I am grateful. This gives me peace of mind.

1 Corinthians 10:13
No temptation has overtaken you that is not common to man. GOD is faithful, and he will not let you be tempted beyond your ability, but with the temptation he will also provide the way of escape, that you may be able to endure it.

1 Peter 5:8-10
Be sober-minded; be watchful. Your adversary the devil prowls around like a roaring lion, seeking someone to devour. 9 Resist him, firm in your faith, knowing that the same kinds of suffering are being experienced by your brotherhood throughout the world. 10And after you have suffered a little while, the God of all grace, who has called you to his eternal glory in Christ, will himself restore, confirm, strengthen, and establish you.

Lord, thank You for Your Word and allowing Christ to be our foundation and salvation. I pray in JESUS' name. Amen

Calm from the Psalm

I used to live my life calm like a bomb.
Now I'm calm from the Psalm.
I put on the Spirit like a Holy balm.
I strive to stay alive: I must survive.
I'm still here, because someone wants me to thrive.
A pro-creation; me plus mine equal five.
No walking in the darkness: I won't take that dive.
Used to be, messing with me was like shaking a bee-hive.
I was a hero, the unsung. You were bound to get stung.
Figuratively speaking, you would get your figurative bell rung.
Those days are behind me; it's no longer inside me.
I released that demon and was given back that freedom:
Freedom to sing praise for the rest of my days in so many ways,
Only hip hop hoorays and jars of clays.
A wonderful fragrance I spray today.
Have you ever broke through a chain and felt how that felt?
Have you ever won back your innocence with a bad hand you were
dealt?
Have you been told by the rose how good you smelt?
If you have an ear, then hear.
Don't live your life in fear.
If you were a lost cause you wouldn't be here.
Will you draw the line in the sand and grab His hand?
Will you look away and sink?
Will your life pass you by in a blink?
Will you try to skate by, like you're in a rink?
What do you think? Your outdated milk doesn't stink.
Continue carrying that burden and your back will kink.
I'll be that, so call me a nerd.
I'm down with the Word. The way you're living is absurd.
I was once told by someone other than a little bird:
Live a life of love and believe in the Father above.
Let that Spirit come over you like a dove and fit you like a glove.

Find that verse that fits you, but live by them all.
Don't matter how small, how big, or how tall.
Find out who you are, but be who you're supposed to be.
Stand in the light, live through JESUS and be free.
I tell you the truth: it'll be for eternity.
I love PSALM 91; I'm a PSALM kind of guy.
I trust in the LORD: I went to combat and didn't die.
There is only one GOD. (You can quote me. My name is Cy.)
Choose any other and you're destined to fry.
I'm calm from the PSALM. You can read it on a Nook.
Don't waste another second. JESUS will come like a crook.
It's a soul-back guarantee, don't be mistook.

f you die without forgiveness, you won't get another look. All of us who struggle with PTSD and have families need to remember that, though we grow stronger in our recovery and develop coping skills and strengthen our survivor skills, we cannot afford to neglect our families. By this, I mean they have suffered as well throughout our conflict: the war within. They have in best cases stood by our sides through our toughest moments and also have wounds in need of healing. Whether one's family consists of only a spouse, a spouse with kids, or even a boyfriend or girlfriend and various other family types, they too have watched us tear ourselves down and many times, these family members suffer from what is known as Secondary PTSD.

Secondary PTSD is not a disorder which is recognized by the Diagnostic and Statistical Manual of Mental Disorders (as of the fourth edition). However, if you lived with someone who suffers from PTSD, you may notice yourself beginning to "mirror" some of their behaviors. This transformation is called Secondary Post Traumatic Stress Disorder. The signs, symptoms and effects of Secondary PTSD are just as varied as the ones exhibited by Veterans with "primary" PTSD.

When you're living with a veteran who has Post Traumatic Stress Disorder, you become his (or her) caretaker. You slip into a role, without even noticing that it has you constantly watching for people or circumstances that might "set him off." You're trying to make sure everything stays in line—that nothing aggravates or upsets your vet—that everything is "perfect." Despite your best efforts, you're still getting screamed at and berated by the person you're trying to help on a much too frequent basis. Your vet is not emotionally "there" for you; when you're upset or happy, angry or sad, you start "protecting" yourself by treating others, especially your vet, the same way. You're also probably handling all household chores, childcare, financial management, etc. You get no help (or very little) from your spouse. You're the cook, chauffeur, secretary, accountant, yard guy, child-care provider, laundry service, etc., etc., etc. Everything in your family feels like it's up to you. It is a 24/7 job, and you constantly feel like you're failing. It's not humanly possible to do everything—or to prevent PTSD from creeping in. This cycle takes its toll on many spouses. You lose yourself. It's impossible to tiptoe around your vet, day in and day out, while taking care of all of life's other duties (duties normally shared between two people), without feeling the strain. And that strain soon transforms into Secondary PTSD.—www.familyofavet.com

The more I became educated on this topic, I not only became aware of the effects my PTSD was having on my wife, I came to realize that a lot of my children's behaviors also mirrored my own. It only makes sense, due to the fact that we as parents are the main influence in shaping our children's personalities. According to the Veteran's Assistant (VA), people who have PTSD often "re-experience" traumatic events through memories or dreams. This can happen quickly and can seem to come out of nowhere. These symptoms often come with strong feelings of grief, guilt, fear or anger. Sometimes, the experience can be so strong that you may think the trauma is happening again.

These symptoms can be scary, not only for you, but also for your children. Children may not understand what is happening or why it is happening. They may worry about their parent or worry that the parent cannot take care of them. Because the re-experiencing symptoms are so upsetting, people with PTSD try not to think about the event. If you have PTSD, you may also try to avoid places and things that remind you of the trauma. Or, you may not feel like doing things that used to be fun, like going to the movies or your child's event.

It can also be hard for people with PTSD to have good feelings. You may feel "cut off" from family and children. As a result, children may feel that the parent with PTSD does not care about them. People with PTSD tend to be anxious and "on edge." With PTSD, you might have trouble sleeping or paying attention. You might be grouchy or angry much of the time. You may be easily scared, or overly worried about your safety or the safety of your loved ones. It is easy to see how these problems can affect family members. For example, acting grouchy can make a parent seem mean or angry. Since they do not understand the symptoms of PTSD, children may wonder whether the parent loves them.

A parent's PTSD symptoms are directly linked to their child's responses. Children usually respond in certain ways:

- A child might feel and behave just like their parent as a way of trying to connect with the parent. The child might show some of the same symptoms as the parent with PTSD.
- A child may take on the adult role to fill in for the parent with PTSD. The child acts too grown-up for his or her age.

- Some children do not get help with their feelings. This can lead to problems at school, sadness, anxiety (worry, fear) and relationship problems later in life.

Some research shows that children of Veterans with PTSD are more likely to have problems with behaviors and school and problems getting along with others. Their parents see them as more sad, anxious, aggressive and hyper than children of Veterans who do not have PTSD. Some research has also found that PTSD in a parent is related to violence in the home and to children acting violent.

But it is important to note that most Veterans have homes without violence. Although not common, children may start to have symptoms like those the parent has, or symptoms that are somehow related to those the parent has. For example, a child may have nightmares about the parent's trauma, or a child might have trouble paying attention at school because she is thinking about her parent's problems. The impact of a parent's PTSD symptoms on a child is sometimes called "secondary traumatization." Since violence occurs in some homes in which a parent has PTSD, the children may also develop their own PTSD symptoms related to the violence. A child's PTSD symptoms can get worse if there is not a parent who can help the child feel better. Teenage children of Veterans with PTSD can also be affected by their parent's symptoms.

One research study compared teens of non-Veteran fathers to those with Vietnam combat Veteran fathers. The teens of the Vietnam combat Veterans showed worse attitudes toward school and toward their fathers. They were more sad and anxious and were less creative. Their mothers also rated them as having more problem behaviors. However, their behavior at school and their social functioning looked like the children of non-Veterans. This might be because the fathers in this study were not actually diagnosed with PTSD. Overall, teens' problems are much more likely when the parent Veteran has mental health issues, such as PTSD. Although not common, it is possible for children to show signs of PTSD because they are upset by their parent's symptoms. Trauma symptoms can also be passed from parent to child or between generations. This is called "intergenerational transmission of trauma." This has been seen in the families of WWII Holocaust survivors. It is also seen in the families of combat Veterans with PTSD. Here is how it happens:

- When a family silences a child, or teaches him to not talk about disturbing events, thoughts, or feelings, the child's anxiety gets worse. He may start to worry about causing the parent's symptoms if he talks about the trauma. He may create his own ideas about what happened to the parent, which can be worse than what actually happened.
- Sometimes parents share too many full details about the events. Children then can start to experience their own set of PTSD symptoms in response to these terrible images.
- A child may begin to share in her parent's symptoms as a way to connect with the parent.
- Children may also repeat or re-do some aspect of the trauma because they see that their parent has difficulty separating the past trauma from the present moment. Parents can help children by using the information provided in this fact sheet and other resources. Parents or professionals can talk to family members about the possible impact of a parent's PTSD on children. It can be helpful for family members to learn how traumatic reactions can be passed from parent to child.

A good first step in helping children cope with a parent's PTSD is to explain the reasons for the parent's difficulties. Be careful not to share too many details of the event(s) with the child. How much you say depends on your child's age and maturity level. It is important to help children see that your symptoms are not their fault.

Some parents want help with what to say to their children, and a counselor could help with this. There are also many treatment options. Treatment can include individual treatment for the Veteran or adult with PTSD, as well as family therapy. Family therapy supports the parent with PTSD and teaches family members how to get their own needs met. Children may benefit from their own therapy as well, which might differ based on the child's age. Each family is different, and decisions about what kind of treatment to seek, if any, can be hard. The most important thing is to help each member of the family, including the children, say what he or she needs. Vet Centers across the country and some VA PTSD programs offer group, couple and individual programs for family members of Veterans. In the same manner that we would not leave a fallen warrior on the battlefield, it is equally important that we not leave our family members behind.

1 Peter 2:2
Like newborn babies, crave pure spiritual milk, so that by it you may grow up in your salvation

Lord, I pray for those of us who have experienced trauma, that we will be mindful that we have negatively impacted those we love unintentionally and will make an honest effort to heal together as loving friends and family. I pray in JESUS name. Amen

Psalm 91

¹ Whoever dwells in the shelter of the Most High
will rest in the shadow of the Almighty.
² I will say of the LORD, "He is my refuge and my fortress,
my God, in whom I trust."
³ Surely he will save you
from the fowler's snare
and from the deadly pestilence.
⁴ He will cover you with his feathers,
and under his wings you will find refuge;
his faithfulness will be your shield and rampart.
⁵ You will not fear the terror of night,
nor the arrow that flies by day,
⁶ nor the pestilence that stalks in the darkness,
nor the plague that destroys at midday.
⁷ A thousand may fall at your side,
ten thousand at your right hand,
but it will not come near you.
⁸ You will only observe with your eyes
and see the punishment of the wicked.
⁹ If you say, "The LORD is my refuge,"
and you make the Most High your dwelling,
¹⁰ no harm will overtake you,
no disaster will come near your tent.
¹¹ For he will command his angels concerning you
to guard you in all your ways;
¹² they will lift you up in their hands,
so that you will not strike your foot against a stone.
¹³ You will tread on the lion and the cobra;
you will trample the great lion and the serpent.
¹⁴ "Because he loves me," says the LORD, "I will rescue him;
I will protect him, for he acknowledges my name.
¹⁵ He will call on me, and I will answer him;
I will be with him in trouble,
I will deliver him and honor him.
¹⁶ With long life I will satisfy him
and show him my salvation."

Cy Mulholland

There You Were

There you were, my LORD, in the beginning;
Amongst the Heavens before any sinning.
A perfect home you created for us to live.
The gift of life is what you give.
A perfect place is what you gave.
Till the fall of man: we misbehaved.
We took the life we had and killed ourselves.
We were deceived, but we did it to ourselves;
A great disappointment, but You love us still.
You gave us promise and law. You said, "Peace, Be Still."
A chance to prosper, to turn from evil with free will—
The choice was not a matter of taking a red or a blue pill.
There you were, Father, providing purpose, direction and motivation.
We were damned by our sin and You offered compensation.
You told us our numbers would be like the stars in the sky.
The choice was ours: to live free or die.
Unconditional love is what You feel for us.
So weak, we are alone, so in GOD we trust.
You never waver. You are always there,
Showing your most loyal servants Your presence, because You care.
As the Father to Your children, You are strict with discipline.
You destroyed those time and again who chose to live in sin.
With a weakness and faulty nature uncontrolled, You gave us a chance.
To pay the price for our sins, You sent the olive branch.
There You were, my Savior, born of a virgin.
With never-ending love, You provided a way again,
Spreading Your word, thus spreading Yourself,
And sharing Your Spirit, the bountiful wealth.
When the time came and the path had been lit
It was time for You to go, but Your forgiveness would never quit.
You hung on the cross and died the worst death,
And when it was finished, opportunity was left.
You broke the bonds: over You, death has no power.

When You rose again, LORD, was our finest hour.
You are the rock, You are the high tower.
You are more beautiful than the finest flower.
You provide the Comforter, the Holy Spirit everlasting;
The ultimate blessing from the Son of Man, the King.
There You are, my LORD, my GOD, my Savior on high.
It's through Your love that I will not die.
I love You so very much!
Thank You, Praise JESUS!
Everything evil, all hell shudders at the mention of Your name.
The evil one and his followers will burn and only they are to blame.
Thank You for Your blessings, oh LORD. I don't deserve a single one.
Thank You, Father, for loving me so much that You sent Your only Son.

PTSD Preventative Maintenance

1. Love and be loved.
2. Seek first the will of GOD.
3. Humble yourself in the sight of the Lord.
4. Remain in prayer daily and read the Word.
5. Allow yourself to receive treatment.
6. Discover the Coping Skills that suit you.
7. Do NOT self-medicate.
8. Self-educate to promote PTSD awareness.
9. Find purpose in further academic education.
10. Remember, 18 veterans take their fate into their own hands every day by committing suicide, which is an eternal mistake for a serious problem. We didn't surrender on the battlefield, so don't give up now. If you know someone in need of help, reach out. There is real, true healing and hope in Jesus, so have faith.

Jeremiah 29:11
11 For I know the plans I have for you," declares the LORD, "plans to prosper you and not to harm you, plans to give you hope and a future.

I Have Arrived

I have arrived at the checkpoint, but the objective is far away. For
spiritual guidance, I will always pray.
I will strive to be the man, husband and father I am called to be.
I will make every effort to be a productive member of society.
I will honor my brothers by accepting the loss.
Remembrance always: never forgetting the cost.
Though times are tough, I will love this nation.
My focus will remain on those I love and salvation.
I will constantly share the message from above:
The calling for us all is to know faith, hope and love.
Recovery without complacency is the focus of my cause.
The goal is to uphold this belief, without pause.
No longer the problem, I'm part of the solution.
Creating peace in my home and sharing with others is my distribution.
I will continue to give and not worry at all about being given to.
My goal is to help way more than a few.
I put my faith in GOD, because I know He is true.
I will focus on my thoughts, speech and actions in all that I do.
With my morals and values, I stand firm on the rock.
The Lord, my Shepherd has power of the clock.
There will be those days that are harder than others.
I now possess the skills to properly remember my brothers.
I mean what I say when I say: "With drinking, I'm done."
I'd rather be bored than have too much fun.
I will not conform for the world: this is my oath.
I won't be torn down; there is only room for growth.
My life is now one of doing more with not much.
At times I'll fall short, but I will not lose touch.
I walk in the light and always strive for what's right.
Positive self-talk such as this helps me keep myself tight.
Pre-plotted sin cannot be an excuse.
Burden is a load that must be cut loose.
We all have hurt or know someone who is hurting right now.

Cy Mulholland

The question is: what are we going to do about it and how?
We who care, reach out—not for personal gain.
I want for all what I have now, instead of a life filled with pain.
The days come and the days go; what is it that you want to show?
Will your light burn out or will it glow?
Do you have the strength and courage for change and all that it brings?
Can you avoid tempting people, places and things?
Will you consider the well-being of more than yourself?
Will you try and preserve your sprimentical health?
I will pray for those like me, that they find their true definition.
After all, we are forgiven through grace: let there be no suspicion.
I thank GOD and it was about time,
I found a way to unwind my Marne Mind.
With clear vision, my free will and its intention I now see.
The message of grace and healing is meant for you and me.
If you start feeling better, then let someone know.
You can help others; you have something to show.
Pay something forward: it doesn't cost much.
Tune into the life-long task that is recovery: stay in touch.
Make use of your skills; survive and cope.
Protect you and yours, stay away from impurity, drink and dope.
I love to rhyme, so I do it all the time:
Find something constructive to do, don't live a life of crime.
Driving under the influence is definitely wrong.
And we men, who are married: avoid lust—be strong.
If we remain positive and focused, we cannot lose.
Adversity is coming, so what path will you choose?
Remember the light and stay out of the shadow.
Our Father in Heaven sees all things through His window.
Opportunity is what we have, to live the life He intended.
A perfect world was apprehended, but salvation has been mended.
Break free from the chains that are holding you down.
Leave isolation to see all the blessings around.
I made it my mission to share with you what works.
Now cross that line in the sand, grab His hand, and enjoy the Lord's perks.
It's the same for you and the same for me.
The key to success is in the Word and it will set you free.
The very same Word who was there before time existed.

Your answers are in the Holy Bible; it is as JESUS insisted.
Adversity is coming, so remember the unce.
We will face resistance so we'll need it more than once.
Responsibly, I will respond to any response given.
Positive reactions and attitude is now by what I am driven.
We do what is good and remain humble, even if we must suffer.
Things could be tougher and remember, Paul had it much rougher.
Great is the reward which we all will receive,
but only if we believe and don't make our own arrangements to leave.
I've been to rock-bottom, but now I aim high.
I don't mean like the Air Force; I'm a Lord's Army kind of guy.
The evil one will come around and whisper his lies.
However, we have been given life when even the world dies.
Instant gratification followed by guilt follows sin.
I will never turn my back on my Savior again.
I can't wait until time is no more and I can look upon His face!
I feel it in my heart and soul. I have been saved by His grace.
The world will do things that will not please us,
but we must remember to have faith in JESUS!

Cy Mulholland